LOVING JUSTICE

Loving Justice

Legal Emotions in William Blackstone's England

Kathryn D. Temple

NEW YORK UNIVERSITY PRESS

New York

NEW YORK UNIVERSITY PRESS
New York
www.nyupress.org

References to Internet websites (URLs) were accurate at the time of writing. Neither the author nor New York University Press is responsible for URLs that may have expired or changed since the manuscript was prepared.

Library of Congress Cataloging-in-Publication Data
Names: Temple, Kathryn D., 1955–   author.
Title: Loving justice : legal emotions in William Blackstone's England / Kathryn Temple.
Description: New York : New York University Press, 2019. | Also available as an ebook. | Includes bibliographical references and index.
Identifiers: LCCN 2018043707| ISBN 9781479895274 (cloth : alk. paper) | ISBN 147989527X (cloth : alk. paper)
Subjects: LCSH: Blackstone, William, 1723–1780. Commentaries on the laws of England. | Justice in literature. | Emotions in literature. | Law—England—History. | Practice of law—England—Psychological aspects. | Law—Psychological aspects. | Law and aesthetics. | Blackstone, William, 1723–1780—Criticism and interpretation.
Classification: LCC KD660 .T46 2019 | DDC 349.42—dc23
LC record available at https://lccn.loc.gov/2018043707

New York University Press books are printed on acid-free paper, and their binding materials are chosen for strength and durability. We strive to use environmentally responsible suppliers and materials to the greatest extent possible in publishing our books.

Manufactured in the United States of America

10 9 8 7 6 5 4 3 2 1

To my delightful daughter, Lucy Frances Slevin

Never forget that justice is what love looks like in public.
—Cornel West, *Justice Is What Love Looks Like in Public*,
lecture delivered at Howard University, April 17, 2011

CONTENTS

Introduction

Shaping Legal Emotions in Blackstone's England

In the best-selling *Commentaries on the Laws of England* (1765–69), William Blackstone—most celebrated as a legal scholar, but also an occasional poet—famously took the "ungodly jumble" of English law and transformed it into an elegant, readable, and easily transportable four-volume summary. Soon after publication, it became an international monument not only to English law, but to English conceptions of justice, or to, as Blackstone put it, "the immutable laws of good and evil" (I:40).[1] The *Commentaries* was celebrated in London, carried on horseback throughout the American colonies, and relied upon across what was fast becoming the British Empire.[2] The first text assigned in America's first law school at William & Mary, it has been reprinted over 200 times in the 250 years since its initial publication, spawning numerous additional abridgements and related works, but also eliciting comment in fiction and poetry, right up to the present day. In recent years, Blackstone's work has newly interested the US Supreme Court, and has been cited in more than 8 percent of Supreme Court cases.[3]

Legal historians tend to regard the *Commentaries* as the first successful modern application of Enlightenment reason to English legal history. But "reason" and "history" alone do not fully explain the crucial role Blackstone's work played in disseminating conceptions of justice throughout the British Empire. While assuming the voice of reason and claiming historical accuracy as the source of his authority, all in the service of presenting a comprehensive yet easily assimilated guide to English law, Blackstone was also deeply invested in what he thought of as "the qualities of the heart" related to law and justice (I:34).[4] In this he reflected his own time, but also prefigured the view that our conceptions of justice are felt conceptions, interconnected to our perceptions of the beautiful and the ugly: they are arrived at emotionally and aesthetically, as well as rationally. Blackstone—a poet who believed that "the only true and natural foundations of society are the wants and fears of individuals"— was ideally situated to condense English law into a form that evoked emotions crucial to promoting English ideas of justice (I:47). Making art of English law, he avoided the typically dry, encyclopedic overview of black letter law common in his time, and instead produced an elegantly written, emotionally saturated treatise that encouraged readers to *feel* as much as reason their way to justice. That *feeling* element in the *Commentaries* is the key to what might be called its "binding" power, the force that attracted readers to the *Commentaries* and made it an icon for English justice.[5] In enlisting an affective aesthetics to represent English law as just, Blackstone created a moving, evocative poetics of justice with continuing influence across the Western world.

It is hard to imagine the state of English law before the *Commentaries* or the magnitude of Blackstone's task.[6] In an early poem discussed at length later in this introduction, Blackstone lamented the unpleasant "noisiness" of Westminster Hall, a noisiness that was vastly overdetermined, standing in for the incoherence of the English way of doing law during this period. As the courts struggled to cope with international trade and its companions, paper credit and a burgeoning insurance industry, the noise of the present could be seen as frightening and threatening, capable of drowning out what must have seemed like the smoother, more harmonious rhythms of the past. Thus projectors and advisors multiplied throughout the century: the law should be methodized; the law should be formalized; the law should be de-formalized because its formal practices were defeating its larger purposes; practices of lawyers should be regulated through the 1739 Society of Gentlemen Practisers; the behavior of those in the Hall should improve; Law Latin should be eliminated (it was in 1733); without Law Latin, legal pronouncements would become even more incoherent, so it should be enforced; court hand should be eliminated; court hand was a lost art.[7] Complaints about the mysteriousness of the law coincided with an equally heartfelt and more depressing realization: the common law was a chaotic mess of inexplicably conflicting written case reports and precedents, half-remembered practices, and adages, while new statutory laws were often passed with little knowledge of precedent or history, as Blackstone commented in the introduction to the *Commentaries* (I:10–

11).[8] Before Blackstone, others had made feeble or incomplete attempts to synthesize the English common law system, but most practitioners or "professors" of law, as they were called, relied on a compendium of knowledge drawn from a bewildering array of sources—oral, manuscript, and print. As early as 1600, lawyers were calling for organizational methods that would classify legal thought and give them practical guidelines (Cromwell himself had described the law as "an ungodly jumble"[9]). And the print revolution only made things worse: understandings of English law degenerated as printers began to spin off a bewildering number of texts, none of which could predict outcomes or explain decisions. Despite the publication of numerous treatises and guides, there was little to help the anxious law student sort through the mass of available literature. Matthew Hale's *History and Analysis of the Common Law of England* was published in 1713, but it was fragmented, uneven, and did not attempt comprehensive coverage. Many legal texts consisted of lists that assumed an "internal logic" but did not articulate it, leaving later scholars to remark that their "major methodological tool was the alphabet."[10] Thomas Wood, the author of an early eighteenth-century attempt to synthesize English law, was only one of many who complained of the "tedious wandering about" that the study of law had become.[11] No wonder law teaching was referred to as the "cobbler method." To the uninitiated it seemed laws were simply cobbled together in order to reach arbitrary results.[12] Responses to this crisis were well meaning, sometimes brilliant, but ineffective. By the middle of the century, "strident attacks" on the law were common, and "many sought to reduce the common law to good order."[13] Commentators despaired of reconciling the vast array of conflicting cases and incidental jurisprudential remarks with prevailing views of the English constitution and of the continuity and integrity of the system. When Blackstone wrote the *Commentaries*, he attempted to solve a problem that many believed insoluble.

Daniel Boorstin, for years the author of the only humanities-oriented study of Blackstone, noted Blackstone's methodical reduction of legal complexity to "short and rational form," but also recognized that Blackstone was more than a reductive classifier or organizer and more than a legal commentator.[14] Instead, as Boorstin argues, Blackstone drew on the aesthetic tastes and tendencies of his time to represent the law. But Blackstone's artful recapitulation of his materials included successfully managing the emotions that had accumulated around the common law, transforming confusion and irritation into admiration, creating desire where none had existed, and inducing readers to become advocates for the English common law. Much of this involved reducing anxiety around change. The *Commentaries*, in its effort to find an authentic past and preserve it, constructed a particular version of modernity that bridged past and present, shoring up beliefs in the common law system, even while demonstrating its value for adaptation and change.[15] While the practice had been to emphasize tradition through focusing on the history of the law, Blackstone joined other "evolutionary theorists" in bringing history to an "explanation of form and evolution."[16] He also bridged the old alliance with "natural law" and the new interest in positivism that came to drive nineteenth-century law.[17] And finally, he reassured readers of the value of the English common law tradition by managing geographical boundaries, avoiding efforts like Samuel Johnson's to fence off Englishness from its non-English sources, instead celebrating the diverse origins of the English tradition, and foregrounding the "mixing" that linked law and language together in what he presented as a triumphant English achievement. As he put it, "Our laws are mixed as our language: and as our language is so much the richer, the laws are more complete" (I:64).

His own contemporaries greeted his achievement with palpable relief, recognizing that by humanizing an archaic system, Blackstone had made the English common law palatable to a wide audience. William Meredith commented in 1770 that the law "til you brought it from darkness into light, had been as carefully secreted from common understanding, as the mysteries of religion ever were."[18] Edward Gibbon praised him for "clearing" jurisprudence "of the pedantry and obscurity which rendered it the unknown horror of all men of taste."[19] And *The Barrister* noted that the *Commentaries* "brought darkness to light, and reduced to system & method a farrago of legal knowledge, scattered over immense volumes of black-lettered law."[20] It is not surprising that Blackstone was, in his own time, compared to Montesquieu, Beccaria, and Voltaire. As the *Literary Fly* said in 1779, these four great thinkers "echoed" each other.[21] By 1826, his work was seen "in the light of a national property."[22] Horror versus taste, darkness versus light, obscurity versus clarity, mystery versus system: these critiques suggest that Blackstone left the dark past behind for a well-lit present. It thus must have seemed a monumental achievement, the equivalent of Johnson's great *Dictionary* or the British Museum. It is not too much to say of the *Commentaries*, as A. W. B. Simpson does, that its achievement goes beyond the law: "Nothing remotely resembling them in execution had appeared in the English language before."[23] In part, this was because the portable, digestible *Commentaries* not only told the English what the law was and where it came from, but how they were supposed to feel about it.

Although Blackstone has been "rediscovered" numerous times by legal historians, he is only now being rediscovered as a major figure for eighteenth-century studies, as well as for Law and Humanities and the history of emotion. This book participates in the current "Blackstone Revival," signaled by Wilfrid Prest's 2008 biography, his collection of Blackstone's letters, three collections of essays, and the publication of a new edition of the *Commentaries* from Oxford University Press.[24] Blackstone was not merely a writer of legal treatises, but a broadly based eighteenth-century thinker, perhaps one of the most understudied writers of his time, writing not only the *Commentaries*, but also poetry, historical tracts, architectural essays, and criticism, all of which formed a subtext to his legal commentary. His imagination was expansive: the footnotes to the *Commentaries* reveal that he drew from history, political philosophy, literature, and many other sources, yet he managed to produce an elegant (rather than distractingly digressive) treatise that exemplified Pope's praise for "what oft was thought, but ne're so well expressed." His influence is hard to overstate; underestimating him flies in the face of his overriding and yet uncelebrated presence not only in Anglo-American law where Blackstone looms large, but in Anglo-American culture as represented by novels, plays, and most recently experimental essays. As the following chapters will demonstrate, Blackstone appears in some unlikely contexts: in a lover's garden in one of Wilkie Collins's novels, on a pitching ship in *Billy Budd*, in an isolated plantation in the pre–Civil War South in *To Kill a Mockingbird*, even in a modern romance novel, *The Blackstone Key*, published in 2008 by Rose Melikan. Recently, Jessie Allen has produced an eloquent, compelling set of personal essays that bring Blackstone's *Commentaries* to contemporary political and personal issues.[25] Sometimes these creative uses of Blackstone invoke the *Commentaries* as a sign for justice, sometimes for injustice, but always for its emotional valence, for its value in telling us something about how we are supposed to feel about justice and the law.

The Mashup: Blackstone's Poetics

To read Blackstone's *Commentaries* for its emotional valence is, in part, to read it as we would read poetry, to "close read" the *Commentaries*, as literary critics say, to tease out the relationships between form, diction, and content, to go beyond the surface. And to understand why this sort of reading of the *Commentaries* is important, we need to understand Blackstone both as poet and legal commentator, as a writer as invested in aesthetics as he was in law. It doesn't take much of a stretch of the imagination to make this leap, for as a young man, Blackstone was a literary prodigy, the author of numerous poems and other short pieces. He was devoted to literature, studying poetry from Horace to Alexander Pope and publishing verse before he was nine, even winning a prize for a poem on Milton.[26] Admitted to Pembroke College, Oxford, in 1738, he not only read classical poetry and studied Shakespeare, but also absorbed the great English poets, particularly Pope. There was no hint that he would one day become one of the great English jurists. But sometime in 1744 when he was twenty-one years old, he wrote a poem extraordinary for its foreshadowing of his later career. Throughout this book I will return to this early poem, investigating the relationship between certain of its emotional moments as well as its aesthetic preoccupations, and their reappearance in various guises in the much later *Commentaries*. For in "Lawyer's Farewel to His Muse," Blackstone staged the aesthetic, moral, and, above all, emotional issues he would later engage with in the *Commentaries*.[27] The close reading I offer here introduces both the poem and a methodology of close reading that I will return to in my various analyses of the *Commentaries*, one crucial to understanding how the relationships Blackstone created between form and content served to infuse his text with emotion and engage his readers in what he took to be the appropriate emotional responses to legal content.

Katrin Pahl asks, "In what sense can a text be emotional?" and argues that emotional texts are "incongruous and (self) transforming." They "put things or people at odds with themselves."[28] Blackstone's poem is emotional in content, in diction, and in form, as I shall demonstrate at length here. It is high-minded yet sexualized, idealistic yet grounded in gritty images of London life. If a poem had feelings, this one would feel confused, maybe agitated. In the poem, Blackstone's protagonist "drops a last tear" as he turns away from a delighted appreciation of literature and poetry to enter the law. He finds law practice at best irritating and at worst gloomy and frightening, a nightmarish arena of disease and murder where stereotypes about urban London evoke fear and disgust. Only justice offers the sort of pleasure associated with poetry, but she, a "venerable maid," is represented in sexual terms that confuse the image. The poem rotates around multiple dichotomies and moves uneasily through several generic, embodied, and emotive realms: literature is set against law, desire against disappointment, harmony against discord, in order to illustrate an idealized, aestheticized, and yet sexualized representation of justice, who represents "the wisdom of a thousand years," yet is admired "like Eastern queens." Saturated with emotion, the poem fuses the literary world to positive emotions and the legal world to negative ones while justice is represented as an unattainable (and yet oddly embodied) ideal.

One could hardly find a poem more dense with what historians of emotion have called "emotives," words that are meant not only to describe emotions, but to change how we feel, to "do emotions" in a sense.[29] Throughout the poem, the poet cycles through a series of emotions: he "dreads," is "pensive," "doubtful," "cheer'd," "lulled," "joyous," awestruck, "admiring," desiring, disgusted, fearful, and sad (he drops that highly aestheticized "last tear") in turn as the occasion warrants. The poem uses, by conservative count, forty-five emotionally descriptive words in about a hundred lines, all set in contexts meant to evoke more than is said directly. These emotions are connected to both aesthetic and moral realms: riding waves of moral sentiment, the poet-lawyer finds only good in the pastoral imagery and harmonic sounds of the poems he admires, only bad in legal imagery. To transcend that dichotomy, the poet yearns for a particularized, embodied, even sexualized version of justice (the poet wants to "pierce the secret shade" to find her) where "parts with parts unite / In one harmonious rule of right" and "countless wheels distinctly tend / By various laws to one great end." Readers who ride these waves of moral sentiment along with Blackstone's protagonist will love poetry and desire what was understood in Blackstone's time as harmonic justice, a concept I will discuss in subsequent chapters,[30] experience the turn to law as loss, and be saddened as the poet-turned-lawyer eases his way into retirement and towards what seems to be an early death. And they will feel these emotions as part and parcel of both aesthetic and moral judgments.

For the young Blackstone who authored the poem, both justice's harmonies and law's discordances are felt as embodied emotional experiences, expressed both directly in emotive diction and formally, structurally. We feel this with him at the basic level of sound in that sound is felt in the body; Blackstone's references to noise are in themselves unpleasantly noisy. Law becomes "wrangling" and "stubborn" as Blackstone uses discordant hard consonants to bring his emotive points home. In the "sounds uncouth and accents dry, / That grate the soul of harmony," he gives us a false anti-rhyme in "dry" and "harmony" that itself suggests the grating nature of legal talk. Even in resigned retirement at the end of the poem, Blackstone returns to these unpleasant noises, valuing his "retirement" precisely because it removes him from the jarring curses of the "harpy tribe" and the more plaintive but guilt-inducing "orphan's cry." Sound echoes sense here as unpleasant emotions are personified: Blackstone repeatedly draws on the ugly hard *r*; the "harpy tribe" also offers a hard *p* and uses the long *ee* to suggest the shriek of imagined harpies. The more plaintive "orphan's cry" that "wounds" his ear draws on the emphatically long *i* of "cry" and *oo* of "wounds" to underscore the invasive nature of sounds that seemingly can injure the organ of hearing. This is emotion embodied on the page, expressed through both words and sounds.

An alertness to formal conventions reveals that Blackstone relies on the compressed tetrameter couplet to contain the many emotional moments he steers us through in the poem. Couplets have often been seen as a way of closing down difference, but here they keep oppositions in close interaction with each other, allowing Blackstone to sustain the poem's divisive stances (literature against law, harmony against discord, fine feelings against disgust and misery) over many lines. He places opposition against opposition, confining them in the closed world of two rhyming lines, and thus forcing connections between them. To indicate his poet-lawyer's ambivalence, Blackstone writes, "Pensive he treads the destin'd way, / And dreads to go, nor dares to stay," bringing the prosaic "tread" together

with the melancholic "dread" and the expansive "way" with the confining "stay." He makes prominent use of the couplet's caesura, a crucial tool
in constructing both oppositions and balance. For example, the second
line of the couplet quoted above, caesure'd with the comma, reinforces
the opposed "pensive" and "destined" of the first line while containing its
ambivalence, leaving the poet-lawyer positioned, even teetering on the
back of the comma. Blackstone relies on the caesura at other particularly
divisive moments in the poem: "Lost to the field, and torn from you—";
"No room for Peace, no room for you—." The caesura magnifies the sense
of irrevocable loss the poet-lawyer feels as he departs from literature; it
breaks but also sustains the connection by containing both the loss of the
other and the other itself within the same line.

The couplet form intensifies the emotional impact of the poem, while
it enacts Blackstone's theoretical and emotional commitment to ideals of
Concordia discors and harmonic justice, ideals that dated back to Plato
and Pythagoras but gained new vigor in the first half of the eighteenth
century. Harmonic justice was based on theories of proportion and
scale. Blackstone's reliance on it in the poem connected the law unevenly
to what were felt to be eternal verities, to the idea that not only the world
but the universe worked through a sort of natural, coherent harmony,
that "beauty and order are founded upon the divinely ordained harmony
of things."[31] But "Concordia," as Bernard Hibbitts points out, conflates
a number of ideas, including that of the "chorda" related to string instruments, as well as that of "cordia" related to the heart.[32] It is thus a
mixed concept, linking abstract musical harmonies to the real world
of the body and affect. Its assumption that "contrarieties are essential
to order," and of a "universe of exquisite harmonies and of nice corre-
spondences between macrocosm and microcosm"[33] offered a compelling way of thinking about the seemingly impossible-to-reconcile legal
material the young Blackstone would eventually sort through as a law
student and then as a lecturer on the common law, yet it also suggested
the implacability of difference, the difficulties inherent in attempting to
make incongruities congruent. *Concordia discors* thus linked harmony
to moral theory while simultaneously suggesting its opposite: in harmonic justice, harmony is not only pleasing but actually *is* moral virtue. Inevitably, the discordant noise of lived life suggests the fragility of
moral virtue so conceived.[34]

The poem embraces this conflict, most tellingly in Blackstone's discussion of "Justice" with its mixed erotic and idealistic imagery. Justice is represented as an object of sexual desire that can be obtained only through penetrative force and yet in herself exhibits ideas of harmonic justice drawn from Aristotle, Plato, and Pythagoras.[35] While Blackstone surely did not subscribe to the precise mathematical and geometrical formulas that had made Pythagoras the butt of Swift's humor in *Gulliver's Travels*, in the poem's discussion of "lady" Justice, he offers us a version of justice that aligns the theoretical (*Concordia discors*) with the formal (tetrameter couplet), and suggests both the commitments that would govern the eventual organization of the *Commentaries* and the eventual unraveling of those commitments. To find Justice, Blackstone's young poet-lawyer must first fight his way through a "formal band" of lawyers who speak in "sounds uncouth," then be led through a "thorny maze" of law, before he can "pierce the secret shade" and encounter Justice, a "venerable maid." It is here Blackstone finds his "pure spring" of what might be called "harmonic justice," the place where law merges with justice and the two seem to co-exist in perfect harmony. The passage is worth quoting at length since it offers us a window into the idealistic and yet desirous vision that drove the *Commentaries*:

> There, in a winding, close retreat,
> Is Justice doom'd to fix her seat,
> There, fenc'd by bulwarks of the Law,
> She keeps the wond'ring world in awe,
> And there, from vulgar sight retir'd,
> Like eastern queens is more admir'd.
> O let me pierce the secret shade
> Where dwells the venerable maid!
> There humbly mark, with rev'rent awe,
> The guardian of Britannia's Law,
> Unfold with joy her sacred page,
> (Th' united boast of many an age,
> Where mix'd, yet uniform, appears
> The wisdom of a thousand years)
> In that pure spring the bottom view,
> Clear, deep, and regularly true,

And other doctrines thence imbibe
Than lurk within the sordid scribe;
Observe how parts with parts unite
In one harmonious rule of right;
See countless wheels distinctly tend
By various laws to one great end;
While mighty Alfred's piercing soul
Pervades, and regulates the whole.[36]

As the most casual reader will notice, the passage mixes poetic and sexual references. Blackstone evokes myriad eighteenth-century poets, most obviously John Denham—early master of the couplet and poetic popularizer of *Concordia discors*—in both diction and theme, by offering us a "bottom view" of a "pure spring" that is "clear, deep, and regularly true." This "bottom view" (and many eighteenth-century readers would have made a ribald joke of it) reveals what *Concordia discors* implies: the struggle between a controlling sense of order and disorderly elements, in essence a world order unified by a history imagined through that "piercing" gaze. We can hear Denham's "Cooper's Hill" here representing the Thames through images of contained masculine sexuality: "Though deep, yet clear, though gentle, yet not dull / Strong without rage, without ore-flowing full."[37]

Harmony, harmonic justice, and happiness are mapped onto each other in this dissonant image, only to be undone as Blackstone's poet enters the discordant world of law practice. We are meant to desire Alexander Pope's "heav'n strung lyre," while Blackstone's reference to Edmund Waller and the diction he borrows from Denham suggest the larger cultural valence of harmony for Blackstone's world. For the eighteenth-century reader, harmony was not simply a matter of sweet sounds that signified congenial feelings but instead marked a system capable of organizing the post-Augustan understanding of politics and society in ways meant to ensure public happiness.[38] *Concordia discors*, the idea that contradictory principles could be aligned harmoniously, had been pressed into use as a way of explaining the cosmos, but also England's political and jurisprudential life. As Earl Wasserman has argued, it "came to be the cosmic rationale for England's parliamentary monarchy and the model for the ideal attributes of the king of such a mixed state: the political harmony arising from the conflict of monarch and populace is but an imitation of the cosmic harmony produced by the clash of the opposing elements."[39] *Concordia discors* theorized what harmony in poetry enacted: it allowed, even celebrated, the incorporation of elements that threatened its smooth surface. In Blackstone's hands, discordant images of law interrupt the smooth harmony associated with justice, and *Concordia discors* is almost undone by the discord represented by law practice.

What does the poem tell us about the emotions that circulated around law practice in Blackstone's time? In the poem, law is represented as discordant and unpleasant, both emotionally and physically, the antithesis of harmony. We are offered, for instance, what might seem a throwaway reference to the "babbling Hall," suggesting that Blackstone anchored the irritation, disgust, and fear he associated with urban law practice in embodied experience at Westminster Hall, a particularized, well-known, and nationally significant space. Today we do not think of Westminster Hall as particularly noisy, but as a monumental symbol of the majesty and permanence of English law. As Blackstone himself would later write in the *Commentaries* (he was complicit in establishing this myth), the establishment of Westminster Hall as "some certain place" to locate the law of the kingdom ended the long battle between "foreign" law and what he felt to be far superior, the common law of England. Westminster Hall, he argued, "soon raised those laws to that pitch of perfection, which they suddenly attained under the auspices of our English Justinian, King Edward the First" (I:23). But in the "Lawyer's Farewel," Westminster Hall serves as a metaphor for the unpleasant noise of the modern, and the fear and disgust that noise evoked. There Blackstone dreaded encountering the "sounds uncouth and accents dry" as well as the uproar of the city, its "loose revelry and riot," sounds that penumbraed out to embrace not only all the noisiness and ugliness of legal thought and practice during his era, but the noisiness of a new urban world of overpopulation, of too much talk, too many controversial print publications, and too much conflict.

As legal historian David Lemmings remarks in his characteristically understated fashion, "the grandeur, solemnity, and dignity which are normally associated with modern high court proceedings were probably not the prevailing emotions in Westminster Hall during the eighteenth century."[40] Instead, this setting provoked frustration, irritation, and anxiety as well as excitement. Maintaining order in the midst of the noise seems to have been a daunting task. The Hall's numerous courts operated simultaneously, in close proximity to each other and at best separated by the thinnest of partitions and curtains only a few feet high. Crowds exacerbated the noise: the Hall was full of all sorts of folks unconnected to the law, as well as the usual barristers, ushers calling out to witnesses, witnesses waiting for hours and days, and even hangers-on called "men of straw," those who would wear a straw in their shoes to advertise their willingness to give false testimony.[41] Peers, the clergy, and members of Parliament used the Hall as a passageway, while others came in to get warm, to watch, or sometimes to steal from those who were watching. Oddly (at least to modern expectations), the walls were lined with shops in open stalls, selling books and other wares. A 1730 painting by Gravelot depicting these shops is accompanied by a verse claiming Westminster Hall as the "house of babel" where "jargon and noise prevail."[42] As Tom Brown noted in 1702, Westminster Hall was "a magnificent building which is open to all the world, and yet in a manner is shut up, by the prodigious concourse of people, who crowd and sweat to get in or out. What a fantastical jargon does this heap of contrarieties amount to."[43] "Babel," "jargon," "noise," a "heap of contrarieties," people who "crowd and sweat": while we cannot hear the noises of the past or feel the bodies, we can imagine the aversive nature of this environment.[44] No wonder the poem urges us to seek the harmony associated with justice.

The poem does not, in the end, suggest that harmony rules or that justice is obtainable. In the final stanza, the poet-lawyer withdraws into retirement, still haunted by the discordant sounds of law practice. Thus, the poem presents us with an unresolved problem. Harmonic justice is a tremendously seductive idea. But if harmonic justice is what we desire, we will despair when we confront the gap between what we want and what exists. English law and legal practice are unpleasant; they result in human misery. The idea of natural and eternal laws offered up in Justice's one monumental book ("unfold with joy her sacred page"), and with it the hope that law's unpleasant discordant elements could be reduced to "one harmonious rule of right," appealed to Blackstone precisely because it was so distant from the practice of law in mid-century England.[45] It is the project of this book to explore how the traces of an affective aesthetics outlined in this early poem served to help Blackstone reimagine the aesthetic and emotional world of eighteenth-century English law. The alignment of English law with harmonic justice offered an effective, compelling way to organize his legal material around an admirable ideal. While harmonic justice did not offer an escape from the emotional, embodied world of law that Blackstone found after leaving literature, it did offer a scaffolding for his efforts to balance tradition against change, precedent against contingencies. And it helped Blackstone organize the nexus of emotions that I refer to here as "legal emotions," emotions that helped readers make sense of both the *Commentaries* and their attachment to English law.

Taking Care of Blackstone: An Interdisciplinary Methodology

This project emerged from both large-scale and narrowly focused questions. First, the large-scale: a long-held curiosity about group loyalty. Given the emotional turmoil most humans experience, what holds high-functioning societies together? In particular, why do people who have little or no investment in and receive minimal returns from a particular national legal system tend to obey the law? Deterrence theories are hardly satisfying; clearly the threat of punishment alone is not enough to ensure lawful behavior. Every person cannot be managed by a universal regulatory force, even in the most panoptic culture. And in fact, most people break the law at least once in a while—even in fairly well-regulated societies. But most people in well-managed societies obey the law most of the time. Why? The answer to this question is, of course, complex, but it seems to be primarily emotional. Through various public and private interactions between legal systems and human beings, most human beings internalize a desire for law-abiding behavior because they rely on the law's relationship to justice. They learn to love justice and to associate the law with justice, and are, in a sense, "bound" to justice ideals. For them, the law becomes "normative," as Tom Tyler puts it: they obey the law because they "feel the law is just" and they "feel that the authority enforcing the law has the right to dictate behavior."[46] Following this line of scholarship, what John Deigh calls "an emotion-based account of the law's authority,"[47] as I do in this book, focuses more on persuasion than force, although there is always the threat of force behind persuasive juridical gestures.

Informed by affect studies, the history of emotion, and new efforts to study the relationship between law and emotion, but also by the relatively capacious and recently developed Law and Humanities movement, this book crosses disciplinary and historical boundaries in its conception and methodology, stretching from eighteenth-century England to the Colonies, the early Republic and to contemporary matters. My approach addresses a gap that results from powerful if sometimes porous disciplinary constraints. While there are always exceptions and offshoots in any discipline, traditional legal historians tend to focus on empirical, doctrinal, legal, and historical truths; literary critics focus primarily on literary texts and tend to see legal texts as sources of information rather than subjects for interpretation; political philosophers have historically operated at a comparatively abstract, decontextualized level; law and literature scholars take up issues involving the impact of law on literature or vice versa; law and emotion scholars scrutinize normative understandings of emotion with largely instrumental goals in mind. To imagine these disciplinary constraints differently, the question for the legal historian might be, *What was the doctrine?* For the legal scholar, *Given what we know, what should the law do?* For the historian of emotion, *How did they feel? What evidence is there for a particular emotion?* For the law and literature scholar, *Where is the law in this literary text, the literary in this legal text?* For the literary critic interested in emotion, *How does this text produce this particular feeling or encourage the reader to try out this particular feeling?* For the law and emotions scholar, *How are particular emotions expressed and how do they play into legal decision-making?* Law and Humanities scholarship draws on and also bridges these disciplinary divides and allows us to ask, *Given its historical and contemporary context, what does this text do to produce this particular feeling about the law and what does this tell us about the pursuit of justice?*[48]

As a major figure of the Enlightenment who profoundly influenced how a wide audience understood Enlightenment law, Blackstone did more than merely persuade people to follow the law. He was engaged in a sophisticated exploration of the appropriate emotions one should have in regard to the law, and not only to individual laws, but to the entire fabric of the English common law. This was part of the much larger English Enlightenment project that promoted English values as a sign of national identity and British morals as a sign of civility.[49] Blackstone took part in all of the advances and advanced all of the problems and contradictory movements that arose from Enlightenment thought.[50] This intermingling of Enlightenment accomplishments and contradictions is captured in the phrase "legal emotions," meant to be double-edged, implying both the emotions associated with law in Blackstone's England and those regulated by the law. To explore this double-edged line of inquiry, I have drawn fluidly from approaches rooted in textual analysis while taking into account generic and cultural contextualization.[51] My work brings together humanist critique, an attentiveness to how we read, a sensitivity to history, and an alertness to the entanglement of aesthetics, emotion, and law. I try to tease out the emotions of the past through examining textual references to emotions in not only their legal context, but their literary and cultural and philosophical contexts. Along the way, I rely on several different modes of interpretation or what are known as "ways of reading," much discussed among literary historians and critics, perhaps less so in other fields. Methodological flexibility is important in part because Blackstone has been radically under-read or even not read at all. Often the *Commentaries* is milked for quotations out of context. Frequently, it is read for its truth value, as if it represented a transparent window into the common law. Casual readers (or those looking for an apt legal quotation to support a point) may fail to realize that what Blackstone produced was not an authoritative treatise for advanced practitioners, but what he called "a general map of the law," a basic introductory guide to the law meant for "students of all ranks and professions," for an audience not only of beginning law students but of many groups of people who might never go into law practice (I:34, 36). The *Commentaries* then should be thought of as a pedagogical exercise, a text for those who would manage estates or go into the professions—maybe law, but also the clergy or the military. Thus, it presents a highly mediated account of the common law of England, one that goes beyond the trope of "representation" so often relied upon by literary critics or the "primary source evidence" that historians speak of, instead to create what Nathan Hensley has called a "productive reconfiguration" and a "critical recoding operation."[52] This does not mean it is not true or not "real," but rather that it hovers between the true and the sort of true, the real and the unreal, the evidentiary and the imaginary, like all depictions of law. Law is always already mediated by its representations, whether those are performed (a clod of earth being passed to a new owner representing the transfer of real property); narrated (the story told about that passing of the clod); treated as custom (a legal requirement that the clod of earth be passed); or become the subject of a lengthy book that attempts to capture all of England's legal history in four volumes. In the case of the *Commentaries*, we find mediation all the way down: what we get is an elaborated, much mediated condensation of previously mediated texts. It is an authoritative mediation, though, one that many have treated as the final word on eighteenth-century English law.

I often read Blackstone appreciatively. I am enchanted.[53] He accomplished something that few could have done and none before him had managed. But this does not preclude critique. In fact, my investment in Blackstone came first from the exercise of what Eve Sedgwick has famously called "the hermeneutics of suspicion."[54] Blackstone staged the contradictions that would appear in his own text, noting early on in the first volume that the study of the law as a science might result in "improving its method, retrenching its superfluities, and reconciling the little contrarieties, which the practice of many centuries will necessarily create in any human system" (I:30).[55] Reading the *Commentaries* for "little contrarieties" reveals nothing "little," but instead vast yawning gaps between the claims Blackstone made for the English common law system and his descriptions of how the law actually worked. Given the claim that liberty was the foundation of English law, what are we to make of English restrictions on women's liberty or its tolerance for slavery? How are we to understand a legal system developed to "the pitch of perfection" that claimed tenderness when it was about to torture a defendant? Casting these fissures as "symptoms" could have led to a methodological dead end, to obvious questions and obvious condemnations, to a Benthamite casting aside of the *Commentaries* as sheer hypocrisy, to what Hensley has critiqued as criticism in a "heroic mode." But these "little contrarieties" turn out to signify emotionally driven, ideological, and moral conundrums in need of detangling and explanation. In making contradictory claims, Blackstone alerts us to disruptions in the smooth surface he wished to make of English common law, disruptions that call out for analysis rather than dismissal. For all that he wanted readers to love the English common law and identify it with a particular understanding of justice that he thought justified such love, he recognized the law as a human creation driven by human emotions as well as by failed human efforts at rationality.

As I have read and reread Blackstone, I have looked for the way his "little contrarieties" intersect with emotions, how they arouse different emotions or attempt to control or negate them. In other words, in a work of exceptional clarity, what do the muddy parts tell us? In doing so, I have become more interested in what Blackstone was doing than in what he was unable to do. He could not paper over the inconsistencies in the English common law, but he could attempt to create emotional bonds between his readers and their legal system. Thus, my reading has become what might be called a sympathetic critique, more curatorial than adversarial, as interested in understanding Blackstone's creative use of emotions as in the usual critical moves. By "curatorial" here I mean to invoke the idea of care: I want, as Hensley puts it, "to restore a positive affective relation" towards my object of study.[56] Mine is thus in part a recovery project. I advocate for Blackstone's centrality in the canon of eighteenth-century prose works, while recognizing his limitations and internal contradictions, including his concern with maintaining hierarchies and justifying an unjust status quo. But the curatorial effort always gestures towards more than "care." It interferes; it is invasive in that it rearranges its objects and points to certain of their features, in essence exclaiming, "Look at this! Look at that!" and "That's how it is!"[57] To the extent that curators create maps towards a better understanding of the objects they arrange, they also un-map, disrupting whatever arrangement they have encountered, displaying it anew, and creating new knowledge as they do so.[58] Blackstone curated the English common law in order to argue that it had reached the "pitch of perfection." Through this action, he invented new knowledge. Thus, to curate Blackstone, bringing into focus the emotionally driven social and cultural arrangements he so skillfully constructed, and thus to create new knowledge as he did himself, seems both a disruptive and a sympathetic approach, even a *just* way to read him, in the sense that Cornel West speaks of justice as "what love looks like in public."

To pursue this kind of curatorial reading, I have drawn on techniques more familiar to literary critics than to legal historians or historians of emotion. As I indicated in the reading of Blackstone's poetry earlier in this introduction, I pay close attention to both macrocosmic and microcosmic forms (the macro and micro suggesting forms themselves). "Forms, measured forms, are everything," Melville says ironically in *Billy Budd*.[59] And while they may not be everything, as some readings of Billy Budd attest, no one could read Blackstone without noticing his preoccupation with form. Whether he is writing a poem or prose, drawing on the imagery of a walled enclosure like a gothic castle or writing a long, periodic sentence meant to hammer diversity into alignment, Blackstone is a consummate formalist. Attentiveness to form suggests analysis on the level of the set of four volumes, but also on the level of each volume, its chapters, its paragraphs, sentences, and individual words. Paradoxically, it also involves reading surfaces: Blackstone has been so under-read that few have noticed how hard he works to appeal to readers.[60] I offer sustained attention to metaphors, symbols, and to the way details and doctrines are presented. This sort of reading and what it brings to formal analysis has only recently become more fashionable in literary studies. But as critics as diverse as Caroline Levine and Eugenie Brinkema have argued, close reading "was always the way to unlock potentialities," even when it has seemed constrained to demonstrations of the unity and integration of canonical works of literature.[61] And the study of form, of "structural patterns and organizational modes," of "the various shapes language takes" when under pressure, offers insights into both the contradictions and confluences a text can offer.[62] Forms "shape what it is possible to think, say, and do so in a given context," Levine points out.[63] They are not static, but instead can be assembled and disassembled, remade, retrofitted to suit different contexts and purposes. An analysis of form thus has special value not only for literary criticism but for understanding social arrangements, both for how they operate and how they can be changed. This connection between form and social change can help inform our understanding of legal culture. It is no accident that Levine relies on legal theorist Roberto Unger for the argument that social life is not dictated by a few intractable deep structures, but instead by multiple sets of forms, all jostling each other. Understanding

forms draws attention to "the artificiality and contingency of social arrangements and so opens up a new set of opportunities for real change
by way of feasible rearrangements."[64]

Across the chapters in this book, I have explored the role of emotions in creating attachment and resistance to a particular version of
justice, to its aesthetics as well as its maxims. Doing so has entailed
navigating the emotional lexicon, determining what precisely I should
call the broad phenomenon I am discussing as well as its discrete mani-
festations. I am alert to emotion historian Thomas Dixon's concerns:
the keyword "emotion" is indeed "in crisis," as he has argued in a recent essay. Blackstone and his contemporaries would not have used the
word "emotion" as historians and theorists of emotion use it today: they
would have used "passion" or "interest" or "moral sentiment."[65] I have,
however, aligned my practice with other historians of emotion, choosing
the more modern "emotion" to indicate the sorts of feelings I discuss.
Meanwhile, I have attempted to put specific emotions in their historical context: "embarrassment," for example, when used in eighteenth-
century England meant something different from (but related to) what
it means today. "Disgust," though often felt, was only beginning to be
called by that name. A second concern—the distinction between "affect"
and "emotion"—has also called for reflection. While affect theory has
been important to my analysis, the reservation of the word "affect" for
"something immediate and automatic and resistant taking place outside
of language," as Brinkema so succinctly puts it, has seemed as limiting
as a decision not to use the word at all.[66] Affect effects have directed my
interpretive gestures here, but like many historians of emotion, I have
chosen to blur the philosophical and theoretical distinctions between
"affect" and "emotion," while suggesting that they operate along a continuum in which affect is more oriented towards the body (but not prior
to and outside of language and thus impervious to interpretive gestures)
and emotion is more mediated by culture and community.[67]

I have gone emotion-hunting with the tools at my disposal: contextual reading, surface reading, close reading, reading for form, curatorial reading, historiography (both general and legal), post-structuralist
theory, and psychoanalytic theory. These technologies of reading have
made it possible to read Blackstone for his emotional valence, for what
we might call his affect effects, to make an emotional sense at times of

what has not seemed to make sense if law is thought of as purely rational. Assiduous hunting often yields its quarry: I have found emotions everywhere, on the surface of the text, buried deep in doctrinal details, in words, in sentences, paragraphs, and volumes, sometimes presented as clichés or conventions—and yet repeated enough to suggest something more than cliché, something both formal and formative and thus worthy of attention. Attentiveness to the genres of romance, comedy, tragedy, and the gothic has alerted me to the ways we are expected to feel about marriage law, property, torture, and the laws around slavery. Placing Blackstone's public performances in a theatrical context has suggested new ways of thinking about the relationship between law's performances and the usefulness of public embarrassment. Noting the narrative structures that underlie Blackstone's defense of the English law's unity has revealed how he wants us to feel about that unity and about its Englishness.

In a different register, the various strategies offered by both historians of emotion and affect theorists have come into play here.[68] One might associate Blackstone's effort to institute particular emotional responses to particular legal situations with Norbert Elias's theory of gradual development. Elias imagines an ever-progressive movement towards a more civilized culture in which violent and passionate emotions are channeled through the legal system, gentled and domesticated along the way. But this would ignore a Gikandi-influenced understanding of the interdependence of civility and brutality during this period, one displayed multiple times in the *Commentaries* and discussed in detail in chapter 5. William Reddy's idea of emotional regimes and refuges, with the theory that cultures dictate certain emotional norms, relegating others to the outskirts, also seems to explain "legal emotions" in the sense that they often seem compelled. But Blackstone's efforts seem as oriented towards the creation of community as to the policing of emotion, as interested in persuasion as they are in regulation. Thus, while you will see echoes of Reddy here, Barbara H. Rosenwein's concept of coexisting, various "emotional communities," and Monique Scheer's interesting work on emotional practices inflect this work as well.[69] Emotions are embodied; they are, as Scheer argues, "themselves a form of practice" in which subjectivity appears not prior to but "in the doing of emotion."[70] In this "doing," they are contagious, as both eighteenth-century moral philosophers such as David Hume and Adam Smith and current affect theorists such as Lauren Berlant and Sara Ahmed have argued. We catch them from others as we attune ourselves to the emotions around us; we experience them when they are performed for us; we feel them through our reading but also as we read. They are also shaped by our environments and social settings: they "encompass a learned, culturally specific, and habitual distribution of attention to 'inner' processes of thought, feeling, and perception."[71] In reading Blackstone we experience this shaping both on the surface of the text and in its deep structures, its congruencies and its contradictions. Blackstone—a consummate emotional manager—uses emotions to focus our attention and in doing so attempts to teach us how we are supposed to feel about English law as an agent of justice.[72]

Law and Emotion and . . .

My reading of Blackstone is rooted in eighteenth-century studies, yet explores the relationship between justice, genre, and representation by working across fields and periods, locating its concerns very specifically in Blackstone's time and place, but also drawing out their implications across historical eras and the transatlantic. As such, the project joins other post-Rawlsian analyses in that it analyzes our feelings about justice not as abstractions, but as socially and culturally constructed and situated.[73] As mentioned earlier, one special feature of the Law and Humanities movement is the merging of methodologies: in this book, the sort of close reading associated with literary history comes together with an appreciation for the relevance of history to present practices and problems. In this regard, I engage in one of the fundamental tasks of the Law and Humanities movement: the effort to examine affective and aesthetic attachments to justice through analyzing culturally embedded narratives in ways that illuminate current preoccupations and practices.

This book begins with desire and ends with a critique of happiness, organizing chapters around specific emotions that link to each other thematically. As Sara Ahmed points out, emotions often create the conditions for new ways of feeling or for the recognition of a layering of emotion: "Our love might create the condition for our grief, our loss could become the condition for our hate, and so on."[74] Such shifts suggest various emotively directed narratives such as that from love to loss, from embarrassment to the need to dominate others through terror, from the assertion of power through terrorizing the public to the recognition that a realm of potential happiness has been lost. Thus, these chapters lead us through a range of the emotions expressed in the *Commentaries*, but also build interrelated narratives: one around the contrast between Blackstone's harmonic idealization of justice and the "little contrarieties" of the common law that he negotiates; a second around the shift from oral to print culture that made the *Commentaries* essential for the study of law; another around nation and empire as Blackstone's text is pressed into service to disseminate English ideas of justice across the globe; and a fourth about the almost osmotic absorption of Blackstone's ideals as his book gradually became not something read, but an icon for a set of internalized values naturalized across much of the West. My reading is not meant to be exhaustive, but rather to provide proof of concept for future work by scholars interested in the history of emotion and eighteenth-century legal history. Thus, each chapter foregrounds a particular emotional matrix as it relates to a particular legal issue while the book as a whole makes no attempt at coverage. To fully address the emotions Blackstone drew on in writing the *Commentaries* is not the work of one scholar, but of many.

Chapter 1 begins with a question Wilkie Collins asked in his popular 1866 novel, *Armadale*: "Is there no love in Blackstone?" By examining various "zones of desire" and "zones of disgust," first in Blackstone's poetry and then in the *Commentaries*, the chapter unpacks Blackstone's reliance on these twinned emotions as instrumental to his efforts to construct a new understanding of and loyalty to the English common law. Marriage law and Orientalism are interrelated here with a discussion of Blackstone's celebration of the trial as a unique English contribution to justice. In these discussions, desire and disgust worked together to suggest an English legal tradition able to accommodate the forces of commodification and expansion that defined modernity. In chapter 2, I examine the flip side of desire, loss, and this leads to a reading of Blackstone's melancholic assessment of the gaps in the English legal historical record as an extended elegy in the graveyard poets' tradition. In his analysis of real property, Blackstone reifies traditions that reinforce lineage and the retention of estates across multiple generations. His preservation of remnants of Saxon property law stands in for the preservation of property as a concept; that property would forever be attached to a genetic heritage would seem an attempt to thwart not only the mortality of the human body, but the mortality of the English common law system.

Chapter 3 operates as a hinge that allows us to see how Blackstone's own embarrassment marked the importance of the *Commentaries* as a written text, a materialized object that came to symbolize the permanence and reliability of written law. Blackstone's "diffidence," his deficiencies as an orator, operated as legible affective signs of discomfort with the orally based theatricality of legal practice. Reading Blackstone's expressive body as a text in itself available for scrutiny in the famous libel case *Onslow v. Horne* (1770) suggests that although Blackstone's "stuttering" affect in Westminster Hall may have seemed to undermine his authority, it instead played a symbolic role in the global dissemination of the *Commentaries*. The inadequacy of his authentic but imperfect performance shifted attention to the text where Blackstone could perfect his style, if not always his content.

Chapters 4 and 5 press historically contingent readings of the *Commentaries* into service for their value in understanding present-day injustice. In chapter 4, I again take up one of Blackstone's contrarieties: the law is never so "tender" as when it contemplates torture. Here I examine what Blackstone referred to as "the tenderness of the law" in light of the English practice of *peine forte et dure* (pressing). By gothicizing his discussion of what was a common English, not French, practice, Blackstone attempts but fails to distance ideas of English justice from the European acceptance of torture. Buried beneath the surface of his text are experiences such as those of Nathaniel Hawes, a young rebel robber "persuaded" to comply with the law through the judicial application of *peine forte et dure*. Blackstone's treatment of *peine forte et dure* offers analogies to recent US discussions of torture at Guantanamo Bay, but also provides an opening for what has in recent years become a new understanding of the value of tenderness as a legal standard.

I pursue that direction in chapter 5, where I circle back to the harmonic justice so much desired in both Blackstone's early poem and in the *Commentaries*, suggesting that its allure is marred by its association with tyranny, with its intolerance for deviations from form. The happiness it promises is undone by Blackstone's efforts to control contingency, as demonstrated by his ambivalent and shifting position on slavery and the uses his text served in the American colonies and later in the young republic. To pretend that harmonic justice could preserve liberty as a major value becomes a form of what Lauren Berlant has called "cruel optimism," in that the promise of liberty was undermined by later equivocations and then undone by the American amendments to the *Commentaries*. Blackstone's reach is demonstrated through a reading of Harper Lee's *To Kill a Mockingbird*, the canonical American novel that has been hailed for its advocacy for racial equality. In the novel, former slaves learn to read from the *Commentaries* as Lee celebrates Blackstone's claims for liberty as a fundamental value of the English common law. But the irony inherent in this argument is as cruel as the cruel optimism Blackstone inspired. The novel inspires not racial justice, but complacent acceptance of glacially slow change in which gradualism cloaks the most brutal racism. Difference here is represented as deformity and deformity is erased by the end of the novel, replaced with a false sense of ease and comfort.

I end with a brief coda that takes up the value of sympathy in the context of resistance. Inspired by Mary Wollstonecraft's agitated reaction to Blackstone, I reread agitation as a trigger for sympathetic review in light of a recent Texas case in which an agitated defendant undermined the court's "decorum." Wollstonecraft was quieted by an early death and the cultural suppression of her work; the Texas defendant discussed in this coda was silenced by the administration of seizure-inducing electric shocks. Both Wollstonecraft and the Texas defendant, the hapless Terry Lee Morris, offered threats to the formal trappings of justice, to its harmonic balance, or to what was termed "decorum" in the Texas case. We can draw on these moments to examine our emotions around the forms that justice takes. Read a bit askew, decorum seems to be just another name for harmonic justice, agitation another word for resistance.

Alison Young argues that to write of law as poetry, "as if law were art," undermines "the standard hierarchy whereby law is able to govern and regulate artistic production."[75] The same might be said for the relationship between law and emotion. We imagine law as regulating art, and in a less doctrinal but much more fundamental way, governing emotion. But in Blackstone, law, art, and emotion are inextricable; art rules law as much as law rules art and both are channeled through the embodied desires and emotions that we generally abject. On the whole, this approach offers hope for the future because it makes visible a rich archive evidencing the irrepressible human drive towards justice as well as the desire to understand it. While the desire for justice may be thwarted, diverted into other channels, cloaked by substitutions and dismissals, my analysis reveals this desire always at work, always purposefully seeking justice. That Blackstone was committed to that ideal in the context of the emotive life of a people helps explain the influence of the *Commentaries*, but also suggests new ways of thinking about emotion in legal contexts. Blackstone's construction of justice as harmonic and his application of that construction to English law suggests the power of the harmonic metaphor for our understanding of one way the law might work, while also revealing it as a metaphor, a human construction that can be changed. We can seek better and fairer metaphors and thus a better, more inclusive form of justice by viewing our loyalty to forms with suspicion, and instead paying more attention to how emotions work, and to what they can motivate us to do.

1

What's Love Got to Do with It?

Desire, Disgust, and the Ends of Marriage Law

One might think that no genre could be further from law
than romance.
—Susan Sage Heinzelman, *Riding the Black Ram: Law,
Literature, and Gender*, xi

In Wilkie Collins's sensation novel *Armadale*, published almost one
hundred years after the *Commentaries* became available in print, we
find Blackstone, or at least his book, playing a cameo role. In a novel full
of evil doers, Collins's two most innocent and likeable characters meet
in a garden, zone of desire, to peruse the *Commentaries*, the one book
that seems "likely to repay [them] . . . for the trouble of looking into
it."[1] Perhaps having read too many sensationalist novels, Collins's sweet
character, Neelie, has suddenly begun to wonder whether her "contem-
plated elopement was an offense punishable by the Law" and whether
this punishment might result in her lover, Allan, being imprisoned or,
even worse, having his hair cut off. "Hang the law! . . . Let's risk it!" her
lover says, but Neelie, resolute, demands that they "find out the law for
ourselves."[2] Into this rich and hilarious scene ("It's no laughing matter,"
proclaims Neelie), Collins has Allan deliver volume I of Blackstone's
Commentaries in lieu of the "wheelbarrow" full of law books Neelie
demands. "It can't be any harder than music," Neelie says, as the two
meet in the park for their legal study session.[3]

Neelie approaches the problem with all the comic rationality that
Collins can muster, pulling out a "smart little pocketbook and pencil"
and creating two columns: "Good" and "Bad." "'Good' means where the
law is on our side," she says, "and 'Bad' means where the law is against
us." (The "Bad" column is what Collins later refers to as "the depressing
side.")[4] But she has trouble keeping Allan on task; his desire for her is

27

greater than his desire for the law. "Don't look at me—look at Blackstone and begin," she admonishes him.[5] The *Commentaries* itself becomes eroticized as the young lovers reach above and around the book towards each other. Still, between stealing kisses, Allan falls "headlong" not into love, but "into the bottomless abyss of the English Law," becoming hopelessly confused by Blackstone's first premise: "Our law considers marriage in no other light than as a civil contract." "Is there nothing about Love?" asks Neelie. "Look a little lower down." But Allan finds "not a word. He sticks to his confounded 'Contract' all the way through." When Allan does discover some relevant passages, they offer no help. Instead they refer to obstacles to marriage, to what Blackstone calls "disabilities" and "incapacities."[6] Finally, Allan comes to a dead stop at the requirement that minors must have the "consent of the father" in order to marry, leading Neelie to jot in her "pocketbook," "Our marriage is impossible, unless Allan commits perjury."[7] At this moment, the two lovers face each other, "across the insuperable obstacle of Blackstone, in speechless dismay," as Collins presses the *Commentaries* into service as a sign of law's repression, its reductive qualities, and its allegiance to a cold, inhuman rationality rather than to human emotion.[8]

In the scene, Allan and Neelie pivot: their desire for the law turns to disgust even when "looking a little lower down" (a not-very-veiled reference to the body) reveals nothing about love. But Collins's chapter title, "Love and Law" (one might have expected the binary, "Love OR Law"), suggests a more complex interaction. Collins juggles multiple registers here, shifting from the sexual to the institutional as he examines the contrast between human desire with its passion and frailty and institutionalized legal systems.[9] In Collins's garden scene, the *Commentaries*, personified as "Blackstone," seems at first a blunt obstacle to desire, youth, speech, love, and harmonious relations among people. In conventional romances, authors use floods, fires, pirates, and parents to keep lovers apart, create suspense, and delay closure; here Collins assigns the *Commentaries* this role. As such, the *Commentaries* seems to operate as a final, closed "Chinese box," an unassailable text, standing against human relations, against interaction, against understanding, rather than yielding cooperatively to interpretation. But Collins's chapter title—with its expressive "and"—as well as the novel's larger plot, suggest that we try to pry open that box a bit, for it is only through the operations of law that the events of the novel are finally resolved, that evil is sorted out from good (the "bad" and the "good" turn out to apply to more than Blackstone's text), and that the novel's marriage plot eventually comes to its "natural" conclusion. Thus, if we read Collins's depiction of "Blackstone" as merely an obstacle to love, or even as the obstacle that keeps love alive, we miss much of the point. Blackstone here operates as an emotional touchstone: the book (as a signifier for the law) creates a zone of desire, then becomes an object of disgust, but finally functions as a sort of holding environment, a capacious container where unruly emotions can be managed, or as Blackstone might have said, harmonized. How are Allan and Neelie seduced into thinking that Blackstone can solve their problems? As I discuss later in this chapter, Blackstone carefully cultivated the belief that the *Commentaries* could satisfy the human desire for closure, harmony, and happiness. This belief, seductive and beguiling, keeps Collins's characters reading, seeking, and desiring right up to the moment of their pivot—at which point, even the ever-optimistic Allan exclaims disgustedly, "There must be other ways of marrying, besides this roundabout way, that ends in a Publication and a *Void*. Infernal gibberish!"[10] In noting the "Void" at the center of desire, Collins could hardly have chosen words more indicative of the problems not just Neelie and Allan, but all desiring humans experience: desire ends at the void; it operates as a fantasy of completion and wholeness that exceeds human possibility. In an effort to fulfill their mutual desire, Neelie and Allan have fallen for the promise Blackstone's *Commentaries* seems to offer, only to be disappointed and finally disgusted with his account of the law. Their disgust creates aversion, a need for distance. Thus, Allan's next step is not to read further in Blackstone, but to accommodate that aversion: he distances himself from direct exposure to the law by going to London to consult with his lawyers. The entire scene is highly ironized; Collins provides a bit of omniscient narration that undermines any promises Blackstone might seem to have offered, instead emphasizing the role of disgust in the encounter with law: "Here again, in this, as in all other *human* instances, the widely *discordant* elements of the grotesque and the terrible were forced together by that subtle law of contrast which is one of the laws of mortal life. . . . The study of the law of marriage . . . was nothing less than a burlesque in itself!"[11] The "human" with its intimations of the human body, the "discordant" with its reference to music, the "laws of mortal life": all conflict with the lovers' naïve idealistic desire that Blackstone provide something "good," something no harder than music (but apparently, something *like* music), something to advance their felt connection to each other. What Collins tags as burlesque is "the study of the law of marriage," and with it not so much Blackstone or his characters' naïve belief in the *Commentaries*, but the contrast between the idealization of English law as an aid to communal human relations and the actual reading of the law as "grotesque and terrible," in short, disgusting.

Throughout, Collins relies on the "formal conventions" of both desire and disgust to motivate his characters. Lauren Berlant lays out the conventional attributes of desire: the recognition of a void, the making of promises that nurture the desire to fill that void, the breaking of such promises, all with the aim of creating the next desire, which again can never be satisfied.[12] Berlant, of course, has taken as her subject "desire and love," not disgust. But a full understanding of desire's conventions involves desire's corollary, that equally embodied and primitive emotion of disgust. Generally described as a physicalized aversion to substances that might make us ill, like parasites, decaying food, and decaying bodies, disgust has in its modern form become a moral emotion, here exercised as aversion against the "discordant," the "grotesque and terrible" words of the law. Desire and disgust are "counterparts," as Winfried Menninghaus, author of *Disgust: The Theory and History of a Strong Sensation*, argues, in that desire involves "a nearness that is wanted" while disgust "is the experience of a nearness that is not wanted."[13] Erotic desires must suspend disgust; when erotic desire ends, disgust can take over. But the relationship between desire and disgust may be closer than Menninghaus suggests. Disgust often arises unexpectedly to stand between us and what we desire: we desire excellent food, we are disgusted if maggots infest it; we desire the body of the beloved, we are disgusted by the physicality of the beloved; we desire the living body of deceased, we are disgusted by bodily decomposition. We are even, at times, disgusted by a surfeit of desire, when getting what we want turns out to be more than we ever wanted. Collins's characters temporarily suspend their disgust for the law in order to pursue their desires, but disgust returns in full at the moment of their disappointment. The recalcitrant text, "Blackstone," thus becomes the locus of both desire and disgust as it entices these readers, but then fails to satisfy them. In failing as an object of desire, it serves recursively as the cause of desire itself as the lovers' disgusted disappointment only creates new and shifting desires that link these desiring subjects to new objects.

Armadale here spotlights a moment when desire appears embattled, blocked by "Blackstone," and by the hyper-rationality of the law. It reveals as well a common way of reading Blackstone, not as a pedagogical summary of English law or as an effort to map English law onto universal conceptions of justice, but as the authoritative last word, as offering a direct entry into the actuality of law itself instead of an intervention or shaping of diverse materials. But what if Neelie and Allan had continued looking "a little lower down," not down in the sexual sense though these passages are full of sexual innuendos, but down in the sense of into the past, and down also generically, from the respected legal tome that Blackstone's *Commentaries* became almost the moment it was published, down to "The Lawyer's Farewel," the short poem I discussed in the introduction to this book, written more than a decade before the *Commentaries*? By looking "a little lower down," they might have found not only the "something about love" that they sought, but an entire emotive-aesthetic zone constructed around desire and disgust, one that evokes the body and sexuality similarly, if less cleverly than Collins does in their fictional world.

My earlier discussion of this poem revealed Blackstone's deep allegiance to eighteenth-century poetic preoccupations with harmony, musicality, the couplet—with its focus on balance and steady rhythms—and *Concordia discors*, demonstrating how these concerns played out in an idealization of first, literature, and then, the justice-law continuum represented as "harmonic justice." As I briefly mentioned, Blackstone juggles desire and disgust, justice and law, suggesting that powerful desires—marked explicitly but not solely by sexual metaphors as in Collins's text—animate the most abstract of legal conceptions, while the law itself evokes disgust and thus undoes the workings of desire. The present chapter focuses on this representation of the contrast between the desire for harmonic justice and disgust for the law as experienced in the world, then takes this dynamic into the *Commentaries*, predictably enough to marriage law, but less predictably to issues involving the importance of the adversarial trial to the English common law system. In both of these arenas, Blackstone relies on desire and disgust to manage the central tension in any system of justice: that between certitude and contingency.

The Power of Desire

In season six of the television series *Charmed*, the Demon Gith (who seems to have been reading Deleuze and Guattari) reveals a central truth about the workings of desire: "Do you know how much energy is contained in an unfulfilled desire?!" he exclaims, while exploiting the charmed sisters' not-so-secret desires. Eventually Gith dies, consumed by an explosion of that twenty-first-century icon of capitalist desire, the SUV, but not before teaching the sisters to respect, but also to curb, their desires. The episode, like the series, stages the tensions displayed in Collins's novel, those between personal desires and "the law," figured as marriage law in Collins's novel and as "duties" in the show. Blackstone's poem "The Lawyer's Farewel" stages a similar tension, but suggests that simply curbing desires cannot offer resolution: in the poem, personal desires are figured through the young poet-lawyer protagonist's longing for literature, a longing that must be given up if the protagonist is to take up the more publicly acceptable desire for law. Thus, the poet-lawyer is forced to abandon literature, that "gay queen of fancy and of art,"[14] by a disciplinary tyranny that seems to pit literature and law against each other. But desires never simply abate: the structural logic and formal conventions of desire, the drivers of its energy and power, step in when the poet-lawyer looks "a little lower" to find a new, compensatory object of desire in "justice."[15] Blackstone's Justice (all caps in some versions) is "from vulgar sight retir'd, / like eastern queens" held in "winding close retreat," hidden in an apparently overgrown garden by a "thorny maze." Because she is veiled, she is "more admir'd."[16] This image is both familiar and odd: familiar in that justice is seen as unobtainable, hidden in the oft-used metaphoric "thorny maze" of the law,[17] and odd because while Justice had often been sexualized for satiric purposes,[18] here sexual imagery delineates an idealized and perfect justice. The eastern queen is approached through sexualized metaphors worthy of an adolescent poet: "Oh let me pierce the secret shade," the young poet-lawyer cries, to describe his desire for "the bottom view . . . deep and regularly true."[19] (As I noted in the introduction, this language would surely have made Blackstone's contemporaries—at least those who tended to look "a little lower"—laugh.) The poem draws on the erotic gaze, but also on internal bracketing to suggest what Berlant calls "an intensified zone of attachment,"[20] through the sequestration of Justice and the further sequestration of a secret writing on a "sacred page." Blackstone creates multiple obstacles—the thorny maze, a secret shade, and brackets both figurative and literal—between the desiring subject represented by the poet-lawyer and his love object. The imagery slips from one desired object to another, as Justice seems not only to *be* "the guardian of Britannia's law," but also to be *absorbed into or merged with* Britannia's law when the poet-lawyer imagines himself able to observe her as she "unfold[s] with joy her sacred page" (*Pamela*'s readers would have picked up on the erotic charge such a reading represented) where "mix'd, yet uniform, appears / The wisdom of a thousand years."[21] This seemingly illegible "wisdom of a thousand years" is doubly bracketed, enclosed in actual brackets while its stanza is itself both bracketed and interrupted by the poet-lawyer's desire to "pierce" in the first line, and Alfred's "piercing soul" in the last couplet. Throughout the poem, Blackstone emphasizes the expansive operations, the sheer inventive energy of desire, represented through rapid substitutions: "sacred page" for "eastern queen," "countless wheels" for "sacred page," and finally "various laws to one great end" still tantalizingly illegible on that "sacred page." That ultimate object of desire, those "other doctrines" that form a "clear, deep, and regularly true" melding of law and justice, is never truly revealed, but only represented as the poet-lawyer's object of desire, as the perspective shifts from his view to Alfred's, one that "pervades, and regulates the whole." Readers (and the poet-lawyer) see this desired merging of justice with law only conditionally, only *through* desire, as "one harmonious rule of right" in which "countless wheels distinctly tend / by various laws to one great end."[22]

Those versed in twentieth- and twenty-first-century theories of desire will find multiple conventions familiar. Desire, as we might expect, is figured as lack, as directed towards a void that "exceeds representation," that "is only ever represented as a reflection on a veil."[23] It wanders uneasily from image to image, first sexual, then oriented around the need to know, first capacious, then rebelling against its boundaries, at one moment uncertain, watching from afar with "awe," at another "piercing," destructive and masterful. Shoshana Felman's famous discussion of desire, promising, and broken promises in her reading of *Don Juan* suggests that this is how desire works: we are promised much, but little is delivered.[24] Blackstone, like Don Juan in Felman's reading, ever leads us on, only to replace each disappointment with a new and more tantalizing image. The poet-lawyer yearns, but is never satisfied; even the image of the eastern queen, so often associated with excessive desire, luxury, ornamentation, and the mystery of the Orient, slips away, abandoned almost as soon as she is evoked for the even more mysterious "sacred page" of the book she holds—a book that in its own turn slips away, overshadowed by the "harmonious rule of right" with its "countless wheels" all turning "to one great end." Each time it is described, desire's object becomes unattainable: in the poem, the poet-lawyer finally and abruptly abandons even the alluring image of the "harmonious rule of right" with its unintentionally funny "one great end."[25] Shifting gears immediately in the next stanza, the poet-lawyer "welcomes" (but is really disgusted by) the depressing and tedious world of "business" that he associates with law practice, described earlier in the poem as one of discord, disease, bad air, and bad sounds, all associated with urban life and with the practice of law at "babbling" Westminster Hall.[26]

Marina Warner, in her magisterial study *Monuments and Maidens*, wryly notes both the difficulty and importance of rethinking sexualized images of justice, such as that of the eastern queen, "as figures of a divinely inspired social law, and not sexual fantasies," adding that, despite such difficulties, "it is worth trying."[27] But I want to linger for a moment on the eastern queen as sexualized object of desire, because I think it worth marking what we might call Blackstone's Orientalism as a container for the impossible and thwarted abstraction summed up in the concept of harmonic justice, for the desire that animated the *Commentaries* and contributed to its formal qualities as well as to decisions he made as to content. For Blackstone and other late Augustan poets, allegorical personifications felt like real presences that implied precise times and places as well as larger ideals.[28] In this poetic environment, an image such as that of the eastern queen was overdetermined: it shimmered with multiple meanings and associations, operating differently than a reasoned argument or even the most carefully described abstraction.

We respond to such images, as Richard K. Sherwin has argued, "quickly, holistically, and affectively."[29]

"You can't cross-examine an image," Martha Umphrey said at the 2010 Association of Law, Culture and Humanities conference. But what happens if we do "cross-examine" this image? In the poem, Blackstone exploits not only the features of this particular image, but the nature of images themselves, by addressing his readers obliquely with a throwaway line ("like eastern queens") that nevertheless becomes a central image in the poem. In choosing an "as if" descriptor, he gives us an image that is both there and not there simultaneously, utilizing a common convention of desire by tantalizing rather than satisfying readers. Thus, he encourages readers to paper over gaps, gaps between the words on the page and the image, between the concept of justice and its personification, but also between the rather strange image of the eastern queen and the more common yet still mysterious image of the "sacred page," and then the seemingly more material image of the "countless wheels," an image that is a bit threatening in that it replaces a human image with that of a machine. In short, through suggesting, but not fully relating, the story of a young poet-lawyer seduced by an eastern queen, and then through multiple substitutions, Blackstone operates seductively, hooking us with an evocative, sexualized image, promising something more seductive in a holistic and harmonious unified law-justice system, then leading us to the final image of countless wheels operating in perfect harmony.

If Blackstone had wanted to offer up a representative image for English justice, he could not have chosen a stranger one than the eastern queen. The eastern queen had many associations in eighteenth-century print culture, none of which easily mapped onto ideals of English justice. As Diane Hoeveler points out, the Oriental tale with its images of Algerian harems and captivity had become so common in the eighteenth century that "it essentially functioned as a blank screen onto which British authors could project their own particular political, social, religious, or sexual anxieties."[30] Writ large, the image of the eastern queen speaks of excessive desire, for goods, for sex, but also for union with an almost unimaginable radical difference. Some accounts offer a relatively benign view of a beautiful woman, surrounded by luxury, a Cleopatra "laden with money, and magnificent presents of all kinds," as John Aikin does in his *General Biography*.[31] Detailing the luxury goods associated with harem queens seemed to have its own poetics. Lady Mary Wortley Montagu's famous depiction of "sultanas" focused on luxury and goods: "This I am very sure of, that no European queen has had the quantity, and the Empress's jewels (though very fine) would look very mean near hers. . . . The knives were of gold, the hafts set with diamonds, but the piece of luxury that grieved my eyes was the tablecloth and napkins, which were all tiffany embroidered with silks and gold in the finest manner."[32] Other references bring excessive sexuality and loose morality to these images of wealth. For example, in *The Secret History of the Loose and Incestuous Loves of Pope Gregory VII* (1722), a character sends a potential lover "a quantity of Pearls and Jewels sufficient to adorn an Eastern Queen," while in Delarivier Manley's *The Adventures of Rivella* (1725), Tim Double's deceitful betrothed demonstrates "all the pomp and splendour of an Eastern Queen; but her pride working to excessive Height, soon turn'd her brain."[33] *Oberon, a Poem* gives us a Sylvia, known to frequent many men, whose "face, in all its parts, was seen / Far to surpass the Eastern Queen."[34] Sometimes eastern queens are represented as desiring subjects themselves, as eastern harems, sexuality, desire, the world of goods, and even prostitution are all conflated with female desire. Thus, we are told in the *History of Lord Stanton* (1775) to "imagine yourself with one of Mahomet's houris. . . . She was supported with the state and dignity of an eastern queen, and being naturally expensive and extravagant, she hurried him on. There were no bounds to her desires, which met with every indulgence from him."[35] As Ros Ballaster reveals in her work on early novels of seduction, a common association would have been with Roxolana, a character in a frequently reprinted story about an "oriental courtesan-turned-queen" who exemplified "luxury, concealed female agency, slave government, cruelty, despotism, the will-to-power, religious hypocrisy, and imposture."[36] Blackstone was familiar with at least some of these associations. In the *Commentaries*, he compares the Queen of England's entitlements—which he finds very costly—to those of queens "in Eastern countries" (I:215). And earlier, in his poem "The Pantheon," he had associated the East with excessive luxury:

> Eastward the sparkling wall with jewels blaz'd
> From Indian quarries hewn; the beaming gems,

Dispos'd in rich variety, display
The gaudy worship of th' extended East.[37]

By all accounts, as Piyel Haldar has pointed out, the "lavish" and "luxurious" seraglios associated with sequestered eastern queens "had been a source of anxiety for the British since the early seventeenth century and came to be regarded as signs of an extravagant, capricious and whimsical government" that disregarded the rights of the subject and had no respect for that English marker of superiority, liberty. Against this "backdrop" "both the figure of the despot, and the theory of despotism emerge."[38] Given these associations with wealth, sexuality, and despotism, Blackstone's use of the eastern queen to represent justice seems very odd. Such an image might provoke disgust as much as incite desire, the disgust that results from excess, from too many sweets, or too much extravagance, or hypersexuality, all intermingled with the English disgust for despotism. And there is some evidence of this in Blackstone's refusal to linger on the image. But for explicit expressions of disgust in the poem, we must turn to his representation of the practice of law—which he locates not with the eastern queen, but rather with the "thorny maze," the "bulwarks of the law" that keep him from reaching her, and thus from reaching the "sacred page" and the "countless wheels" where harmonic justice implies a higher, better realm of laws that work towards higher aims.

The modern concept of disgust, a relatively new word for an old visceral reaction, surfaced in the late sixteenth and early seventeenth centuries in English, and by Blackstone's time had multifaceted meanings, from the highly physicalized "aversion of the palate from any thing" to "ill humour; malevolence," and to an "offence conceived."[39] Despite the word's rather late emergence, neuroscientists and historians of emotion agree that our feelings of disgust found their origins in our very survival. Thus, it has quite primitive beginnings: we feel "disgusted," even nauseated, by spoiled food, certain insects, parasites, sewage, human waste, and the physical incidentals related to death such as maggots and decaying flesh. But we also feel disgusted by moral lapses, by behaviors we consider outside the realm of the accepted, leading theorists as varied as Martha Nussbaum and Norbert Elias to argue for the value of disgust in the civilizing process. Although the use of our feelings of disgust to police moral boundaries presents some obvious problems because of the overgeneralization of the disgust instinct (we tend to feel "disgusted" by the "other," and thus "disgust" frequently comes into play when policing racial, national, or sexual difference boundaries),[40] the turn towards disgust as a moral emotion in Blackstone's time seems to have represented a slight advance in humanitarian attitudes: like Adam Smith, Blackstone preferred "disgust" to rage in the moral arena. Such a view marked him as more evolved than those who, for instance, wished to use the criminal law to exact revenge on evildoers.[41]

In Blackstone's poem, everyday law (law as practiced in Westminster Hall and other venues) functions as justice's other, a form of intellectual contagion in which legal knowledge is constructed as a disagreeable black hole, as "mystic, dark, discordant lore," and practicing law involves working in "wrangling courts," handling "tedious forms," engaging in "the pert dispute" and "the dull debate." Blackstone was to echo this idea in the *Commentaries*. He uses the word "disgust" there sparingly, but it is notable that he warns against the "fraud and corruption" of "attorneys and solicitors, who are also officers of the respective courts," because "if frequent or unpunished, [it] creates among the people a disgust against the courts themselves" (IV:281). The mendacity of lawyers and the dullness of law study and practice were already old ideas when Blackstone wrote. William Ian Miller, in his book on disgust, points to lawyers as particular objects of disgust in that they are "moral menials": "They perform functions in the moral order similar to those played by garbage men and butchers in the system of provisioning. . . . Moral menials deal with moral dirt, or they have to get morally dirty to do what the polity needs them to do."[42] In Blackstone's poem, disgust for the debased intellectual work of legal practice is matched by disgust for its moral failures as the young lawyer anticipates "the guilty bribe" and curses of "the harpy-tribe." Whereas justice is positioned in a garden, law is located in the eighteenth century's most ready metaphor for filth, the overcrowded and dangerous city made familiar to readers through Swift's "Description of a City Shower." Blackstone's "pure spring" of justice, with its "bottom view, / Clear, deep, and regularly true," both hints at and operates in opposition to the flood of sewage in Swift's anti-pastoral poem, where "streams" contained all sorts of disgusting objects, "filths of all hues and odours," and could never be imagined as happily "merging," since any "merger" would have involved contamination.[43] Picking up on this common theme, Blackstone describes the city as a place that evokes both physical and moral disgust, a place of "smoak, and crowds," where

> diseases taint the murky air,
> And midnight conflagrations glare;
> Loose Revelry and Riot bold
> In frighted streets their orgies hold.[44]

Blackstone thus creates a complex emotional zone in the poem: desire and disgust jostle for position. In opposition to those who thought disgusting images lessened aesthetic enjoyment, Blackstone increases our aesthetic satisfaction through his representation of disgusting images: his descriptions of diseased air and moral disorder mark "justice" as all the more desirable, but also create interest in themselves, a phenomenon Blackstone plays upon by returning to them repeatedly even while leaving justice pristine and untouched, bracketed in the middle of the poem.

The eastern queen is offered to create a zone of desire: her purposes are largely pedagogical in the sense that pedagogy involves seduction, as Blackstone leads us on through her alluring image to his dearest desire, that of a holistic and harmonic marriage between justice and law. But she is also part of the larger dynamic of disgust and desire that governs the poem. Felman, in her foundational work on desire, on promising and the failures of promising, speaks of the "slip" we encounter in reading J. L. Austin, the slip between his theoretical language and his more prosaic and often humorous or sexual examples. This "slip," Felman says, works like a pratfall; it involves a disparity of levels, a thwarting of expectations as one is suddenly dislodged from high theory and tumbles into a "low" example from real life.[45] In Blackstone's poem, we at first "slip" not down, but up, from the embodied sexuality in the image of the eastern queen to the "book," with its abstracted language of "harmonious right," and then to the "countless wheels" that "distinctly tend / By various laws to one great end." We then "slip" down into a disgusting representation of the practice of law, aversive both physically and morally, depicted as leading ultimately to death. What are we to make of these upward/downward "slips" organized around the celebration of a perfect, timeless, self-contained system where justice and law work together as "countless wheels" under the penetrating gaze of Alfred, but are contained in the image of the eastern queen who apparently holds the "sacred page"? As David Goldberg and his colleagues argue, romantic longing can exceed the personal and biological, to represent "the desire for conceptual unity, linear models of social change, and the resolution of conflict."[46] In this light, Blackstone draws on the odd image of the eastern queen to make a rather radical suggestion, to seduce us into considering an old idea, that of harmonic justice, in a new context. Rather than defining justice in terms of redress, retribution, and reparation, as his peers frequently did, he reaches for something larger, something holistic and of potentially universal value. For though he rejects law practice as disgusting, Blackstone remakes it in the image of the "sacred page" where "countless wheels distinctly tend / By various laws to one great end," and where we find *Concordia discors* in action, the promise of a marriage between law and justice that Blackstone figures as harmonic justice. Throughout the poem, desire and disgust are closely linked, as Blackstone uneasily shifts from representations of the desirability of justice to those of the disgusting nature of law, and yet attempts to map each onto its other. And it is these images, this desire with its consecutive disappointments, marked by disgust, that drove Blackstone as he wrote the *Commentaries*.

Look a Little Higher: Desire, Thwarted Desire, and Marriage Law

From the very beginning of volume I of the *Commentaries*, Blackstone pours energy into seducing his readers, readers who were not professional lawyers and who—perhaps like Allan and Neelie—wanted a clear, coherent statement of the law. He had embarked on a highly original and unprecedented project: to "sell" English common law to an audience that revered the civil law but, as Edmund Burke put it, thought of the common law as "dry, disgusting, heavy."[47] Thus, in "On the Study of the Law," offered as a preface to the *Commentaries*, we find him hard at the work of seduction, telling his prospective readers of the beauty of English law and of its virtues, especially when compared to the law of the "East," the "despotic monarchy of Rome and Byzantium" (I:5). This first section offers a primer on pedagogical seduction. Blackstone announces that "persons of inferior condition" don't really need to learn English law. He flatters his readers who have "more abilities" than the average person (I:7) and are "noble and ingenuous" (I:37). He issues a call to public duty in that his readers "cannot . . . discharge properly their duty either to the public or themselves, without some degree of knowledge of the laws" (I:7). He appeals to their selfishness, arguing that his readers need to know the law in order to manage their own landed property (I:7); issues threats, noting that "An ignorance of [the law of wills and testaments] must always be of dangerous consequence" (I:7); calls on the power of emulation by offering examples of "the ornaments of this seat of learning" (I:13); and, finally, offers enticing descriptions of the object of desire: the common law of England, a system at "the pitch of perfection" (I:23) that "distinguishes the criterions of right and wrong; which teaches to establish the one and prevent, punish, or redress the other; which employs in its theory the noblest faculties of the soul, and exerts in its practice the cardinal virtues of the heart; a science, which is universal in its use and extent, accommodated to each individual, yet comprehending the whole community" (I:27). What Blackstone promises is an over-the-top solution to the world's ills, a technology that can manage every problem while providing a moral compass, exalting both "the noblest faculties of the soul" and "the cardinal virtues of the heart"—in short, a system that brings reason and emotion together, marries them, and then further marries them to an ideal of communal harmony. This section ends with a specific appeal to desire, with the hope that the "rising generation" will be infused with "a desire to be still better acquainted with the laws and constitution of their country" (I:37). Who could resist?

One legal issue that many hoped to be "better acquainted with" might very well have been that of marriage. Marriage was a hot topic in mid-eighteenth-century England, addressed in thousands of pamphlets, journalistic accounts, plays, and novels. And marriage (and marriage law) appears at crucial turning points in the narrative structure of desire. It provides an end point, but then in its dissatisfactions allows the formation of new desires, operating at the juncture of promising, of the failures of promising, and of the creation of new expectations. It is no accident that Felman maps her theory of desire onto *Don Juan*, a text that tantalizes with promises of marriage, one that had found a ready home on eighteenth-century stages across Europe and in England. For eighteenth-century readers, the concept of marriage offered closure *and* flexibility, akin to that offered by *Concordia discors*, and thus had an aesthetic as well as an emotional, legal, commercial, and personal value. The association between marriage and *Concordia discors*, between *Concordia discors* and justice, was commonplace as both marriage and justice held out some hope for harmony in the world, for the reconciliation of differences in support of the common good. True justice operated as an imagined happy marriage, where all the rough edges have been worn away and wheels turn within wheels harmoniously. To offer only one of the most famous of many eighteenth-century examples, Samuel Johnson in *The Rambler* 167 emphasizes the importance of unity in marriage. It is worth looking carefully at the fictionalized letter on marriage that makes up this entry. There, the happy couple claims that

> tho' our characters beheld at a distance, exhibit this general resemblance, yet a nearer inspection discovers such a dissimilitude of our habitudes and sentiments, as leaves each some peculiar advantages and affords that *Concordia discors*, that suitable disagreement which is always necessary to intellectual harmony. Our thoughts like rivulets issuing from distant springs, are each impregnated in its course with various mixtures, and tinged by infusions unknown to the other, yet at last easily unite into one stream, and purify themselves by the gentle effervescence of contrary qualities.[48]

In *The Rambler*, at least, a good marriage, like harmonic justice itself, operates through an "easy" unification of the "rivulets" of intellectual and emotional difference, through the merger of difference into a single stream of harmonic thought. We might then expect or at least hope, especially given the expectations Blackstone created in first the poem and then the prefatory material in volume I of the *Commentaries*, that marriage law might provide a showcase for these ideals. But when we turn to Blackstone for a primer in marriage law, whatever promises marriage law might offer eventually lead to disappointment and disgust, a disappointment almost as dramatic and as comic as the one described in Collins's *Armadale*. Putting ourselves in Allan's place, we can imagine that he would have first turned to Blackstone's index to find references to marriage (this is what would have allowed him to bring only one volume when he meets Neelie in the garden). Seduced by the promises of textual paraphernalia, Allan would have found nine entries under the general category "Marriage": three overtly discouraging, even disgusting, citations ("Marriage, clandestine or irregular"; "forcible"; "licenses and registers, forging or destroying"); one esoteric reference ("socage"); three that focus on the business of marriage ("contract"; "property by"; "settlement"), and only two that might seem of slight interest to potential lovers ("in chivalry"; "its antiquity"). Alas, the one positive reference ("Marriages, when good") turns out *not* to be "good" (in Neelie's terms), but rather to be very bad.[49] When we turn to this reference at volume I:440, we find we are not in the marriage chapter, but rather in chapter 16, "Of Parent and Child." Here we find one of the many instances of the "void" that Neelie and Allan found so discouraging: "The consent or concurrence of the parent to the marriage of his child under age, was also *directed* by our antient law to be obtained: but now it is absolutely *necessary*; for without it the contract is void" (I:440). As if to hammer home the point, Blackstone then launches into a discussion of the importance of parental authority, using such intimidating phrases as "the legal power of a father" and "the empire of the father" to illustrate the principle that fathers control children until the children reach the age of twenty-one (I:441). The corollary of this parental "empire" is that of the child's obedience: "The *duties* of children to their parents arise from a principle of natural justice and retribution," Blackstone tells us. "For to those, who gave us existence, we naturally owe subjection and obedience during our minority, and honour and reverence ever after; they, who protected the weakness of our infancy, are entitled to our protection in the infirmity of their age; they who by sustenance and education have enabled their offspring to prosper, ought in return to be supported by that offspring. . . . Upon this principle proceed all the duties of children to their parents, which are enjoyed by positive laws" (I:441). Whereas Blackstone had promised at the beginning of volume I that England was "perhaps the only [land] in the universe in which political or civil liberty is the very end and scope of the constitution" (I:6), what we find towards the end of the volume is not liberty, but imperial power, despotic dominion, and hierarchy, quite literally as well as figuratively the law of the father.

Backtracking to "Chapter the Fifteenth. Of Husband and Wife," we might again be excused if we hope to find a unified, holistic description of marriage law, for Blackstone is famous for reiterating the famous proposition that "By marriage, the husband and wife are one person in law," a proposition objectionable to modern ears, but simple and straightforward (I:430). But like Allan and Neelie, the reader finds that the introductory paragraph focuses not on love or union, not on making two into one, but on "duties," and on the "legal effects and consequence of marriage." The first sentence of the first paragraph likely evoked Allan's exasperated outburst about contract law: "Our law considers marriage in no other light than as a civil contract" (I:421). Yet this passage is probably the most holistic, well-integrated section, incidentally supportive of Allan and Neelie's desires, in that Blackstone treats us to the basic elements of contract law: contracting parties must be "willing to contract"; "able to contract"; and "actually did contract" as "the law treats [marriage] as it does all other contracts" (I:421). At this point we should be done with marriage law as Blackstone has mapped it onto contract law in a way that satisfies his desire for harmonic congruence, for those "countless wheels" that "distinctly tend by various laws to one great end." "Willing," "able," and "did" express a theory elegant, simple, and easily understood. Two parties, both of sound mind, both willing, able, and then actually saying "I do" (the classic example of performative speech in J. L. Austin's world), should be able to marry. Body, mind, and then again body (in that last performative gesture) are all united here in law. Blackstone offers couples all of the promises contract law held out for equitable agreements among free legal subjects, for contract law promises that our promises will be kept, or as Hannah Arendt puts it in *The Human Condition*, contract law creates "islands of security without which not even continuity, let alone durability of any kind, would be possible in the relationships between men."[50]

But despite the simplicity of this principle, marriage law in Blackstone's *Commentaries* turns out to be just as "disgusting" as reluctant law students might have feared. Confused and riddled with inconsistencies, it resists even Blackstone's efforts to make of it a unified creature. Indeed, the bodily metaphor is apt here, for instead of that hallmark of a happy marriage, "the suitable disagreements that unite into one stream," we find no unification, but a sort of battle between common law, ecclesiastical law, and statute, one that focuses on the problems caused by recalcitrant and potentially disgusting bodies rather than the delights of harmonic justice with its harmonic unions. Following the promising clarity of Blackstone's reference to contract law, we are not a page into the discussion before we find Blackstone introducing numerous complications: there are the complications of "holiness" and of "sin," which, although Blackstone first submits is "left entirely to the ecclesiastical law," we discover plays a role in the common law as well. Such "sins" as "relation by blood" fall under ecclesiastical jurisdiction, yet still create "voidable" marriages under the common law "by sentence of separation" (I:422). After this confusing discussion, in which sin matters not at all, and then does matter, we are treated to a list of "disabilities," or of all the restrictions on marriage: a prior marriage with husband or wife still living; "want of age"; "want of consent of parents"; and "want of reason" (we can imagine Collins laughing here, as reason clearly had little to do with Allan and Neelie's desire to marry).[51] The physicalized, embodied nature of these issues need hardly be pointed out. Further complications can be blamed on statutory law: we are only two pages into the discussion when Statute 32 Hen.VIII.c.38 seems to help our young lovers, for it allowed that "all persons may lawfully marry, but such as are prohibited by God's law; and that all marriages contracted by lawful persons in the face of the church and consummate with bodily knowledge and fruit of children, shall be indissoluble" (I:423). But a half page later, this statute has been repealed by 2 and 3 Edw.VI.c.23, and yet possibly and partially (Blackstone isn't sure) revived by 26 Geo.II.c.33, the famous Lord Hardwicke's Marriage Act of 1753, purportedly enacted to reduce the perceived frequency of "clandestine" marriages and the threats they seemed to present to society. Only after his listing of "disabilities" does Blackstone reveal this change in the law, the shift that must have most impacted Allan and Neelie, in that it eliminated the private performative speech that in itself had once served as, if not an actual marriage, an enforceable contract to marry.

Let me explain: prior to the 1753 act, according to Blackstone, "any contract made . . . in words of the present tense, and in case of cohabitation . . . between persons able to contract" was "deemed a valid marriage." But, also according to Blackstone, the 1753 act effected a major shift, for "these verbal contracts are now of no force, to compel a future marriage. Neither is any marriage at present valid, that is not celebrated in some parish church or public chapel." Blackstone goes on to detail the other requirements of the 1753 act in terms that suggest a newly theatrical and public display: marriages must be "celebrated in some parish church or public chapel," they must be "preceded by publication of banns," and the failure to observe any number of other requirements, though it may not void the marriage, is now punishable through criminal sanctions (I:427–28). These complications and equivocations suggest that anyone reading Blackstone's marriage law sections in a search for harmonic justice, of those "wheels . . . that tend by various laws to one great end," will find only disappointment, a disappointment made striking and obvious by the disjuncture between his concise statement of contract law and the far longer and more confusing discussion of the ways that the 1753 act had altered previous practices.

If one thinks of Blackstone as the foremost arbiter of mid-eighteenth-century law, then it feels odd to discover that Blackstone's views have been challenged by recent scholarship. Rebecca Probert's "reassessment" of marriage law in *Marriage Law and Practice in the Long Eighteenth Century* provides a recent, deeply researched account of the causes and effects of the 1753 act.[52] According to her archival work, the act caused much less disruption to marriage practices than most scholars have suggested because couples had never been able to affect a marriage through a mere exchange of vows.[53] In fact, the 1753 act, Probert argues, simply formalized existing procedures. It is interesting then that an act that simply formalized procedures already in place would inspire as much controversy as the 1753 act did. What Probert calls "the sheer diversity of dissent" included the story (possibly untrue or exaggerated) that an enthusiastic crowd carried Henry Fox through the streets to celebrate his opposition to the act, and another that a congregation walked out when their minister began the required reading of the act.[54] Meanwhile, couples rushed to "clandestine marriage" to beat the act, while pamphleteers raised the possibility of dire consequences like "fornication, concubinage, and (not entirely consistently) depopulation."[55] Probert's discussion itself suggests how disruptive the conversations around the act must have been: despite digging deeply into the primary sources, she is unable to find one convincing and unifying rationale for the passage of the act in 1753. Instead, justifications came from all sides: from those against the "great Mischiefs and Inconveniences [that] have arisen from Clandestine Marriages,"[56] including wealthy landowners who needed to control their children's marriages, those who thought private marriages signified immorality, those who worried about adolescents making hasty decisions, and those who wished for "legal certainty."[57] But that "clandestine marriages" were a greater problem in 1753 than they had been in previous eras seems unlikely according to Probert. And, in the end, the act seems to have been passed as part of a larger effort to systematize customary law and to reinforce provisions that were already in place rather than as an effort to effect real change.

Blackstone's account of a disrupted situation then seems to reflect not the actual impact of the new act, but the sociocultural tumult that occurred around it. He provides example after example of confusing changes in the law, of the idea that prior to the act, couples could effectively marry simply through words, while after the act, they were required to perform a number of public behaviors designed to put others on notice of their intent to marry and thus to prevent individuals from making the private decisions implied by contract law. And, in fact, a bare reading of the language of the act, without context, would seem to suggest that he was correct, for the act in its language seemingly performs a radical change: it claims to have been passed to avert those "great Mischiefs and Inconveniences [that] have arisen from Clandestine Marriages." It operates not only prescriptively, but performatively, both in the technical sense of Austin's performative speech acts, but also in the larger sense that Eve Sedgwick refers to as "thickened."[58] That the document is sprinkled through with the phrase "it is hereby further enacted" suggests its performative function in Austin's technical sense. Meanwhile its focus on embodied public performances in front of audiences ("the presence of two or more credible witnesses"), after "banns," which were required to "be published in an audible manner" in a place where the couple has resided, suggests the larger sense of the performative, that "thickened" sense that Sedgwick refers to. For instance, the act goes into great detail on the issue of residency, emphasizing the embodied presence we associate with performance. The materialized, embodied nature of the act's requirements is underscored in that creating a written record is addressed in detail, with ministers being required to record a marriage immediately after the fact in a "proper book[s] of vellum, or good and durable paper." The act also provided specific instructions for page numbering, spacing, and composition, and mandated capital punishment for those who would "falsely make, alter, forge or counterfeit" such entries. Finally, the act required a public reading of its five dense pages, not once, but four times a year, in essence requiring all of church-going England to become audience to the act (and potentially to be disgusted by it, if Probert's example of people walking out during the readings is reliable). Thus, to say that the act tracked common practices and customs and represented no change at all (as Probert implies), although true in one sense, is entirely untrue in another. The act was a performative gesture: it created a new world for marriage on the page and on the stages on which it was read, while emphasizing marriage as an embodied, flawed, human construction, one as likely to evoke disgust as satisfy desire. In doing so, it was calibrated to manage urbanophobic and imperial anxieties provoked by a newly urban shifting and transient population. In this new world, diversity jostled against itself, no man could be said to know his neighbor or trust his claims to property, class structures were breaking down, and both the lying, seductive suitor and deceitful, scheming bride had become common tropes. These anxieties were reflected in debates around the passage of the act, debates that leaned on expressions of disgust related to sexuality, profligacy, and venereal disease, whether propagated through marital rebellion thought to be common in upper-class life or marital impulsiveness, supposedly engaged in by the poor. In short, the act was passed to manage the emotions around these changes, to legislate, regulate, and effectively channel desire and disgust in a new world in which sexual and marital mixing represented a threat to both class and national status. In doing so, it created a new object of disgust: the law itself. The act's spurring of numerous new regulations, sites of administrative oversight, and potential areas of disagreement and litigation remind us of Blackstone's disgust for "solemn prate" and "dull debate." Ironically, Blackstone's representation of the confused state of marriage law post-act might have sent many young lovers, less naïve than Allan and Neelie, running to lawyers for advice and counsel.

If the act itself is performative, then perhaps Blackstone's account of the act is simply constative, a description of the present state of the law. But to read Blackstone's description of the act as merely descriptive is to err. We should note not only what Blackstone *says*, but also what he *does*, thus treating the *Commentaries* as offering not only knowledge, but also a particular sort of performance associated with desire and with disgust, that of the pratfall, or in Felman's words, the slip. That slip lies at least in part in Blackstone's willing display on the page of both informative language and performative language, each elbowing the other for prominence.[59] Textually, his inclusion of the provisions of the act interrupts his desire for the holistic, harmonious version of law represented by his simple expression of contract law, creating disgust rather than satisfaction. This inclusion reflects the "real" world of law, at least according to Blackstone, in that the act interrupted the gradual development of common law with the external force of statute. Felman points out the "problem of the relation" in English of three meanings of performance, all of them pointing towards embodied emotions: the erotic, the theatrical, and the linguistic.[60] In Blackstone's description of marriage we get all three: an erotic attempt to seduce us into a better understanding of marriage law through claims for its simplicity, in other words, an erotics of pedagogy; a close-to-theatrical display of confusion and disruption that plays off the sociocultural context that resulted in the act; and a linguistic "performative" that does more than simply declare the law of marriage to be confused, conflicted, and disrupted, but actually makes it so through words. We are truly in Felman territory here, in the world where desire and the promises that elicit it result in slippage, the slip of broken promises and broken connections that she delineates so brilliantly. Blackstone is then like Don Juan in Felman's account, and like all humans, "the promising animal, incapable of keeping his promise, incapable of not making it, powerless both to fulfill the commitment and to avoid committing himself—to avoid playing beyond his means, playing, indeed, the devil: the scandal of the speaking body, which in failing itself and others makes an act of that failure, and makes history."[61]

Blackstone's representation of the new act as new, rather than simply a formal standardization of existing custom, is fundamental to that performance, in that the act—with its emphasis on public and publicized marriages, on performance, and demonstrable evidence of those performances—operates as a microcosmic performative exemplar. Indeed, the entire section works not through fulfilling promises, but through breaking them; it is organized around (as Felman says of the play *Don Juan*) a "continuity of breaches," leading us from the desirable bright clarity of contract law, its promise, on to that breach of promise that seemed to doom Collins's characters, ending with the ultimate breach, a discussion of divorce and dissolution of marriage, further punctuated by the penultimate paragraph in the chapter, Blackstone's discussion of the husband's right to give his wife "moderate correction" (I:432–33). Indeed, the only optimistic, forward-looking passage in the chapter is the initial setting out of marriage as contractual: half a page of a thirteen-page chapter. If one counts the references to parental authority regarding marriage in the following chapter, Blackstone's efforts to explain marriage constitute an even more elaborated version of the slip that Felman outlines, raising us quite high with the "promise" that contract law will not only clarify all things marital, but also foster individual freedom. Then, he drops us dramatically to a disappointing and rather unconvincing reaffirmation of the workings of authority, the importance of duty, and the need to subordinate individuality to the greater good, all wrapped up in a confusing tangle of regulations, made more complex by the addition of exceptions piled on exceptions.

Throughout, Blackstone has performed the dynamics of desire, offering us promises, followed by failures of promising, followed by the failures of marriage itself in his discussion of divorce, and finally capped off in the next section with a reassertion of despotic authority over the free will of the young and the desiring. Marriage law has then failed to satisfy. Law and justice cannot be married here; justice is left standing at the altar, while law, in all its disgusting complications, controls the plot. Throughout, Blackstone's representation of marriage law has mapped not onto harmonic justice, but directly onto the images of law he had drawn on in his early poem: law here is "mystic, dark, discordant lore," organized more to profit lawyers and create conflict than to resolve human problems.

We Hate What We Love: The Return of the Eastern Queen

Marriage law, it seems, cannot satisfy the desire for harmonic justice. Contingency—represented by the body, by political motives, by commercial forces, by statutory law, by ecclesiastical law—intervenes, introducing with it various objects of disgust, including the poor, unrestrained sexuality, the suffocating density and alienation of the city, but also law and law practice. This dynamic suggests we shift focus, returning to the poem for a moment in order to rethink the relationship it constructs between desire and disgust and to entertain the possibility that the binary Blackstone constructs in the poem is one he must later complicate in the *Commentaries*. As we have seen above, Blackstone puts the image of the eastern queen to use to represent the merging of justice and law that he imagines as harmonic justice, and sets up that merging against law practice, represented as disgusting, both physically and morally. But he quickly dismisses the image of the eastern queen as he weaves and bobs, first to her "sacred page," then to the "countless wheels" of harmonic justice, overseen by Alfred's penetrating gaze. In the larger scale of the poem, he abandons *all* of the images related to harmonic justice: eastern queen, sacred page, and countless wheels are all left behind and the poem ends with a return to the ugliness of law practice and the suggestion of the poet-lawyer's death. Such movement signals aversion, or perhaps the ambivalence we hold for all objects of desire. While the eastern queen is not a suitable candidate for marriage, but merely a means towards the end Blackstone desires, "harmonic justice" as represented by the "sacred page" and the "countless wheels" also seems not to satisfy, but rather to devolve into the disgusting arena of law practice.[62] Rejected then, or at least set aside, the eastern queen and with her, harmonic justice, become part of the detritus of the poem, not quite "filth" as William A. Cohen and Ryan Johnson define it in their influential 2004 collection *Filth: Dirt, Disgust, and Modern Life*, but rejected bits of throwaway imagery, used once and forgotten, left behind as the poet-lawyer abandons the idea of a literary career and succumbs to the contingency-laden, disgusting world of law and law practice.[63]

Is there something disgusting in the eastern queen, something as Aurel Kolnai's 1929 foundational essay on disgust asserted that one "clears away," but also something that can be repurposed?[64] We cannot rid ourselves of those things we find disgusting. Our mere encounter with the object of disgust changes us; by the time we have defined it and rejected it, we are already tainted, having, as Cohen puts it, "rubbed up against it."[65] Thus, often we repurpose it, making it not filth or waste, but a recyclable bit of trash, available for use elsewhere. We might look again to Blackstone's *Commentaries*, searching quite literally for images of the "East," of the harem, and even of eastern queens, to examine this repurposing, as well as to trace on a larger scale the shifting operations of desire and disgust in Blackstone's work and in his larger world. While charging Blackstone with a crude form of Orientalism is not my ultimate aim here, I want to linger a minute on his comments in the *Commentaries*, particularly on how they evoke the Eastern body as a locus for disgust. It is commonplace by now to argue that Blackstone's England defined itself in opposition to the "East." Thus, when Hamid Dabashi remarks towards the end of *Post-Orientalism* that various twenty-first-century commentators make it their mission to convince "their readers that Muslims are backward and diabolic while 'the West' is the principal source of good in the world," he is not speaking of a recent phenomenon, so much as one rooted in the history of and even crucial to our understanding of the Anglo-American world.[66]

It is not surprising then that Blackstone draws on images of the "East" to engage his readers loyalty to English law. Whereas in the poem, the "East" represents desire, in the *Commentaries*, Blackstone posits the East and the Muslim world as objects of disgust, primitive places of "ignorant barbarity" (IV:337), "where little regard is shewn to the lives or fortunes of the subject, all causes are quickly decided: the basha on a summary hearing, orders which party he pleases to be bastinadoed, and sends them about on their business" (III:423). "Bastinadoed," of course, takes us directly to the body, to the feet and to images of debasement and torture. In another example, Blackstone alludes to the sexuality associated with the Eastern harem, but not to eastern queens: discussing the fortunes of soldiers, he compares them to "eunuchs in the eastern seraglios" who "live in a state of perpetual envy and hatred towards the rest of the community" (I:404). Other examples argue that Turkey (often compared to France) represents whimsical and irrational government, where unrestrained despots can "dispatch or exile any man that was obnoxious to the government, by an instant declaration that such is their will and pleasure" (IV:343). His belief that in "adjacent countries in East India" creditors were allowed to collect a debt by "disposing" of the debtor and his family and could "even violate with impunity the chastity of the debtor's wife" makes the English system of imprisonment for debt seem humane by comparison (II:472–3, note g). Overall, Blackstone's expressions of conflated disgust for the Eastern body and Eastern despotism seem to operate dichotomously: English law emphasizes liberty, process, and monarchical power balanced by constitutional duties and the parliamentary system, while Eastern law is no law at all, but rather the erratic and tyrannical exercise of personality, a slave system in which the only non-slave is the resident despot and others are reduced to mere bodies, tortured, castrated, traumatized, and abused.

But is the East really the "other" as Blackstone seems to assert? Disgust is a boundary-shoring emotion, as theorists as diverse as Sartre and Mary Douglas have argued: porous boundaries must be avoided, as they result in contamination and "anomalous, indeterminate states of being."[67] Expressions of disgust reveal the fear of contagion, contagion from something that has become too close to the self, something that represents a danger of being incorporated by the self and causing disease and death. As Ros Ballaster points out in her study on oriental romances, the critique of Western monarchies tended to dwell on their similarity to oriental despotism. A "plurality" of voices from Montesquieu to the *Turkish Spy*, a popular work throughout the eighteenth century, offered "a critique of oriental despotism and the failure of Western monarchy to differentiate sufficiently from it."[68] If we turn to Blackstone's section on "the king" and "the crown," we can see exactly why Blackstone needed disgust, needed the foil of Eastern despotism, to shore up his argument for England's monarchical republic. Paul Halliday's brilliant essay "Blackstone's King" notes Blackstone's vacillation between two points: the king as having "sacred" and embodied power versus the king as "crown," in other words, as a disembodied role constructed by law and hemmed in by duties to the people and by his relationship to Parliament. Halliday points particularly to an extended discussion in volume I of the *Commentaries* where Blackstone argues that it is a sign of English liberty that limitations on the king's power can be discussed; Blackstone was highly conscious of a time not that far in the past when England had not been much different than the maligned East, a time when English kings forbade the discussion of limitations on their power.[69] If, as Halliday says, Blackstone's "pen drew the bounds around the king," it was in part to mark the mid-eighteenth-century English legal system as progressive, tolerant of change, and responsive to many different voices.[70] One of those boundary-drawing acts involved the disgust Blackstone directed at "Eastern" government, the government of despots, associated in a much broader symbolic sense with the deadening effects of a closed system, in which the eastern queen represented a shutting down of options, a repetitive return to the same "countless wheels" of the poem, and a figurative death worthy of moral disgust. In drawing a boundary around the rights an English king could exercise, Blackstone drew a protective boundary around Englishness and English law as well, uniting it in a shared disgust directed at the Eastern other.

Is There No Love in the *Commentaries*?

Reading the above, one might become convinced (as Allan was) that there's no love in the *Commentaries*, "not a word." And if Blackstone relies on disgust more than desire, he might be excused for doing so: disgust, some theorists argue, better serves community building than desire. Desire is more private, more difficult to experience vicariously: we can understand why someone else feels desire for a particular object without sharing that desire. Disgust, on the other hand, is "felt" when described by others. Our stomachs turn when another describes rancid food; similarly, we become outraged when we read about or hear of disgusting moral behavior, a phenomenon Samuel Johnson recognized when he argued that vice must naturally disgust us.[71] As Sianne Ngai points out, disgust "seeks to include or draw others *into* its exclusion of its object, enabling a strange kind of sociability."[72] Perversely perhaps, disgust can then engender love for those drawn "into its exclusion of its object," thus bringing us full circle in the desire–disgust continuum.

But Blackstone's interweaving of desire and disgust is more complex than this suggests. Tracking the eastern queen as first an object of desire in the poem, then rejected detritus in the *Commentaries* reveals that rather than positioning desire and affiliation against disgust and aversion, Blackstone creates space in the *Commentaries* for their Mobius-strip-like interaction. In the *Commentaries*, we are permitted our desires, but taught to subordinate them, to contain them in a larger economy where mixed emotions, like the various streams in *Concordia discors*, can run together. Turning to volume III of the *Commentaries*, we find Blackstone unexpectedly more sympathetic to the allure of the eastern queen, to the allure of despotism, than his distaste for Eastern tyrants might suggest. Oddly enough, he expresses this sympathy in the introduction to the section that focuses on one of the most central images of English justice: that of the adversarial trial. In a discussion that takes up almost six full pages, Blackstone begins chapter 22 of the third volume, "Of the Several Species of Trial," with what might seem like a peculiar argument having nothing to do with trials, an argument he introduces almost as a joke: "The uncertainty of legal proceedings is a notion so generally adopted, and has so long been the standing theme of wit and good humour, that he who should attempt to refute it would be looked upon as a man, who was either incapable of discernment himself, or else meant to impose upon others" (III:325). Uncertainty, wit, and humor: we are again in the world of the pratfall here, the world of disappointments and disillusionments, often taken to be funny. Yet we are also about to see Blackstone attempt to refute this humorous notion, and in doing so, position this pratfall world of desire and disappointment in the context provided by despotism and the image of the eastern queen. "People," he says, "are apt to be angry" (perhaps even disgusted, as critics of the common law often argued) "at the want of simplicity in our laws: they mistake variety for confusion, and complicated cases for contradictory." And this anger fuels a desire for despotism, as these very critics value "an arbitrary, despotic, government, where the lands are at the disposal of the prince, the rules of succession, or the mode of enjoyment, must depend upon his will and pleasure." These critics even "bring us examples of arbitrary governments . . . and unreasonably require the same paucity of laws, the same conciseness of practice" (III:325–26).

Blackstone tells us that while arbitrary despotism may have served past, simpler nations, it cannot be trusted to manage a nation invested in change and growth. And thus Blackstone argues that such critics fail to realize that "a tyrannical sway" holds many disadvantages for a "nation of freemen, a polite and commercial people" with "a populous extent of territory." Blackstone collapses these disadvantages, backing into a very attenuated reference to the eastern queen: under tyranny, he says, commerce will suffer and "the commonality" are "incapable of either right or injury," while "marriages are usually contracted with slaves; or at least women are treated as such" (III:326). Here he comes close to erasing his image of the eastern queen, replacing her with that of a seraglio-bound marital slave. In doing so, he creates an oxymoron that contrasts directly with his description of marriage law in volume I, for if marriage is a contract and the definition of contract is a freely made agreement, then slaves cannot enter into contractual arrangements: one cannot contract with a slave. Through a slippery association and substitution of images, slavery has come to be associated with harmonic justice, with the simple machinery of "countless wheels," in that the despotism of the East offers only a closed, clockwork system, one ultimately disgusting because it represents the death of contingency. The image of the harem, or its women, might remain a focal point for desire, but it could not serve as a helpful metaphor for English justice, as it signifies a "space of narrative" in which the same tales are to be told again and again, and the lives of subjects reduced to "endlessly circulating stories" designed to pass time, but not advance it.[73] In contrast, the English investment in "science, in commerce and in the arts" demands a complex, flexible, and responsive legal system that can change with changing circumstances and respond to multiple voices. If English laws are many, various, and sometimes in conflict, this is caused by "the extent of the country which they govern; the commerce and refinement of its inhabitants; but, above all, the liberty and property of the subject. These will naturally produce an infinite fund of disputes" (III:327). We might desire a "perfect" justice system, one "deep but clear," but Blackstone tells us that the perfect is indeed the enemy of the good: it comes with built-in disadvantages. The easily executed, efficient justice of the East, of the harem, would avoid a proliferation of laws, true, but it would also close down meaning, and dictate a predictable, self-limiting, machine-like, and endlessly repeating world, just as eighteenth-century ideas of the "East" posited "a discursive process that transforms a changing history into a set of unchanging and repetitive images."[74]

Thus, almost two decades after writing his poem, Blackstone recognizes and even validates the fantasy of the eastern queen, our desires for her and with her the simplicity and aesthetic rewards of harmonic justice (to "contract" marriages with slaves would surely have simplified marriage law), but folds that recognition into an historical understanding of the English common law. While Blackstone relegates the idea of Eastern despotism to the past, he yet allows the fantasy of harmonic justice a bit of continuing life in his claims that "the English law is less embarrassed with inconsistent resolutions and doubtful questions, than any other known system of the same extent and the same duration" (III:328). In defending the integrity of the system, he allows harmonic justice to continue to function as an object of desire, but in the context of the pratfall and the lapsed promise, the world of difference, rather than that of the perfectly performed oath, the inviolable contract, and the closed system of turning wheels.

It is no accident that after this lengthy commendation of the English system, Blackstone lists the seven "species" of civil trials, as if their number and complexity represented a virtue rather than a point of confusion and complexity, remarking that this complexity is related to England's devotion to "truth"—in other words, to contingency and particularity—over system. What is surprising is that he then creates what might seem an odd gap between the first six types discussed and the main meat of his discussion, the Trial by Jury, abruptly ending chapter 22 without covering all of the seven "species" in order to give trial by jury—that most contingent of contingent processes—a place of honor in chapter 23. It is almost as if trial by jury, "the principal bulwark of our liberties" (III:350), has escaped careful categorization, escaped into the world of contingency that he feels is necessary to discovering the truth, yet has tried to control by creating a list of "species." Never mind, though—Blackstone quickly shifts in chapter 23 from praising the trial by jury to initiating "the dissection and examination of it in all its parts . . . since, the more it is searched into and understood, the more it is sure to be valued" (III:350). This dissection though quickly breaks down into one of Blackstone's more convoluted sections, as he shifts from current practice to ancient practices, to fine points of jury empanelment and empanelment failure, then suddenly breaks into a "pause" to again consider "how admirably this constitution is adapted and framed for the investigation of truth" (III:355). Promises, promises! For after this brief "pause" we are once again thrust into a world of confusing contingency, treated to a number of paragraphs explaining various technical requirements and then to a section on "challenges" to juries, either to panels or individuals (III:359–65). A juror may be challenged for being a lord or a slave, a woman or too poor. He may be partial, biased, or have committed a crime, be sick or "decrepit" or over seventy or under twenty-one. Such exclusions may result in a call for more jurors, and then these jurors in turn can be challenged. This catalogue of human frailty, of what must be eliminated to protect the "scrupulously delicate" English system meant to ensure impartiality, both reassures and creates anxiety: efforts to circumscribe jury service may serve only to remind us of contingency and particularity, of the impossibility of the task. Despite these problems, Blackstone ends the section with yet another reassurance of how "excellently contrived" the challenges are despite their "prodigious multitude" (III:366).

Without belaboring the point, this is Blackstone's method throughout the chapter: his promises of systematic exposition are followed by dense passages of confusing contingencies, always summed up as absolutely necessary to the perfection of the system. After the final lengthy discussion of evidence and verdict, one readies oneself for the close of the chapter when Blacktone magisterially proclaims that "trial by jury ever has been, and I trust ever will be, looked upon as the glory of the English law. . . . It is the most transcendent privilege which any subject can enjoy, or wish for" (III:379). The jury system, he argues, stands between England and "the most oppressive of absolute governments," between England and despotism (III:380). Alas, we are only to be disappointed again, as Blackstone then launches into a lengthy discussion of the jury system's defects, finally ending the chapter on the rather flat note of "sober reflection," able to say only that the system, despite "all its imperfections," is better than those of other countries.

As Berlant points out, Freud argues that "to love an object is to attempt to master, to seek to destroy its alterity or Otherness."[75] Felman makes the same point when she quotes Don Juan, who says, "Once you are master, there is no more to say, nor anything left to wish for."[76] Attaining one's perfect desires leads not to happiness, but to the death of desire. To imagine a perfect resolution of conflict, of difference, of contrarieties, is in itself a form of violence, one that does violence not only to the object of desire, but to desire itself. In escaping from an ordered list of "seven species" and then proving itself to be less than ideal, the trial by jury resists efforts at systematization, but leaves room for desire, partly through bringing in a bit of disgust for the defects of human error. Blackstone's account incorporates the human where to be human is to have human flaws. In fact, it is remarkable how often Blackstone references the "human" in these passages meant to justify, even celebrate, the institution of the adversarial trial: "the defects of human laws" and "the natural imbecility and imperfection that attends all human proceedings" are his theme throughout (III:328–29). This preoccupation, though seemingly negative and even evincing disgust for human failings, references a living system, a system in which human emotions, "intentions" (which cause much of the confusion in law), flaws, and complexities, are folded into the dream of harmonic justice. In Blackstone's world there are no slave marriages; instead, one values "the liberty and property of the subject," embraces change, and accepts the "natural" occurrence of "an infinite fund of disputes" (III:327). While this embrace of the "infinite," one which creates a "multitude" of new rules and cases and is so imperfect that its imperfections must be catalogued, may create confusion, it also speaks to the law's responsiveness to individuals, to the humanity of the system: it arises from the efforts of what Blackstone presents as a relatively stable system of laws that respond to "the intentions of individuals" and attempts an understanding and integration of human eccentricities and foibles, an understanding Blackstone performs through revealing the inextricable interweaving of desire and disgust within the *Commentaries* itself.

Blackstone's "Last Tear"

Productive Melancholia and the Sense of No Ending

Pensive he treads the destin'd way,
And Dreads to go, nor dares to stay;
'Till on some neighb'ring mountain's brow
he stops, and turns his eyes below;
There, melting at the well-known view,
Drops a last tear, and bids adieu.
—William Blackstone, "The Lawyer's Farewel to His Muse"

As I noted in the introduction to this book, Sara Ahmed reminds us that our shifting emotions create narratives: "Our love might create the condition for our grief, our loss could become the condition for our hate, and so on."[1] This chapter turns to grief, to feelings of loss that result from disappointment in love, to loss as the inevitable companion to desire's idealizations.[2] As we have seen earlier, loss played a major role in Blackstone's early poem "The Lawyer's Farewel," where Blackstone had reluctantly dragged himself away from poetry "As, by some tyrant's stern command, / A wretch forsakes his native land." There, "Adieu" became a repetitive lament as Blackstone shed one "last tear" and "bid adieu" to poetics, to harmony, to justice, and even to "King Alfred." What are we to make of this aestheticized, clichéd "adieu": with its "last tear"? As Eugenia Brinkema points out, the tear has long been "the supreme metonym for the expressivity of interior states, a liquid volley in countless debates over whether emotion is an active production or a passive subjection," in short, "the tear is something that must be read."[3] To read Blackstone's tear is to realize that this is not the "tear" Brinkema brings to her analysis, a tear suspended in a visual image from a Hitchcock film. Nor is it one of the performative tears that judges shed throughout the early modern and Victorian period to demonstrate their compassion.[4] Instead, it is what we might call an "artificial tear," one used conventionally to suggest a pleasant sadness—similar to but not as intense as those feelings David Hume describes in "Of Tragedy." This artificiality should not preclude analysis. As Barbara Rosenwein explains in her helpful discussion on reading emotions in history, "artificial sentiments tell us about conventions and habits; these have everything to do with emotion."[5] Blackstone's tear then suggests sadness, but also something torn, just as Blackstone's young lawyer is torn away from the law. The tear becomes a physical sign of an embodied emotion that yet leaves the body, meanwhile pointing to a conventional, habitual, historically contingent way of organizing feelings about the relationship between literature and law. This was an old trope as Peter Goodrich has demonstrated, well-known to Renaissance lawyers who associated law with sensory deprivation, harsh discipline, and harsh words.[6] In the poem, Blackstone draws on this tradition, imagining literature as offering a fullness of emotional and aesthetic experience in which beautiful sounds and beautiful emotions conjoin to create pleasure; law, meanwhile, becomes the depository of all that is unpleasant, disgusting, and to be avoided. The loss of literature thus merits a tear as Blackstone's young lawyer turns away from it for the poor substitute of the law.

But neither Blackstone's "last tear" nor his "adieu" were truly final. Blackstone never left poetry or the emotions associated with it behind but instead maintained his interests in literature throughout his lifespan, engaging in debates over Pope's poetry and contributing to an edition of Shakespeare that was published soon after his death.[7] In bringing the poetics of his time to the *Commentaries*, he brought as well the melancholy aesthetic associated with that "last tear," less devastating than our Freudian-influenced modern understanding of melancholia as a psychological state, yet serving some of the same cultural functions. As Anne Anlin Cheng argues in her work on affect, "melancholia does not simply denote a *condition* of grief but is, rather, a *legislation* of grief."[8] Legislation implies not simply regulation, but planning and purpose. As legislation, melancholia has a form; it takes the past into account, consolidates it, and makes of it a set of rules for the future. And thus in the *Commentaries*, when Blackstone "legislates" a particular version of grief, he chooses one that memorializes the past, but also encourages readers to move forward, to integrate the lost past of English law into new formulations that support progress and embrace modernity. This chapter focuses on how the aesthetics of mourning and melancholia that appear in Blackstone's poetry resurface in the *Commentaries*—in perhaps the most influential, but also most esoteric, most technical, and thus least expected of Blackstone's legal arenas: property law.

In Emily Brady and Arto Haapala's oft-cited essay, "Melancholy as an Aesthetic Emotion," the authors note that "melancholy" shares a family resemblance with sadness and depression but is distinguished by its reliance on narrative, its complexity, and its reflective qualities. They argue that melancholy is "fascinating in itself," identifying this feeling or complex of feelings as not only something we can feel, but something we can observe, and thus in itself an aesthetic object. The features of the melancholy aesthetic object include complexity (when in a melancholic state we feel both negative and positive emotions) and the development of an "overall harmony" among our differing emotions. As the authors put it, "the reflection constitutive in melancholy makes it a rational, controllable emotion. We have been able to take some distance from our previous experiences; we have given them a place in our own history."[9] Reading Blackstone's work on the laws of inheritance and property in this context alerts us to melancholic operations in the *Commentaries*, specifically to the ways that an intensified nexus of complex assertions and counter-assertions attempts to stand in for the lost bodies of the past. Blackstone's mournful history of landed property regulation assigns all that has been lost to "time immemorial," while the technical precision of his discussion of the laws of inheritance substitutes for both the embodied wishes of the voiceless dead and the lost culture of the Saxons that he argued formed the basis of English property law. And this dynamic speaks to the larger movement of the *Commentaries* itself, a text erected on the remnants of an idealized oral tradition of customs and memory that must be repeatedly marked as lost, and yet repeatedly invoked. Working through melancholic incorporation, Blackstone writes not so much a technical exposition of English inheritance laws, but an extended elegy for an ancient oral (and poetic) tradition imagined as communal and harmonious, one that was in the process of being undone by statutory innovations even as he completed his work.

A Poetics of Legal History

As with the historians Walter Benjamin critiqued in "On the Concept of History," Blackstone strove to make the course of legal historical events run "through his hands smoothly, like a thread" as part of his argument for English law's specifically English nature and for its contribution to progress. Thus, for Blackstone, legal history was essentially melancholic: no one can read his sections on property without recalling Benjamin's elegiac "In the voices we hear, isn't there an echo of now silent ones?"[10] Tracing Blackstone's historical aesthetic back to his poetry reveals the full context for this view of history. Like other poets of his generation, the young poet Blackstone emerged in a time when melancholy had become faddish.[11] What Thomas Warton called "the soft thrillings of the tragic muse" by 1745 came to stand in not only for refinement, for a heightened sensibility, but also for the creative spirit in poetry.[12] The poetic vogue for melancholy musings—the association of melancholia with poetic creativity—swept through 1740s and 1750s England; it included James Macpherson's Ossianic mania as well as those poets literary historians later began to refer to as the Graveyard poets, particularly Robert Blair, Edward Young, and Thomas Gray.[13] Both the more generalized "melancholy" and a more pathologized "melancholia," of course, had a long pre-history. This tradition went back to Aristotle, who had asked why so many statesmen, philosophers, and poets tended towards melancholic feelings.[14] Richard Burton's *Anatomy of Melancholy* (1621) had offered a keystone text that bridged the classical world and the world of the Enlightenment.[15] By Blackstone's time, it was difficult to find a poet, philosopher, or scribbling doctor who had not commented on the emotion or the condition. As Sanja Bahun points out, melancholy (the immediate emotional sign of the condition) and melancholia (the condition) were malleable concepts that "could be defined as an affect or an affective disorder, a conceptual construction, a type of behavior . . . and a mere descriptive, thence a discourse, perception, and interpretation . . . a sorrow without a cause, and a condition that mysteriously triggers the powers of imagination and cognition."[16] Depictions of melancholia ran the gamut, with some describing it as a serious mental illness that we might now call depression or agitated depression, while others likened it to what Thomas Gray called "a good, easy sort of state."[17] Tellingly, physician William Stukeley included Anne Finch's dark poem *The Spleen* in his 1723 medical treatise on melancholia, thus bringing aesthetic efforts to describe a mood together with medical explication.[18] A related strand of thought recognized melancholia as a "fashionable" illness, linking it to aesthetics: Jonson mocked this, while James Makittrick Adair argued against the fad for melancholy in a 1790 polemic against quackery.[19] Nevertheless, Frances Burney, sobbing over the *Vicar of Wakefield* in 1769, was seen as exhibiting a fashionable sensibility rather than a severe (even bizarre) depression.[20] Overall, it seems a catchall term, one that uneasily straddled body and mind, poetry, the imagination, and medical disability.

As a very late "early modern," Blackstone inherited the melancholic tradition, but his work also prefigured later Freudian and even post-Freudian understandings of the human response to loss. Following Freud, many theorists have separated unhealthy, medicalized melancholia from states of "healthy" and "natural" mourning by reference to propriety. "Proper" mourning in Freud engages in a "linear process of restoration" in which the lost object is replaced by another object. By the end of the process, the mourner has moved on and a substitute has been found for the lost object. For the traditional Freudian, improper mourning—the "bad" sort—becomes melancholia, a state typified by an investment in an unhealthy continuing obsession with the loss that the patient has incurred. Melancholia, at least in the earlier Freud, involves an ongoing engagement with loss, perhaps not a conscious engagement, but one that intersects or is entangled with all that is new.[21] Tammy Clewell emphasizes this opposition in her work on trauma: healthy mourning "introjects" the lost object and then accepts a substitute as adequate compensation. Unhealthy melancholia "incorporates" the lost object, encrypting the loss in the body, or, as Jonathan Flatley puts it, "internalizes the lost object into his or her very subjectivity as a way of refusing to let the past go."[22] In explaining one of the classic strands of psychoanalytic thought in this area, Clewell uses the example of the child who must give up the mother (at least symbolically) in favor of language: "The child negates the loss of the mother and accepts its own linguistic mastery as adequate compensation."[23] Failure to manage mourning means failure to enter into humanity, to fully participate in what it means to be human. In the unhealthy melancholic, the lost is never really lost, but instead becomes part of the mourner's subjectivity, interfering with healthy functioning and preventing the melancholic from engaging with life as an ongoing process.

Of course, the mental disorder melancholia sometimes refers to is not the same as a melancholic aesthetic. And yet they are interrelated, each informing the other, as art borrows from both its tradition and from its embodied present and as humans attempt to understand their melancholia through art. Thomas Gray's *Elegy Written in a Country Churchyard* offers a convenient touchstone for understanding the functioning of melancholia in Blackstone's era.[24] Gray's *Elegy* has been heralded as the harbinger of the modern age both because of its melancholic embrace of a lost past and its claim for a central authorial identity that sees from a distance, absorbs what it sees, and awards it a transcendent meaning. It has been called the "standard English poem" and "continuously the most popular of mid-eighteenth-century English poems," making it as canonical in literature as Blackstone is in law. It thus functions as a sort of generic map to the conventions in Blackstone's "Lawyer's Farewell," not only because it was published in 1751 by Robert Dodsley as the lead poem in the same volume in which Blackstone's "Lawyer's Farewel" appeared, but also because it did so in a much broader arena where concerns about loss, death, the past as exemplified by ruins both literal and figural, and the historical losses endemic to a lost culture and a lost tradition were not limited to the legal world.[25] As Eric Parisot points out, in the *Elegy*, Gray created a "landmark poetic experiment" that became the "model for sympathetic response."[26] It also became a model for legal parody: by 1770, we find William Woty publishing "The Pettyfogger, a Parody," a long joke comparing the ribald, sexualized, commodity-focused world of Westminster Hall to Gray's romanticized country churchyard. It must have made the rounds in Westminster Hall as it was reprinted at least ten times in the next ten years, and in later years was plagiarized, reprinted without attribution, and otherwise abused.[27]

In his poem, Gray lays out a particular emotional regime meant to be taken quite seriously, one reliant on an aesthetic of containment akin to entombment as well as on a meta-poetics that oddly (but aptly, given the poem's melancholic concerns) positions the poet as witness to his own death.[28] The poem begins by offering us a poet's view of the fading light over a rural landscape including "leas" and "rugged elms, that Yew-

Tree's Shade," much as Blackstone lingers on a fast-receding landscape in "Lawyer's Farewel."[29] Also like Blackstone, Gray gives us the sounds of an idealized pastoral past, its "drowsy tinklings," "swallow twittering," "moping owl," and "lisping" children.[30] Soon, though, Gray focuses on the ancient graves of poor farm laborers, now reduced to "many a mouldering heap."[31] These poor lie beneath rude stones, "far from the madding crowd," silenced not only by death, but by their orality, their illiteracy, and the lack of historical records.[32] "Some mute inglorious Milton here may rest," Gray remarks, reminding his readers that the poor have ample abilities, yet lack access to knowledge, learning, and reading, and that poetry has been lost with their deaths.[33] What is left for them?

> Their name, their years, spelt by th' unletter'd muse,
> The place of fame and elegy supply:
> And many a holy text around she strews,
> That teach the rustic moralist to dye.[34]

What is lost is not simply the lives of the poor, but their stories, their history, their potential for creativity, detailed knowledge of their lineages and desires. Just as Blackstone does in "The Lawyer's Farewel," Gray here idealizes writing: the "ample page / Rich with the spoils of time [that] did ne'er unroll" could have, but did not, speak for these uncelebrated dead.[35] The poem's primary formal convention is that of entombment: as the "rude Forefathers of the Hamlet" sleep in their graves, accounts of their lives are buried in the unknown past, their stories as lost as a gem's "ray serene" unseen in "dark unfathom'd caves."[36] The dead, their experiences, their potential are all buried, even "their crimes confin'd" by their lack of any opportunity for learning.[37] By the end of the poem, as Margaret Doody notes, "the Poet disappears into the dusty ground he has been celebrating."[38] He seems to be observing his own doubly aestheticized death, a death accompanied by "dirges" and memorialized by a "lay, / Grav'd on the stone beneath yon aged thorn."[39] The poet mourns the loss of poetry, buried in the graves of the illiterate dead, and then proceeds to further entomb this loss by silencing his own voice and joining the very illiterate dead he has immortalized. This suicidal move intersects with our understanding of melancholia as an illness—a symptom of an underlying un-grieved or badly grieved loss, and a condition that taints the melancholic's very existence as he "takes on the emptiness . . . and in this way participates in his/her own self-denigration."[40] The urge towards self-denigration, though expressed as sadness, contains anger as well. As psychoanalysts argue, the melancholic's self-doubt, even self-hate, arises from resentment and anger towards the lost other, whether person or ideal, an "other" that has been absorbed by the self. Cheng puts it quite bluntly: the melancholic is a cannibal who "eats the lost object," but then chokes on it, in a not-very-efficient digestive process.[41]

Blackstone's poem "The Lawyer's Farewel" operates on a smaller scale than Gray's *Elegy*, but reflects a similar emotional regime. In becoming a lawyer, his protagonist has joined the "selfish Faction," taken on "pride and avarice," and engaged the noisy "wrangling" that he simultaneously rejects.[42] Ultimately, he sentences himself to retirement, eventually imagining his own death, both an escape from and a punishment for the choice he has made. In this retirement-unto-death Blackstone returns to the very poetry he has left, as in the final lines, he draws on the imagery of retirement reminiscent of the pastoral poems he loved. Yet he is still unable to banish the anti-poetic noise of law. As Cheng suggests, in the melancholic mind, self and other—represented in Blackstone's poem as the harmonics of poetry and the discord of law—have become "intrinsically (con)fused."[43] This sentiment is reinforced by the poem's form. Emphasizing loss, the poem marches in melancholic time, its beat reminding the reader of the passing of time and the necessary losses the poet-lawyer (and the reader) must endure.[44] Its couplets offer further formal advantages for the representation of melancholia.[45] Whether heroic as in Gray or tetrameter as in Blackstone, couplets provide the potential for melancholic incorporation, for the containment of loss within their enclosed lines, especially when they join loss with the desired other through the caesura. So, in Blackstone's poem, closed couplets in the sections discussing law seem to box the poet-lawyer in, creating a sort of death within the poem, while Blackstone relies on the caesura at particularly wrenching moments to keep the desired other in play: "Lost to the field, and torn from you, —," "No room for peace, no room for you."[46] The caesura magnifies the sense of an irrevocable break—that tear or rending that Blackstone's "last tear" suggests—as the poet-lawyer leaves literature for law, while both caesura and couplet sustain the connection by containing both the loss of the other and the other itself within the same line, and eventually within the same couplet.

In Blackstone's poem, the sounds of the poem reinforce both loss and self-hatred. Buried are the remnants of a lost tradition of harmonic sound, now mourned. "Sounds in poems," according to Susan Stewart, "are never heard outside an expectation of meaning."[47] The sounds of nature that Blackstone associates with his lost poetic world (and the poetic world equates with the oral world, the world of the bard and of nature) are actually the sounds of humans listening to nature, sounds assigned to "natural" noise, "humming" and "warbling."[48] In contrast, when Blackstone turns from poetry to law, he finds only "wrangling" and "babbling"; he has lost the meaningful and beautiful, what we might refer to as the harmonics embedded in human names for sound and instead finds only the cacophony of law's noise, which had begun to seem increasingly removed from what he saw as the harmonious roots of English law.[49] In the poem, that harmony is contained in the cloistered figure of justice with "her sacred page," a page in which we find "the wisdom of a thousand years."[50] But Blackstone's poet-lawyer's world is populated by ghosts: first, the ghost of the poet-lawyer, already imagining his own death; second, the ghosts of those lawyers who could, in some better past, remember and thus harmonize the "discordant lore" that the poet-lawyer is left to ponder; third, the ghost of poetry that haunts "justice"; and fourth, the ghost of Alfred.[51] In the final stanza, we find three lines, enclosed in the middle of Blackstone's final "retirement unto death" stanza, that describe the legal setting that the poet-lawyer supposedly evaded through rural retirement and the grave:

> Untainted by the guilty bribe;
> Uncurs'd amid the harpy-tribe;
> No orphan's cry to wound my ear.[52]

"Uncurs'd," "harpy," "cry," "wound"—at the very moment Blackstone offers an escape through death to a peaceful arena free of law's disagreeable sounds, he reintroduces the law's painful, injurious noise, noise that both interrupts and forms the core of his retirement imagery. An

avoided curse still evokes a curse, while in the avoided and yet incorporated "wound," the poet-lawyer's melancholia suggests hypochondria, a
playing out on the body of a psychic injury. Entombment and encryption merge, as the poet's losses become encrypted in bodily wounds.
The poet-lawyer's abrupt departure from well-loved poetry to a world of
law that seems unrewarding, even deadly; his resignation; and his final
acceptance of a death-like retirement all suggest that mourning is never
resolved. Instead, it has evolved into melancholia, or in Dana Luciano's
words, "the pathological refusal of time's discipline."[53]

Blackstone's poem—with its numerous references to sounds now in
the poet's past, its ghosts, and its silenced depiction of Justice—offers a
veiled commentary on the loss of law's ancient tradition, on the loss of
"the illiterate and silent" mourned in Gray's poem and in the image of
the illegible "sacred page" Blackstone introduces. The focus on this sort
of loss suggests Blackstone's preoccupation with what we might call the
problem of the deep past where lost oral pronouncements mingle with
a partial written record.[54] This image of loss was not confined to poetry,
but rather haunted all of law practice. As Peter Goodrich argues, "The
law simply expresses what had always been done, and so assumed the
consent of the people through being, in legal fiction at least, no more
than the description of the illiterate and silent consent of its subject
manifest in custom and use."[55] This spectral theme plays out in the *Commentaries* where the ancient legal tradition that Blackstone associates
with Alfred haunts the modern Enlightenment project that Blackstone
undertakes.[56] Such ghosting suggests a problem with boundaries of
time, of genre, and of emotion in which the past refuses to stay dead and
buried, but instead insists on a continuing existence. As Cheng points
out, "In the landscape of grief, the boundary between subject and object,
the lover and the thing lost, poses a constant problem."[57] Yet this is not
always a negative, not always a "problem." In the *Commentaries*, the failure to transcend the past affectively binds readers to the law by bringing
the most mourned object of the past into law's modern consciousness.
By implying an ongoing process of mourning structured as melancholia, the *Commentaries* indicates a special relationship with legal history,
most immediately present in volume II on property, and particularly in
Blackstone's sections on real property and inheritance.[58]

Legal Melancholia, Productive Melancholia?

I take seriously Jerome Neu's argument that "a tear is an intellectual thing," especially when the tear invoked is an aesthetic tear.[59] As Sartre argues in *Sketch for a Theory of the Emotions*, when facing insoluble problems, expressions of emotion can work strategically to contain conflict while keeping it alive.[60] How might the "intellectual thing" at the heart of this emotional strategy manifest in the *Commentaries*? If the thought of studying law had depressed Blackstone's poet-lawyer, the tasks Blackstone himself faced in writing the *Commentaries* may have seemed even more daunting.[61] It was one thing to write a young man's poem full of melancholy observations, but quite another to resolve the contradictions English law had developed by the 1760s. Legal melancholia already had a long history by Blackstone's time: as a discipline, law had been associated since Horace with the loss of pleasure, of color, of all that was considered beautiful and life-affirming.[62] What had to be repressed in favor of "order, science, reason, and justice" was beauty, or, as Peter Goodrich puts it, "flowers, ornaments, aesthetic judgments, tastes, emotions, lifestyles, and fantasies."[63] Eighteenth- and nineteenth-century comments about the law suggest a continuing association between law's melancholia and the aesthetic losses that Blackstone regretted in "Lawyer's Farewel." Thomas Roscoe's *Westminster Hall: Or, Professional Relics and Anecdotes of the Bar, Bench, and Woolsack* (1825) repeated the old maxim that "Lady Common Law must lie alone," and it was common knowledge that successful law students gave up all forms of pleasure, including women, fashionable dress, and rich food, in the pursuit of knowledge.[64] Typical was poor Jonathan Belcher, a hapless barrister, who, after failing to find business in Westminster Hall, went to Dublin in 1742 only to find that he was "after all [his] studies, fatigue, and expense in a very melancholy situation."[65] As Blackstone notes in his preface to the *Commentaries*, law students faced a "tedious lonely process" and a "dark and puzzled" fate, given the law's lack of organized written resources and the inadequacy of its debilitated oral tradition (I:31). Like Blackstone, Lord Hardwicke framed the law's failures as aesthetic ones, claiming that the law's "notions are so bulky & ill shapen that when they once enter the Brain they jostle out everything else."[66] In Blackstone's early lectures, he wrote about the law's aesthetic decline over time: "The common law of England has fared like other venerable edifices of antiquity, which rash and unexperienced workmen have ventured to new-dress and refine, with all the rage of modern improvement. Hence frequently its symmetry has been destroyed, its proportions distorted, and its majestic simplicity exchanged for specious embellishments and fantastic novelties" (I:10). The law was now full of "insensible and disagreeing words"; it had been "altered and impaired by the violence of the times" (although it had "weathered the rude shock of the Norman conquest"); its study had been "neglected" by the very gentlemen who relied on its protections and made its laws (I:11, 17). Destruction, distortion, violence, neglect: the association of the law with the negative imagery of loss was matched by its "insensible and disagreeing words."

How then does Blackstone manage these losses without succumbing to the malignant melancholia of the poem, without in the end retreating into death? For in the *Commentaries* he incorporates loss into a text that, as William Holdsworth said, displayed an "intelligent satisfaction with the present."[67] This complacent tone has given rise to complaints that Blackstone displayed an "indiscriminate optimism" that has been read as "conservatism"[68]; it might lead one to think that in the effort to avoid a melancholia leading to death, Blackstone had truly shed his last aestheticized tear in "Lawyer's Farewel." And yet, this reading does not take all of the *Commentaries* into account; it ignores Blackstone's treatment of history, his efforts to merge past and present in order to offer readers a satisfying narrative that celebrated England's unique contribution to Western law. All affect serves a function. Even Freud, generally negative about melancholia, held that it attaches us to objects, and motivates us to move towards what we need and away from what hurts us. As David Eng, co-editor of one of the most influential recent collections on loss, argues, melancholia can be "productive rather than pathological, abundant rather than lacking, social rather than solipsistic, militant rather than reactionary."[69] In part, this is a matter of recovery: as we make ourselves whole after some sort of loss, we again become happy. Thus, we are motivated towards improvement. But melancholia, despite interrupting our progress towards wholeness, is productive beyond the new meanings and new attachments meant to help us escape the past. As Eng and Kazanjian posit, melancholia creates "an open and ongoing relationship with the past—bringing its ghosts and specters, its flaring and fleeting images into the present."[70] As a result, melancholia—at least in its aestheticized form—in itself always retains something of the lost past, while offering us something we need: a way of building a future out of that past without ever truly losing it, a way that might even be seen as progressive. This version of melancholia has thus begun to seem to be part of what makes for healthy societal functioning, for progress rather than revolution (in this sense it is conservative), but also for social stability and predictability in the face of the rapid changes brought on by modernity. Less pragmatically, in the realm of aesthetics, productive melancholia creates interest: instead of giving us a flat present—always different, yet always the same since there is nothing to compare it to—it provides us with a rich, layered, interesting world, one with meaning beyond the mere comfort level a presentist perspective might have to offer. Indeed, as Flatley points out, melancholia might "produce its own kind of knowledge."[71]

To understand Blackstone's *Commentaries*, it seems that we need this different understanding of melancholia, one that focuses neither on simple mourning in which the lost object is relinquished and replaced with something new, nor on how melancholia hurts the "patient," leading to a suicidal withdrawal, but instead on what these emotions do for both texts and readers. Such an understanding could mark the violence the melancholic worldview does to history, the ways it destroys accurate understandings of history and replaces them with convenient, powerful narratives that support whatever the present status quo might be. But it could also focus on how melancholia might lead not to hopeless illness, depression, malaise, even suicide, might not involve self-denigration and rage against the lost other, but might instead prove to be a productive, even ethical, force that incorporates losses, remembers them, and bears them homage, while integrating them into a narrative of progress, into what could be referred to as a "new normal" for Enlightenment law.[72]

The Ends of Loss: History, Property, and Identity

If loss was all we had and the past was gone and done for, English law could appear to be mere fiction, something made up to fill the void, offering only an arid, dense codification divorced from the history that it claimed as its authoritative base. Instead, Blackstone strategically invokes loss as a way of avoiding devastation, drawing on melancholia's ability to manage historical change, to fold in what is being mourned, to contain it, even as its absence is noted. Melancholia as exercised in the property volume of the *Commentaries* is thus a formal device: while the melancholic mood established by the property law context (property is not theft here, but loss) helps bind readers to certain ideas about the law, formal devices related to melancholia allow Blackstone to preserve the emotional life of the past by entombing and encrypting it, containing it in a larger future-oriented narrative. In particular, Blackstone relies on melancholic incorporation to preserve the embodied, emotion-laden practices of what he imagined as the free feudal people who provided the foundations of English justice. And he buries this idealized historical past—that of King Alfred and the ancient constitution with its hybrid oral-literate tradition and set of customs from "time immemorial"—in what seems to some readers an obsessive detailing of doctrine, nowhere more manifest than in Blackstone's discussions of property law, particularly of hereditary rights involving real property.

Twenty-first-century readers may find the idea that the power of Blackstone's property sections relied on emotional pleas amusing: this area of law is often seen as the least interesting and most daunting. But property law, like property, is uniquely tied to identity, and identity involves a complex of emotions around all that is associated with it.[73] Blackstone's aesthetic choices mitigate the dullness and dryness commonly associated with property law. In comparison to earlier writers, his prose was considered a joy to read; a long opening portion of the property law volume was collected as a sample of the best English prose had to offer in works such as *The Beauties of English Prose* (1772) and *Elegant Extracts* (1785).[74] Part of that readerly enjoyment resulted from his management of emotion. In the beginning of volume II, he frames property law as an aesthetically organized emotional arena when, in this opening passage, he claims, "There is nothing which so generally strikes *the imagination*, and *engages the affections* of mankind, as the right of property or that sole and despotic dominion which one man claims and exercises over the external things of the world, in total exclusion of the right of any other individual in the universe" (emphasis added, II:2).[75] Moving quickly from imagination and affection to a range of other emotions in what turns out to be a long paragraph, Blackstone evokes pleasure, fear, and satisfaction as possible responses to issues involving property law. In fact, throughout the real property discussion in chapter 2 (and real property takes up over two-thirds of the volume, as Blackstone paid much less attention to personal property or what he called "Of Things Personal"), Blackstone repeatedly invokes a whole network of emotions: contentiousness, greed, jealousy, loyalty, suspicion, possessiveness, impatience, as well as affection, even love and happiness. But the most prominent emotion here is embedded in the very concept of property. Whereas the ownership of property cannot occur without life, it also cannot occur without loss, often loss figured as the death of an ancestor, of family. As Ravit Reichman argues, property can be the object of our desire and also that of our "grief, disappointment, dispossession and guilt."[76]

Other scholars have noted the aesthetic nature of Blackstone's approach to property law, perhaps following his lead when he announces early in volume II that the origins of property law as ordained by God had been preserved in "memorials . . . in the golden age of poets, or the uniform accounts given by historians of that time" (II:3). In her 1999 article, "Canons of Property Talk, or, Blackstone's Anxiety," Carol M. Rose brilliantly addresses Blackstone's understanding of real property and argues that he "set out a range of argumentative moves that can be recognized even today as the canonical strategies for scholarly property talk."[77] Focusing on Blackstone's expressions of anxiety, Rose points out that Blackstone seemed to have little faith in his magisterial opening remarks about the power of man's "sole and despotic dominion" over property.[78] As Rose notes, Blackstone almost immediately begins to qualify this striking, oft-quoted claim, suggesting that even if we allow possession to define ownership, there is no justification for allowing ownership to pass to one's heirs after one's death. In this section of Blackstone's discussion, dead is dead; the dead have "abandoned" their property, for "naturally speaking, the instant a man ceases to be, he ceases to have any dominion. . . . All property must therefore cease upon death, considering men as absolute individuals" (II:10). Death puts an end not only to an individual's intentions and desires, but to their very utility. Sentimental judgments about honoring the intentions of the dead have no place in the law: if the deceased "had a right to dispose of his acquisitions one moment beyond his life, he would also have a right to direct their disposal for a million of ages after him; which would be highly absurd and inconvenient" (II:10).[79] This assumption is crucial to Blackstone's argument for real property law as an artificial construction: "There is no foundation in nature or in natural law, why a set of words upon parchment should convey the dominion of land; why the son should have a right to exclude his fellow creatures from a determinate spot of ground . . . ; or why the occupier of a particular field or of a jewel, when lying on his death-bed and no longer able to maintain possession, should be entitled to tell the rest of the world which of them should enjoy it after him" (II:2). Given the "unnaturalness" of extending an owner's desires beyond death, how then, Blackstone asks, has our elaborate, complex understanding of property law, including the laws of inheritance, developed? Is it possible that our claimed titles to property—titles that have been passed on for generations—are indefensible? Rose deftly explains Blackstone's efforts to deal with this destabilizing insight, what she calls "Ownership Anxiety," as involving a "just so story" followed by "a veritable flood of doctrine," both designed to "smooth the waters and steer the great ship of the common law back on course."[80] As Rose sees it, Blackstone describes property law in three parts: after initially laying out the absurdity of the "exclusivity principle" in what we might call part one, in part two, he explains the origins of real property law in utilitarian terms, using the just so story to explain why property law has evolved into its current state, and in part three, he buries that story in a mass of technicalities.[81]

Without undoing Rose's astute analysis, I want to suggest that Blackstone's just so story is not the only story being told in his discussion of real property. As Wolfram Schmidgen remarks, "the political and social functions of property and place indicate a rich mine for stories about how objects constitute subject."[82] In fact, both the utilitarian just so section and the doctrinal sections owe much to multiple narratives, and Rose's just so story pops up repeatedly throughout the entire property volume.[83] Just so stories claim access to origins in cases where true origins cannot be ascertained. It is no accident then that Blackstone's earliest examples are drawn from the originating story of the Old Testament; for instance, Blackstone cites Genesis 15:3 to note that there was a time when servants could inherit because they tended to surround the death bed. Just so stories also extrapolate from the point of origin they claim; in Rudyard Kipling's just so story about how the elephant got his trunk, he imagines that the impact of an alligator stretching an elephant's trunk could be inherited by the elephant's offspring. Thus, in the world of the just so story, we learn of justifications for the exclusivity clause, such as the need to avoid conflict (conflicts would be inevitable if ownership terminated on death); the importance of husbanding the land (which no one would do if ownership was vested in the most aggressive taker); and finally the gradual development of class structures in which "a part only of society was sufficient to provide by their manual labour, for the necessary subsistence of all; and leisure was given to others to cultivate the human mind, to invent useful arts, and to lay the foundations of science" (II:8). Blackstone's just so story leans heavily on pragmatics: such and such was the logical thing to do, so our distant ancestors must have done it. But this flat pragmatism is invigorated throughout volume II by moments when Blackstone brings the past to life, allowing us to feel as property owners in medieval times might have felt, or at least as Blackstone imagined they felt. In fact, even in the final passages of the most pragmatic section of the just so story, we see glimpses of a more romantic narrative, less ruled by pragmatism and claims to common sense, more familiar to us from chivalric romance or even fairy tales. Merging images from legends and fairy tales with pragmatics, Blackstone asks, what would happen if various unclaimed forms of property could not be owned? "Such are forests and other waste grounds. . . . Such also are wrecks, estrays, and that species of wild animals [termed] game" (II: 14). Here we are in the world of the unclaimed, the uncategorized, hinted at by the fabulous unclaimed jewel of the just so story—so much more exciting than a "particular field"—the world of all that's romantic: wild animals, shipwrecks, lost pets, and mysterious forests. But like a Disney fairy tale ending in marriage, Blackstone soon domesticates these wayward images, locating their disruptive potential firmly in the past. As he puts it, to avoid "disturbances and quarrels," the law has wisely vested ownership of anything unowned in "the sovereign of the state or else in his representatives (II:15). We are meant to be comforted by the closing words of the just so story: "The legislature of England has universally promoted the grand ends of civil society, the peace and security of individuals, by steadily pursuing that wise and orderly maxim, of assigning to every thing capable of ownership a legal and determinate owner" (II:15). There is no longer room for anything wild or free in England; everything is subsumed under ownership.

When we turn to what Rose terms "doctrinal deflection," where Blackstone buries us in "a veritable flood of doctrine," we find another related story gradually surfacing.[84] Rose argues that a close reading of the "doctrinal" section of volume II reveals that Blackstone buries not only the past, but also the reader in doctrinal details. But Blackstone cannot bury the past without revealing where the bodies lie. Instead, his account contains the traces of both the Norman past and the dimly understood Saxon past, an effort at inclusivity on Blackstone's part. This gesture revises England's past so as to suggest that it had one continuous lineage, only slightly interrupted by the Norman Conquest, and traceable back to what Blackstone saw as the Saxon world of liberty and cooperation.[85] Much of that world could only be guessed at; it resided in the lost oral past, in "time immemorial," as legal historians put it. But as Charles Montgomery Gray has demonstrated, Blackstone's "ability to imagine urged him on despite uncertainty. . . . He said enough about Anglo-Saxon England to tantalize, without gathering up the loose ends."[86] And we are tantalized: buried in masses of doctrine is a simpler, braver, less restrictive world of rugged knights and lords, of first-born sons pledged to their lord, of a communal people in solidarity against their enemies. The real story of property law in the *Commentaries* thus lies not in the short, introductory just so portion of the volume, but in the doctrinal sections, where feudal England as Blackstone imagined it lies entombed, encrypted in the intricacy of doctrinal law.

Although all property involves loss as one cannot hold property without someone else being excluded, the macrocosmic losses of Blackstone's volume II extend beyond the individual property owner to encompass the losses of history, the loss of oral culture, and in the largest sense, the loss of communal agreements about meaning and practice that can only occur in a true community of kindred souls. Representing what has been lost, Blackstone offers us the fantastic lost world of King Alfred and the Saxon ancient constitution, filtered through the lens of the Norman refinements that Blackstone found so reprehensible. Whereas Alfred had established laws that were straightforward and easily understood, the "Norman interpreters," who were "skilled in all the niceties of the feodal constitutions . . . took a handle to introduce not only the rigorous doctrines which prevailed in the duchy of Normandy, but also such fruits and dependencies, such hardships and services, as never were known to other nations" (II:51). Buried in Norman doctrine are hints of the deep past of the Anglo-Saxons, a past shrouded in the paucity and obscurity of written records, clouded by changes wrought after the Norman Conquest, brought alive not primarily by Blackstone's references to doctrinal law, but by reference to the body, to embodied and emotive practices woven into the very fabric of the doctrine that he carefully attempts to elucidate. The "antient simplicity of feuds," which Blackstone refers to as "a plan of simplicity and liberty, equally beneficial to both lord and tenant, and prudently calculated for their mutual protection and defence" (II:58), is associated with a fantasy of communality, as Blackstone's imagined lost world seems to hold more in common with Raymond Williams's idealization of the culture of the country as "a celebration of a community of people who share the same assumptions and live in kindness and mutuality" than with any real understanding of the brutal and most likely short lives of the Saxons.[87] What had been lost is a world Blackstone represents as one of mutual interdependence, the world of the "middle course" (II:214). As we have seen earlier, Blackstone had idealized this version of community in his poem; there harmony reigns under "Alfred's piercing soul." But in the Commentaries, instead of a "harmonious rule of right," Blackstone struggles with a web of elaborated, almost incomprehensible doctrine that resulted in part from development once England began to be "considered in the light of a civil establishment," but, he argues, was made more complicated and impenetrable by the Normans. In Blackstone's version of legal history, the Normans destroyed the simple rules of their earlier feudal cousins through "the subtilty of the scholastic disquisitions, and bewildered philosophy in the mazes of metaphysical jargon," which resulted in the "most . . . oppressive consequences" (II:58).[88]

To manage this material, Blackstone frames his account of the "Feodal System" with the melancholic image of the ruin. For him, studying the "obsolete" rules of the past offered the same rewards as observing the ruins of Rome. The image of "the majestic ruins of Rome or Athens, of Balbec or Palmyra" with which he begins chapter 4, while suggesting losses accrued over time, also delights: such study "administers both pleasure and instruction to compare them with the draughts of the same edifices, in their pristine proportion and splendour" (II:44). Ruins are not only "loaded with narrative," as Robert Harbison points out; they invite interpretation, and thus form a fitting image for opening up a discussion about a feudal system known more by its fragments of text and claims of memory than through any comprehensive written records.[89] The comparative pleasures inherent in contemplating ruins were melancholic ones: ruins suggested death, decay, and deterioration, the eventual reduction of even the greatest societies to mere relics and remnants. Blackstone thus suggests here both the pleasures and pains of historical scholarship, of comparing remnants to the reconstructions of remnants, all the while knowing that no reconstruction can fully capture the original.

Out of these ruins and relics of the mostly oral Saxon culture, Blackstone constructs the following story, one focused on oral culture and thus on the body: originally, the King owned all the land, and granted parcels to his knights in exchange for their service. These transfers occurred "at a time when the art of writing was very little known: and therefore the evidence of property was reposed in the memory of the neighbourhood" (II:53). Among others, Pierre Legendere has pointed out that "wherever writing is in issue, so too is the body"; "even though the law has no body, it speaks."[90] In Blackstone, the extended metaphor of the body helps the law speak; his careful historical exegesis offers a window into the development of this dynamic over time. Before the law spoke through writing, it spoke through embodied rituals: for instance, "the delivery of the turf," where objects stood in for bodily possession of land. As Blackstone explains it, "A symbolical delivery of possession was in many cases antiently allowed; by transferring something near at hand, in the presence of credible witnesses, which by agreement should serve to represent the very thing designed to be conveyed; and an occupancy of this sign or symbol was permitted as equivalent to occupancy of the land itself." Some of the objects that stood in for land were objects closely attached to bodies: a shoe, a "cloak of the buyer," a "staff or wand" (II:312–13). But the "mere delivery of possession, either actual or symbolical," eventually grew unsatisfactory because it was subject to "the ocular testimony and remembrance of the witnesses, was liable to be forgotten or misrepresented, and became frequently incapable of proof"

(II:313). Thus, in what seems to have been a lengthy, attenuated process, written deeds developed to stand in for physical deeds, becoming in Blackstone's view "the most solemn and authentic act that a man can possibly perform, with relation to the disposal of his property" (II:314, 295). Interestingly, the *writing* rather than the "deed" is fetishized in these passages, as Blackstone rhapsodizes about the requirement that property transfers be recorded in writing: "The deed must be *written*, or I presume *printed*; . . . it must be on paper, or parchment. For if it be written on stone, board, linen, leather, or the like, it is no deed. Wood or stone may be more durable, and linen less liable to rasures; but writing on paper or parchment unites in itself, more perfectly than any other way, both those desirable qualities: for there is nothing else so durable, and at the same time so little liable to alteration; nothing so secure from alteration, that is the same time so durable" (II:297).[91] Blackstone records with seeming delight the early practice called syngrapha by the "canonists" and chirography in the common law, which preserves the integrity of deeds made by several parties: "It was usual to write both parts on the same piece of parchment, with some word or letters of the alphabet written between them; through which the parchment was cut, either in a strait or indented line, in such a manner as to leave half the word on one part and half on the other" (II:295–96). Durability and inalterability, both qualities of things, but not of human bodies, are here meant to stand in for the ephemeral nature of human transactions, for the vagaries of memory, and the losses that time bestows.

These passages suggest the striking contrast between the vulnerability of the body and the durability of writing. Here we have blood, sex, food (the "hotchpot" as a way of describing the portioning out of real property to daughters), even crying babies.[92] This oral, embodied culture sustained itself through ceremonial moments, including rituals of the body, such as the "homage" when "the vassal or tenant upon investiture did usually pay *homage* to his lord; openly and humbly kneeling, being ungirt, uncovered, and holding up his hands both together between those of the lord, who sate before him . . . and then he received a kiss from his lord" (II:53). Obligations to the lord were physical, potentially violent: "to ransom the lord's person, if taken prisoner"; to go to war for the lord; and to sacrifice one's family if necessary. The lord claimed, for instance, the right to make his vassals' first-born sons knights, a right exercised to provide protection, but also "a matter that was formerly attended with great ceremony, pomp, and expense. . . . The intention of it being to breed up the eldest son, and heir apparent of the seignory, to deeds of arms and chivalry, for the better defense of the nation" (II:63). Body and land were intertwined in these tales, for the lord had the right of wardship of underage heirs should their father die before they became of age, since "the wardship of the body was a consequence of the wardship of the land" (II:68). Grants of land were related to the personal, embodied ability of the grantee to defend the grantor in battle, and thus fathers could not inherit from their sons, even if their sons predeceased them, because lords did not wish to grant land to a "decrepit grandsire" who "would be but indifferently qualified" to serve in battle (II:212). Similarly, women could not inherit, not because they were women per se, but because due to their relative weakness and frequent pregnancies they were unable to serve in battle. Blood is all important here, the key to inheritance and to the "unalterable maxim" that "none was capable of inheriting a feud, but such as was of the blood of, that is, lineally descended from, the first feudatory" (II:56). Such a person is referred to as a "kinsman of the whole blood" (II:227). The blood metaphor plays out in many different contexts: for instance, it is possible for one's "blood" to be "attainted" by being convicted of a felony, for the "inheritable quality of his blood" to be "extinguished," a disability that cannot be removed even by act of Parliament (II:252–54). Reliance on the blood metaphor can lead to absurd results, including the rule that "Bastards are incapable of being heirs. Being thus the sons of nobody, they have no blood in them" (II:247). To this Blackstone adds, as if realizing the attenuation of the blood metaphor, "at least no inheritable blood" (II:247).[93] Land, body, and bloodlines were mutually constitutive of identity: one could lose one's land or one's body or one's bloodline because each stood in for the other.

Of course, there are no real bodies in the *Commentaries*, and no real blood—only virtual bodies and virtual blood or bloodlines. It's all representation everywhere, as the body and blood serve as a highly extended metaphor for a constellation of rights, and instead of actual bodies, we get the language of bodies, words that stand in for bodies. To offer only one of many examples, one from the description of the much-maligned "entail" with its "in tail male or tail female," "the word *body*, or some other words of procreation, are necessary to make it a fee-tail" (II:114–15). And crucially important in creating a fee tail (rather than an estate for life) are "words to ascertain the body out of which [the heirs] shall issue . . . if the words of . . . procreation be omitted . . . this will not make an estate-tail" (II:115). Many of the most important legal terms involving property are terms of embodiment. "Fee-tail," for instance, "signified any mutilated or truncated inheritance, from which the heirs general were *cut* off; being derived from the barbarous verb *taliare*, to cut" (II:112, n.*m*). "Heirloom" derives from "loom," which Blackstone calls "of Saxon original," adding "in which language it signifies a limb or member; so that an heirloom is nothing else, but a limb or member of the inheritance" (II:427). And what of the body that is not a human body? "A monster," Blackstone tells us, "which hath not the shape of mankind, but in any part evidently bears the resemblance of the brute creation, hath no inheritable blood, and cannot be heir. . . . Yet if it hath human shape, it may be heir. This is a very antient rule in the law of England" (II:246–47). As here, Blackstone takes pains to bring the oral world of embodied speech to the textualized world of his own time, the fabulous "ancient" rule of the "monster" to its present application.

This powerful association between Saxon bodies, Saxon customs, and property law persists in the *Commentaries* in the proliferation of technical specifications that eventually came to stand in for the loss of bodies, and with the death of the body, the death of intent and dominion. From the "delivery of the turf" to signify property transfer to the use of the concept of socage, the Saxon practices lived on in Blackstone's version of eighteenth-century England.[94] In fact, according to Blackstone, it was the loss of the body in the body-equals-land equation that destroyed the feudal system. Over time, knights began to offer payments to their lords rather than services, a development that Blackstone refers to as "degeneration" (II:75). And with this "degenerating of knight-service . . . into . . . pecuniary assessments, all the advantages . . . of the feudal constitution were destroyed, and nothing but the hardships remained" (II:75). Worse yet from Blackstone's perspective, embellishments, such as those that characterized the doctrine of uses, destroyed the beauty of "the plain simple rules of property established by the antient law," which made it impossible to untangle, or at least "impracticable" to explain, the current state of the law to educated readers (II:331). The body becomes merely an extended metaphor created by words, words no longer spoken but written, and in an even further attenuated relation to the body, printed and widely disseminated. But in "standing in," writing also marked the loss of the body with its oral expressions, its failure to persist over time. By marking the loss of the oral origins of English law, Blackstone foregrounded the loss of law's authoritative grounding in custom and tradition, in the Saxon bodies of those original creators of English law.

The erasure of law's oral origins was not only a matter for antiquarians, but an ongoing problem still of note to Blackstone's contemporaries. Orality is written into the language and practice of law from its very origins: the word "jurisdiction" contains the word "diction," and as Michel Foucault has pointed out, the court has always been "a site of enunciation."[95] Bernard Hibbitts provides numerous examples of the importance of orality in medieval English law, suggesting the conflation of the oral with poetry when he notes that early English legal representatives were called "conteurs," or "singers of tales." As Hibbitts argues, early law "depended . . . on an orchestration of diverse sensory experiences . . . that enabled transactions to be remembered months, years, and even decades after the fact. Jurisprudence thrived on oral stories and vaguely poetic phrases."[96] The written law marked the loss of that oral world; writing was not necessarily a gain, not necessarily "progress." Indeed, the very modernizing forces that Blackstone celebrates are accompanied by losses in the sense that modernity erases traditions that can only be recounted but not truly experienced in writing. As moderns we mourn that writing can never fully convey what we wish to convey, that writing can never completely stand in for the lost real, that in writing we are relegating our words to the page and thus to others who may never understand them (or even worse, may never read them). Writing represents the quickening pace of modernity, as we are rushed from word to word, pulled from one sentence to the next, from one text to another. To move forward across the page is always to leave something behind. While sound, especially the sound of oral speech, connects us to others who feel it in their bodies as we do, writing separates us from not only the bodies of others, but from our own bodies.[97] The sounds of oral speech are natural; writing is artificial, constructed. In relying on writing for communication, we affirm and reaffirm that we have lost our connection to the oral world of direct communication, of embodied understanding. A story from Albert Lord's *Teller of Tales* illustrates this beautifully: Lord tries to imagine how we might have shifted from oral to written culture. He suggests that we would have needed a scribe to take down the singer's words, but that scribe would have had to ask the singer to slow down, to stop between phrases, to sing the work several times so gaps could be filled in. Perhaps two scribes could have worked together, each filling in the gaps of the other.[98] In any case, no number of scribes could have fully preserved the embodied nature of oral performance. Something is always lost in the recording.

Lord's elaborated description of the technology needed to create a surrogate for the lived oral experience relies on an elaborated process. Similarly, English law relied on extensive doctrinal elaborations, a different sort of technology, to fill in the gaps left by dead bodies and ephemeral oral statements of intent. Much of volume II is consumed by an ever more elaborate effort to explain past practices and align them with present practices, to manage change. In a passage marked by melancholic regret, Blackstone ends his discussion of real property and the law of inheritance with a reference to complexity, to the infinite elaborations that have never proved sufficient to fill the gaps left by the silent dead who originally created the system he strives to preserve. "Vast alterations," he says, "infinite determinations upon points that continually arise and which have been heaped one upon another for a course of seven centuries, without any order or method; and the multiplicity of acts of parliament which have amended, or sometimes only altered, the common law; these cases have made the study of this branch of our national jurisprudence a little perplexed and intricate" (II:382–83). He apologizes for the extensive use of "terms of art," difficult to understand because "of the different languages which our law has at different periods been taught to speak. . . ."[99] He has done what he could, he says, to select the "most simple" principles where practice was the "least embarrassed" (II:383).

The Sense of No Ending

As Frank Kermode tells us, "it is not expected of critics as it is of poets that they should help us to make sense of our lives; they are bound only to attempt the lesser feat of making sense of the ways we try to make sense of our lives."[100] In this effort to make sense of Blackstone's sense-making effort, I turn to Jessie Allen, who has pointed out that it is a cliché to say that inheritance rights allow us to live beyond our own death.[101] But it is not, I think, equally clichéd to say that the proliferation of written inheritance laws regarding real property—so complex that they often tied real property up in the courts for generations—served to extend life after death and to memorialize the dead through ensuring a lack of closure and thus the impossibility of forgetting. People may die, and entire cultures such as that of the Saxon "ancient constitution" may die out, but land persists and claims involving land can, as Rose points out, "go on and on, in layer after layer, to be lost, found, banished, restored, relished, then lost again."[102] The complexity of property law in general, particularly of inheritance laws, seems related to both loss and the denial of loss, to the desire to extend not only individual lives but also cultural lives that might otherwise have been extinguished.

In speaking for the muted dead, Blackstone spoke for England's oral past, for a tradition he imagined as communal and cooperative. The idealized past he imagined seems incompatible with his most cited stand on property law: the right of "sole and despotic dominion" (II:2). Can "no trespassing" signs ever be a sign of communal cooperation? As Duncan Kennedy argues in his famous critique of the *Commentaries*, the effort to organize English law was "an effort to discover the conditions of social justice."[103] But it was also "an attempt to deny the truth of our painfully contradictory feelings about the actual state of relations between persons in our social world."[104] Following Kennedy, we can see that Blackstone's strategy was not benignly rational and optimistic, as so many commentators have claimed. Instead, it involved psychic losses, Kennedy's "pain" and "feelings," the exercise of an emotional economy that does not seem to appear on the surface of the *Commentaries*. The losses Kennedy references are the losses Blackstone associated with the people, with the "social relations" of the old oral world that was seemingly erased by modernity and print, and yet continually evoked in Blackstone's references to the Saxons, and ultimately, in the web of references to Saxon and Norman feudal practices that characterizes much of the volume on property. What Rose calls "a veritable flood of doctrine" can thus be seen to be overdetermined.[105] While impenetrable doctrine serves to deflect readers from the insufficiency of the just so story of property law's origination, doctrinal complications do more than that:

they create a fictional world of web-like interrelations, of time periods, languages, and statements of "will," that in their complexity attempt to compensate us for the imagined wholeness and simplicity of the lost past, despite our pragmatic realization that no contemporary construction can ever give us access to the reality of that past or to its voices.[106] Several of Blackstone's explanations of property law hint at this deep desire for wholeness, for interrelatedness, for community. When Blackstone remarks that "all men are to some degree related to each other," providing us with the lovely, balanced "Table of Consanguinity," he points to the continuity of relations over time, given that after twenty generations, "every man hath above a million of ancestors, as common arithmetic will demonstrate" (II:202–3, see footnote II:203–4). Like the "Table of Consanguinity," the beautiful "Table of Descents" (II:241–42) with its elegant clasped hands, expresses relationality, the ties that bind us together. Such textually inscribed moments reinscribe Blackstone's refusal to divorce 1760s England from its past, either Norman or Saxon, and attempt to affirm community persisting over time, to bring the Saxons and the Normans into solidarity with Blackstone's present.

The assurance of continued rumination on the dead is what psychoanalysis associates with long-term mourning and its supposedly sick cousin melancholia. In Gray's churchyard, the dead lie mute, their memories preserved only through Gray's somewhat self-interested remembrance. Gray's writing stands in for the bodies of the poor and illiterate, allowing us to imagine them in memory. It also entombs them; our pleasure in the work is attained only through their deaths, which ultimately benefit Gray's narrator as he imagines his own highly aestheticized death. As in Gray's poem, what stands in for the dead in Blackstone's *Commentaries* is words, mountains of words that attempt to compensate for the missing human body with its intentionality. Paradoxically, these words, while always pointing towards the missing bodies of the dead, also offer a substitution for those bodies. They provide a link between the lost pronouncements of the dead of the past and the present, keeping human intentionality alive and thus allowing time to move forward, to progress, but without forgetting, without erasing the memory of those who have gone before. In Blackstone's imagined legal world, as in Gray's poetic one, the mourned lost dead stand in for a much larger loss, for the loss of a community imagined as oral in the sense of the oral tradition with its communal solidarity, its integrity, or as Blackstone would have it, its harmony. R. Clifton Spargo tells us in *The Ethics of Mourning* that "solidarity with the dead is an impossible standard," yet one that truly ethical mourning attempts.[107] Unresolved mourning attempts to keep the dead "other" alive in the present, to preserve not only memory, but presence, despite the impracticality of doing so. "When mourning sides with the impossible as though it were standing against the injustice of the death of the other, it demands from its society a reconfiguration of the very idea of ethics itself."[108]

From at least one perspective, then, Blackstone's stance is a profoundly ethical one, suggesting that, with recent theorists of mourning, we celebrate aesthetic melancholia for its ability to keep the memory of the dead alive even as we move forward in time. Blackstone hints at this relation when he associates gains with losses in his examination of landed estates: "We must first of all observe, that (as gains and loss are terms of relation, and of a reciprocal nature) by whatever method one man gains an estate, by that same method or its correlative some other man has lost it. As where the heir acquires by descent; the ancestor has first lost or abandoned the estate by his death" (II:200). Loss and gain are bound together here; every gain has buried within it a loss, and the losses associated with radical change remain, incorporated into the whole through melancholic identification. No matter then how rapid the changes that modernity forced on the English legal system, melancholia compelled incorporation of not just any past, but a heroic, communal past in which writing had been unnecessary because a united people operated in a culture of mutual understanding. By incorporating that past with its vulnerable bodies, Blackstone humanized the technology of the law, asserting its essential grounding in a human frame subject to human effort and sometimes human failure.

In the final pages of the last volume of the *Commentaries*, Blackstone again turns to the past, and to the human, to explain the current state of English law. We may mourn the lack of "authentic monuments" that would have allowed us "to search out the original of English laws," he notes on the last page of the last volume of the *Commentaries*. But "nor have [law's] faults been concealed from view; for faults it has, lest we should be tempted to think it of more than human structure" (IV:436). This "human structure," though faulty, contains not only "antient simplicity," but also "the more curious refinements of modern art," suggesting that the law can accommodate both the oral past and Blackstone's artful manner of containing it in a modern story of progress. Reading Blackstone for an affective aesthetics of melancholia as I have attempted here suggests that more than repression of the past, of loss, and of death is at work; the common law engages its public and claims its authority through the complex aesthetic management of an affective matrix that includes, as in Blackstone, a melancholic understanding of the past. Making visible this management of affective aesthetics reinforces Blackstone's claim that property law is constructed rather than natural, a manmade product, designed to reduce conflict and maintain hierarchies. And yet the meshing of affect with law also asserts law's relationship to human nature, to the natural and normative emotions that we recognize through personal experience. In the end, Blackstone's manipulation of the melancholic losses of orality brings his readers back to the life of the emotions and the senses, back to the body, back to their own feelings, and back to a sort of binding affection that unites them with what might otherwise be regarded as an alienating and repressive legal system.

3

The Orator's Dilemma

Public Embarrassment and the Promise of the Book

It almost seems that legal performance is a legal embarrassment.
—Bernard J. Hibbitts, *De-scribing Law: Performance in the Constitution of Legality*, paper presented at the 1996 Performance Studies Conference, Northwestern University, March 1996, http://law.pitt.edu

The previous two chapters presented a linked effort to explicate the internal workings of Blackstone's *Commentaries* from two different but related emotional perspectives. If a text creates certain kinds of desires that can never truly be met, how then does it manage the inevitable disappointments that result? To explore this dynamic, I largely treated the emotions Blackstone elicited as embedded in text. While these emotions travelled within the text, between the text and other texts, and between the text and its readers, the evidence for them was words on the page, words that at times referenced embodiment and that in themselves imply a sort of materiality, yet still, words. In this chapter, I flip the focus, beginning with the historically situated body in order to complicate the relationship between body and text, between oral expression and print culture. Here emotional mobility finds its fulcrum in the body which itself shifts between materiality and textuality: Blackstone's body with its expressiveness communicates emotion through becoming a sort of text that can be "read," while also remaining a physicalized body, one that inter-communicates with other bodies. Meanwhile, the reading of Blackstone's body that I offer intermingles with the actual text of the *Commentaries* and with other sorts of textualities, including court records and reports. To say that "emotions oscillate between discursive patterns and embodied practices," as Benno Gammerl does, comes close but not close enough to the phenomenon I am interested in here: "oscillate" implies a regular movement, and the movements we see here jerk restlessly around, stutteringly so, as Blackstone himself stutters and stammers in his efforts to shift attention from failed bodies to perfectible books.[1]

Blackstone emerged on the national cultural stage in the 1750s when he was appointed to deliver the Vinerian lectures, the first university-sanctioned lectures on the English common law. Few men could have been less suited for such public visibility. He launched the lecture series with what reads today like a ritual apology, an affective commentary that notes his "great diffidence and apprehensions" in light of the high stakes involved in a public attempt to synthesize and explain the intricacies of the law (I:3). Was Blackstone following Pope's rather conventional advice to "Be silent always, when you doubt your sense; / And speak, though sure, with seeming diffidence"?[2] If so, he seems to have overdone it, for if the printed text of the lecture is to be believed, he held forth on his "great diffidence and apprehensions" for a full two minutes, downplaying his own abilities, yet speaking officiously, even pompously, in the third person. In response to the "honor" of his appointment, the Vinerian lecturer "feels by experience how unequal his abilities are" (I:4). No matter how unequal, though, the Vinerian lecturer is crucial to the future of the nation: should the first appointed Vinerian lecturer fail, Blackstone says, still speaking of himself in the third person, the entire enterprise will fail, and the English common law—"the laws and constitution of our own country"—will continue to be thought of as "dry and unfruitful," even be abandoned as a field of study. These comments seem to connect oral performance to textual efficacy, as Blackstone critiques both his own inadequate embodied presence at the lecture podium and his inadequacy to accomplish the "extensive and arduous task" of "methodizing" the common law, a task that lay ahead of him and would make his career. In fact, both embodied oral and disembodied textual efficacy were at issue.

Blackstone's embarrassment during public performances manifested itself differently at different stages of his career. Throughout, he seems to have had problems with tone, often alienating his listeners with his formality, at other times startling them when he stammered and gaped. Bentham, for instance, found the delivery of the lectures, oral performances that he read from carefully prepared texts, "formal, precise, and affected," the work of a man uneasy with extemporaneous speech.[3] Regarding his appearances at the bar, Blackstone's brother-in-law James Clitherow described him as having "a certain Irritability of Temper, derived from Nature, and encreased in his latter Years by a strong nervous Affection," and to be characterized by "a natural Reserve and Diffidence."[4] Overall, he was "not . . . happy in a graceful Delivery or a Flow of Elocution (both which he much wanted)."[5] In Parliament, he was judged to be "an indifferent speaker."[6] Even his close friends were critical. The poet Richard Graves, a friend and mentor, noted that he "lacked that plausible superfluity of words, which gives some pleadings a show of eloquence." Graves seems to have seen the problem as one involving the filler phrases and expressions that allowed other, more accomplished speakers to fill in gaps:

> [He] never used those supplementary phrases, of "I humbly apprehend;" and "I beg leave to insist on it; or I can take it upon me to prove; with all imaginable ease and facility, to the perfect satisfaction of your lordship and the court," &c.[7]

Sometimes he was damned with faint praise. As Prest notes, a Rev W Palmer found that Blackstone "spoke excellently well . . . in a manner much like that of reading a lecture in college."[8] Others were overtly unkind, suggesting that his deficits were so great that he should have avoided becoming a barrister.[9] Summing up his career on the bench, legal historian Emily Kadens concludes that Blackstone was a "fussy, by-the-book pedant," ill-spoken and perhaps actually ill-mannered.[10] Blackstone himself was under no illusions: as he put it, "there are certain Qualifications for being a public Speaker, in which I am very sensible of my own Deficiency."[11]

Diffident, disfluent, a man without eloquence in an age that valued eloquence: these traits clash with not only Blackstone's literary style, but with his judicial philosophy, with the desire evinced in his poetry and in the *Commentaries* for a justice imagined neither as hesitant or uncertain, but as harmoniously interweaving a culture and its history, just as God had woven all of nature together into one harmonious whole. Various explanations for his inability to express these harmonies in speech have been offered, including an innate shyness that may even have resulted in a near breakdown after he gave his first lecture as Vinerian Professor.[12]

Perhaps Blackstone's humble origins and the loss of his father before he was born undermined his confidence. Bad experiences at school may also have contributed to his later self-consciousness.[13] But glimpses of personal inadequacy found in the historical record will never allow us to plumb the depths of Blackstone's psychology with any confidence. They occur at moments of public performance, and as Peggy Phelan has so compellingly argued, "Performance always teases its spectator with his incomplete access to the subject he gazes upon."[14] Thus, I focus not on Blackstone's personal psychology, but on how these representations of Blackstone as an embarrassed, disfluent public speaker operate to suggest a legible affective sign. To make Blackstone's "diffidence" speak we need to read it in its performative context—as anti-performative as his awkward utterances may seem—as a public, theatricalized performance that was also performative in Austin's sense. As my discussion of Blackstone's anti-performative performance in the famous 1770 *Onslow v. Horne* libel case will demonstrate, these embarrassed, interruptive disfluencies do have a performative value: through a very particular type of performance of the natural, they call the opposition between legal theatricality and the natural into question. More specifically, a disfluent, halting, or oppositional "by the book" style pushes observers into impatience, into desire for the unimpeded word, away from courtroom theatrics and towards the certainty and security of the book. We can thus read Blackstone's awkward self-presentation not only as a symptom of intense discomfort with what had become a highly theatricalised legal environment, but also, and perhaps more importantly, as a performative rejection of orality in favour of the book and the priority of writing. His over-expression of affective discomfort highlighted the comforts offered by the *Commentaries*, comforts more consistent with the new world of print than with the older legal world of oral presentations. Blackstone's embarrassment thus marks not so much his own deficits, but the shift from a no-longer-effective theatrical and oral culture of law to the culture of the book and particularly to the primacy of the *Commentaries*. Going forward, print, not men with their ephemeral performances, would play the key role in Anglo-American law.

Dropping the Teacup: Diffidence, Embarrassment, Bashfulness, Shame

To understand this legible affective sign, we need to know a little about how "diffidence," "bashfulness," shame, and embarrassment were read during Blackstone's time as well as how they are understood today, for they turn out to be crucially important emotions for understanding social relations, and thus intimately related to how we understand justice.[15] These were oft-discussed emotions, partly because mid-eighteenth-century England offered a highly self-conscious arena for public performances, magnified by the expansion of print and literacy. Public performances on the stage, in court, or in the lecture hall were amplified by the spread of newspapers, as now everyone could read about what might once have been minor private embarrassments. Accounts of what happened in court were newly and widely distributed in unofficial reports and compilations printed primarily to entertain the reading public. Both theatrical and legal performances were evaluated not only for their entertainment value, but for their moral value, their authenticity, and their adherence (or lack of adherence) to conventional self-display. No one could escape this culture of performance: it is no accident that during this period Adam Smith wrote embarrassment into moral philosophy with his invention of the "impartial spectator," a spectator we must internalize and whom we can thus never elude.[16]

Although twentieth- and twenty-first-century psychologists debate the difference between shame, shyness, and embarrassment, such distinctions seemed of little importance to Blackstone's contemporaries. Samuel Johnson's *Rambler* 157 essay on "The Scholar's Complaint of his own Bashfulness," published in the early 1750s, offers a prime example, easily mapped onto Blackstone's situation. Johnson's fictionalized letter writer, like Blackstone, has studied "with incessant industry, and avoided every thing which I had been taught to consider either as vicious or tending to vice."[17] But, on suddenly coming into sophisticated company, he is "quelled by some nameless power which I found impossible to be resisted. My sight was dazzled, my cheeks glowed, my perceptions were confounded. . . . The sense of my own blunders increased my confusion, and . . . I was ready to sink under the oppression of surprise; my voice grew weak, and my knees trembled."[18] In short, he suffers an intense attack of embarrassment. He recovers, then decides to join "the ladies" at tea, only again to be "confounded by the necessity of encountering so many eyes at once."[19] Mortified and "ashamed of silence," he pays "too much attention to my own meditations," and drops his saucer, spilling his tea. "The cup was broken, the lap-dog was scalded, a brocaded petticoat was stained, and the whole assembly was thrown into disorder," he says. In response, he slinks away "in silence." While the letter writer refers to his dilemma as "this conflict of shame," Johnson refers to it as "bashfulness" and "diffidence," and recommends the same "medicine" that the Stoics had prescribed, further exposure and the application of reason.[20]

That Johnson primarily relies on "bashfulness" to refer to what we would call embarrassment today makes sense given that the word "embarrassment" was only beginning to come into use in the modern sense when he wrote his *Rambler* essays.[21] Most historians of emotion point out that only in the 1750s did embarrassment stop referring to entanglements and confusion and begin to refer to feelings of awkward self-consciousness related to shame.[22] Blackstone himself uses the word in the *Commentaries* in its earlier sense, to mean confusion or difficulties (I:123, II:202, II:383), as Johnson does in the *Dictionary* where he defines it as "perplexity, entanglement."[23] In the *Commentaries*, the law is often embarrassed, not because it is ashamed, but because it is confused or resistant to explication. In contrast, the modern use of shame as we generally construe it today, as "the painful emotion arising from the consciousness of something dishonouring, ridiculous, or indecorous in one's own conduct" or, as Samuel Johnson put it, "the passion felt when reputation is supposed to be lost; the passion expressed sometimes by blushes," was well established.[24] In the *Commentaries*, shame is reserved for those who should know the law but are ignorant of it or for a government who fails to punish criminals appropriately (I:12; IV:369). The first case invokes the ridiculous; the second something dishonoring.

Many scholars today lump shame and embarrassment together. Take, for example, Martha Nussbaum's comment that embarrassment is simply "a lighter matter than shame," and W. Ray Crozier's concept of the "domain of shame, embarrassment and shyness" as indicating related emotions with differences in intensity and circumstance.[25] Others see embarrassment as something that can only happen in public or in the memory of a public event, while shame can be felt internally in the absence of the public gaze. Shame has received a great deal of attention from both literary theorists and moral philosophers, while embarrassment is an under-theorized emotion that yet provides a crucial link between two theoretical camps in the study of the history of emotion. This is because a primary characteristic of embarrassment is that it is a communicative emotion: it interrupts relations among people through the public display of intense discomfort. Historians of emotion often debate whether emotions are "natural" or "cultural," whereas embarrassment seems almost to embarrass that dichotomy in its simultaneous engagement with the body and the world. It is not surprising then that we find the word "embarrassment" undergoing transformation during a period when public performances became so important. In its essence, it marks breaches in civility, whether those of the embarrassed or of those who have created embarrassment, interruptions in the smooth flow of discourse and the genial celebration of communal agreement through the creation of a non-violent but aggressive, visible and sometimes auditory, punctuation. As Erving Goffman's work suggests, this interruptive quality is at odds with embarrassment's secondary effect, that of offering a bridge to overcome error, of apologizing, in essence, for the very interruption it imposes.[26]

Johnson's dropped teacup serves to make the point: insignificant as the event is, it interrupts all social relations and throws everyone into "disorder." The embodied connotations of the speaker's halting speech are played out in the sexual signs of the scalded lapdog and the stained brocade, as well as in the speaker's inability to communicate with "the ladies." Johnson amplifies the incident to make a point: to serve its social functions, embarrassment must be manifested broadly, must be visible and easily recognised. Thus, from the first cognitive recognition that one has deviated from social norms and been observed, an embarrassed person begins to exhibit symptoms such as restlessness, abrupt gestures, even, as Goffman points out, "stuttering . . . quavering speech, or breaking of the voice," symptoms that operate as a barrier to fluid communication.[27] The speaker may become "rigidly immobile" (as Blackstone once did when challenged in public to align his legal views with the *Commentaries*) because he or she "cannot for the time being mobilize his muscular and intellectual resources for the task at hand. . . . He cannot volunteer a response to those around him that will allow them to sustain the conversation smoothly."[28] Thus, social intercourse is interrupted.

But Johnson designs the teacup incident to highlight its solution. In his response to the fictionalized letter from the embarrassed scholar, he prefigures Goffman, explaining that "diffidence may check resolution and obstruct performance, but compensates its embarrassments by more important advantages: it conciliates the proud, and softens the severe, averts envy from excellence, and censure from miscarriage."[29] If embarrassment silences a speaker, it also prevents him from making a fool of himself and thus reconciles him with his audience. Johnson suggests that all the scholar needs is a little more practice and a lot more humility, and that such embarrassing incidents are typical in the lives of the young and inexperienced. To be embarrassed is to recognize one's faults in order to develop opportunities to overcome them.

"This Learned Theatre of Law": High Stakes and Stuttering Lawyers

By the time Blackstone first entered Westminster Hall as a barrister in the 1740s, it had become a popular venue for proliferating performances that competed noisily for the attention of the spectators, a place where both justices and lawyers were evaluated for their performative potential just as actors were on theatrical stages.[30] The theatrical power of juridical arenas has been a long-running theme in political and cultural theory. We find examples in medieval displays of legal power, in Bentham's assertion that "publicity" was essential to justice, and in Shoshana Felman's more recent observation that "the legal function of the court . . . is in its very *moral essence*, a *dramatic* function: not only that of 'doing justice,' but that of '*making justice seen*' in a larger moral and historically unique sense."[31] Alan Read's recent work on the relationship between theater and law suggests that lawyers may have been the first actors, operating in the Classical world as figures that entertained the public. Juridical venues had always served theatrical purposes, bringing communities together and both displaying and purging emotions in a relatively safe and contained space. And the old argument that law acts on the world while theater merely represents it could be unravelled in both directions: theater clearly influences things in the world, while law both represents and creates what counts as reality.[32]

What may have changed by Blackstone's time was the dissemination of reports of legal performances by the popular press. Given an active, interventionist press, performance at Westminster Hall had become a high-stakes activity; every major trial drew a physical, embodied audience, but also an audience of readers and critics who commented on trials as readily as on the plays they saw at the theater. Given the new reach of speech, lawyers and judges must have felt that all eyes were upon them. In one tract on marital legal practice, Nicolas Venette admonished young lawyers to control their speech and appearance: "If the lawyer displeases, if his voice is harsh, or that he stammers, or has an ugly countenance . . . the Lawyer [may] lose his cause."[33] Boswell worried that he "could not contend with those whom I heard speaking with a perfect English accent,"[34] while a young barrister writing in 1826 explained in exquisite detail the state of nervousness that these expectations raised in him: "The court was crowded. . . . It was a dreadful moment—the ushers stilled the audience into awful silences. . . . It can hardly be conceived by those who have not gone through the ordeal, how terrific is this mute attention to the object of it."[35] There had always been show trials, but now they began to seem more like shows than trials. Major trials like that of Sacheverell in 1710 raised a "demand for seats so great that it provoked a slump in the theatre,"[36] while the 1776 trial of the Duchess of Kingston for bigamy involved, as Hannah More put it, "the bustle of five thousand people getting into one hall." In her letters, More critiqued the Duchess's behavior as if she were on stage: the Duchess "affected to write very often, though I plainly perceived she wrote only as they do their love epistles on the stage, without forming a letter," and the Duchess "was taken ill, but performed it very badly."[37] In the end, she "was mightily pleased with herself for so brilliant a house. People fought and struggled for their places just as they do at the Opera on a great night."[38] That Samuel Foote wrote a play on the event further blurred the lines.[39] Similarly, at the Warren Hastings trial late in the century, seats sold for fifty pounds. Among other attractions, famous orator, playwright, and theater manager Richard Brinsley Sheridan's prosecutorial performance excited an unprecedented flood of press coverage and critical commentary that focused as much on acting style as on the legal aspects of the case. Commentary suggested an audience aware of the metaphorical as well as the immediate stakes. Describing it as "a spectacle of the most exalted nature," journalists said that it "gave us the idea that justice herself sat upon the vacant throne."[40]

Clearly, rapid advances in print culture contributed to this overheated environment. While print may have lessened the memorial value of courtroom performances, it also created a new need for the creation of media events, to be immortalized in print, reported on and argued about in the periodical press, and thus communicated to the far reaches of British rule. Thomas Sheridan said in 1780 that "it is by speech that all affairs relative to the nation at large, or particular societies, are carried on,"[41] but although national affairs might be settled orally, they were communicated throughout Britain by print. An 1825 description of Lord Mansfield reveals the minute level of inspection justices endured, the blurring of lines between the court and the theater, and most importantly, the role of the judicial body in legal performances: "This nobleman was now in the decline of his life . . . but the roses and lilies had not yet forsook his cheeks, and the lustre of his complexion was augmented by means of eyes that seemed to sparkle with genius. His person, if somewhat below the exact standard of beauty, was yet exquisitely formed; his motions were graceful. . . . He also possessed a voice replete with music in all its various modulations."[42] The description focuses on the theatricalised operations of the judicial body, its cheeks and eyes (and through its eyes, its living brain and soul), its complexion with its visible blood, its motions and vocal modulations, all within the space of Westminster Hall, reminding us that legal decisions were made in a physical context by real human beings who were observed by other human beings to be breathing, speaking, and feeling. It also speaks to the theatricalization of the juridical world, a theatricalization that emphasized the "charms of sound" and "music" of the law as much as its visual aspects. Such an emotional and visceral display made justice and the law come alive to an audience, while this sort of publicity was beginning to be seen as essential to judicial authority. As Bentham was to argue, this was an age that brought home the idea that "publicity is the very soul of justice. . . . It keeps the Judge himself, while trying, under trial."[43] Oratory associated with legal performance had become overdetermined, serving both low and high ends: it entertained the public, meanwhile influencing decisions of national and local import while maintaining the integrity of the system.

But the theatricalization of law was a double-edged sword; it could easily be overdone. A highly theatrical oratorical style could be equated with inauthenticity, as is clear in journalistic responses to both the Duchess of Kingston and Warren Hastings trials.[44] Given the connections between theatricality and instability, disguise and false appearances, theatricality could tarnish the juridical world "with the artifice, dissimulation, effeminacy, and luxury" popularly associated with the theater.[45] Critiques span the century, with Pope's 1727 *Peri Bathous* proposing sarcastically that Westminster Hall be turned into a massive theater with room for 10,000 (including the judges), while a 1794 advertisement mocked the "grand display" of "astonishing and magnificent deceptions" to be held at the "grand Hall of Exhibitions at Westminster." These were to include "an enchanted drum," which, rather than promoting harmony, would "set all the company a fighting, for the avowed purpose of preserving order and tranquillity."[46] This sort of commentary suggests that while eloquence was expected, anything too obviously oratorical could draw criticism, even ridicule. These high stakes for public oratory—the requirement for an oxymoronic "authentic performance"—reflected and refracted changes occurring in the theater; both were under radical revision. Beginning in the middle of the eighteenth century, the old "formal" acting style lost its effectiveness and began to be replaced by what was thought of as a "natural" style. A challenging double bind evolved as orators came to be closely scrutinized for their "natural" expression of feelings. As Jay Fliegelman reveals, oratorical texts read like instructions to actors, while actors, as they adopted this supposedly more natural style (most obviously exemplified by Garrick), began to seem more like orators. James Burgh's *Art of Speaking*, first published in 1764 and frequently reprinted during Blackstone's career, is "nothing less than a theatrical text committed to the physiognomy and tonal semiotics of over 75 passions," as Fliegelman points out.[47] According to Burgh, the best natural and spontaneous public speaking could have a profound impact on the listener through its extraordinary qualities: "Like irresistible *beauty*, it *transports*, it *ravishes*, it *commands* the *admiration* of all, who are within its reach." And yet because it subordinates reason to affective presentation, it also reveals "the nakedness of truth, a true beauty, a self-evidence that required no judgment."[48] One can well imagine the stress resulting from an attempt to speak "naturally" while drawing on a memorized performance of over seventy-five passions. This association between oratory and performance, combined with the emphasis on the truth value of fine oratory, on the ability of oratory to stand in for evidence and eliminate the need for judgment, raised the stakes for both oratory and justice. If it was true, as the author of an instruction manual for young barristers opined, that "the perfection of speech depends upon beauty of thought and beauty of expression. As the excellence of speech is thought, so the value of thought is truth," then the manner in which one spoke could be taken to reflect one's deepest values.[49]

Blackstone, of course, came under additional pressure due to the popularity of the *Commentaries*. Adding to the societal pressure for a natural and yet performed oratory to signify if not truth, at least authenticity, was Blackstone's status as first an academic lecturer on the law and later, by the time he was on the bench, the author of the *Commentaries*. For, as much as his person, his works were on display when he sat in Westminster Hall; all who came to observe were ready to critique the consistency of his opinions with the *Commentaries*. Even before Blackstone became a judge, he had been attacked in Parliament for espousing a position that seemed at odds with the *Commentaries*. Blackstone's response suggests the extreme discomfort accompanying such an attack:

> Instead of defending himself upon the spot, he sunk under the charge, in an agony of confusion and despair. It is well known that there was a pause of some minutes in the house, from a general expectation that the Doctor would say something in his own defence; but, it seems, his faculties were too much overpowered to think of those subtleties and refinements, which have since occurred to him.[50]

The very idea of a print representation of the law seems to have been on trial here; much of the conversation around the importance of oratory made unfavorable comparisons to writing. Did Thomas Sheridan have Blackstone in mind when he complained that "our greatest men have been trying to do that with the pen, which can only be performed with the tongue"?[51] Sheridan certainly reinforced the dichotomy when he asserted that "all writers seem to be under the influence of one common delusion, that by the help of words alone, they can communicate."[52]

To complicate matters further, by the middle of the eighteenth century, the use of the new natural style was linked by many to ideas of natural law. Fliegelman has pointed to the mid-century development of the idea that one could find "a natural spoken language that would be a corollary to natural law."[53] Paradoxically, making natural speech represent natural law created an equal if not greater need for theatricality. Over time, the natural became not only as frustratingly artificial as the artificial had been, but also far more difficult to perform.[54] We can see these forces at work in Samuel Foote's *The Orators*, an extremely successful play, performed thirty-nine times in 1762 and on numerous occasions in 1765 and 1766 just as the *Commentaries* was coming out. Here all sorts of ill-speakers find themselves under review.[55] The play satirises *both* the overly eloquent, overly theatrical new oratory with its supposedly "natural" style *and* what we might call the disfluent or "stuttering" style—a style that we think of as truly natural in that it seems to emerge unmediated from the body. In the first act of the play, Foote hammers Thomas Sheridan and his advocacy of the new oratorical style. As Murphy explains it, in Foote's view this new oratorical movement "overemphasized voice and gesture and appealed to the imagination and the passions rather than to the understanding."[56] But in Act II, Foote turns to a "Hall of Justice," obviously Westminster Hall, where he mocks the "stuttering" style, which he denaturalises with his stage directions and over-the-top dialogue. The players are admonished to remember "your proper pauses, repetitions, hums, has, and interjections: now seat yourselves and you the counsel remember to be mighty dull, and you the justice to fall asleep."[57] The actual dialogue is so interrupted as to be painful to read. One lawyer speaks as follows:

> I have an objection to make, that is—hem—I shall object to her pleading at all.—hem—it is the standing law of this country—hem—and has—hem—always been so allow'd, deem'ed, and practis'd that—hem— all criminals should be try'd *per pares*, by their equals—hem—that is— hem—by a jury of equal rank with themselves.[58]

Here Foote turns what we commonly think of as the natural on itself, making of it an artificial performance subject to mockery.[59] Such disfluencies impede effective communication because the more difficult ideas are to process, the less intelligent the speaker seems to his audience and the more likely the audience is to doubt what the speaker says to be true. Thus, halting and repetitive speech marks more than the stupidity or awkwardness of the speaker. As social psychologists Adam Alter and Daniel Oppenheimer have demonstrated, "fluency influences judgment independently of the retrieved content that accompanies the experience of fluency. . . ."[60] Stumbles and stammers, badly handled complexity, sudden reversals, and agonized pauses create processing problems in listeners, making them work harder to understand content and suggesting not only that something is wrong with the speaker, but that something is wrong with the ideas he is attempting to convey. Disfluency "functions as an alarm" calling for heightened suspicion and critique of the speaker's ideas.[61] In *The Orators*, interruptive dashes, the unnecessary piling on of multiple synonyms, the repetitive "hems" of a speaker who makes a speech out of multiple disfluencies all suggest a turn to "the standing law," perhaps even the written law, but any law more reliable and easily processed than that enunciated so poorly by Foote's stuttering lawyer.

Truth, the natural, and oratory were conflated in the public mind with a highly desirable "harmony," thought to be natural, but also ideal. In reading Fliegelman's description of the purposes of late-eighteenth-century elocution and its relationship to "harmony," one is reminded of the harmony Blackstone associated with the idealized form of justice he sometimes called natural law and tried to explicate in the *Commentaries*.[62] But harmonizing texts and voices created a disharmonizing disjunction of their own, as they highlighted the sometimes complex relationship between text and body, between the natural body and the body that lived only to be interpreted for its authentic—or inauthentic—expression of feelings. Both *embodied*—in that self and body were held to be identical—and *disembodied*—in that the surface of the body became a textual surface subject to interpretation—the speaking body of a prominent justice in Westminster Hall must have been under considerable pressure to reproduce the harmonies that the English common law supposedly represented. That Blackstone seemed to have been afflicted with some form of disfluency, that his utterances were interruptive if not precisely abrasive, seems particularly unfortunate given his commitment to the smooth, harmonious representation of English law, but also particularly evocative. His disfluency suggests an anti-performance as performative in its own way as any oratorically sophisticated performance could have been. To make Blackstone's disfluency speak—rather than to pathologize it or dismiss it as incidental—is to begin to understand the complex relationship between legal orality and print culture during his time.

Given the twisting meanings of natural and artificial in this context, it seems important to focus on Blackstone in all his particularity, on the performative nature of his anti-performative style. For when associated with the author of the *Commentaries*, an anti-performative performance must have taken on a very specific meaning. We have evidence of four kinds of disfluency that Blackstone exhibited: first, the marked formality with which he presented the lectures; second, a reticence or "stammer" while attempting to develop his practice at Westminster Hall; third, a paralysis of articulation when challenged in Parliament; and fourth, a sort of oppositional disfluency while on the bench. Such disfluencies—what I call his "stuttering" style—mark his performance as both natural and awkward, a departure from the harmonies of nature as both memorable and undesirable, as uncomfortable, and as anti-performative. When we read of Blackstone's "diffidence," his silence when challenged, his formality, we can imagine both his own embarrassment and observers becoming impatient and embarrassed, even wishing for an escape from orality into writing. Blackstone's style brought others up short, interrupted proceedings, and called into question the authenticity of oratorically sophisticated juridical performances.

On Not Knowing Where to Stop: Performing Obstruction

Legal performance and anti-performance, public embarrassment, disfluency, and the oral-print continuum collided in *Onslow v. Horne* (1770), a libel case, and thus a case that reflects the period's concerns with what has been called "impression management."[63] As in most libel cases, public embarrassment was at issue, here in regard to George Onslow, the first Earl of Onslow (1731–1814), who had been accused in the *Public Advertiser* of accepting a bribe. In response to what he called "a gross and infamous lie from beginning to end," he sued, thus kicking off one of the great technical cases of the century, one in which both Blackstone's disfluency and his regard for print played important roles.[64] Legal scholar Emily Kadens draws on this case to demonstrate Blackstone's desire "to avoid exercising discretion" while on the bench, noting that this libel action showcased Blackstone's adherence to a precedent that may have seemed overly precious. But while Kadens focuses on Blackstone's preoccupation with precedent, a closer look at her examples reveals that print and precedent are often conflated. For the precedent Blackstone insisted on here was that of the requirement that a print libel be reproduced in the pleadings exactly, to the letter, as it had appeared in its original publication.[65]

Blackstone's insistence on the priority of print reveals a lifelong preoccupation. As Kadens puts it, Blackstone came to the bench with a reputation for his "knowledge of the black letter law . . . primarily from books."[66] This bookish orientation, the faith in the power of print that had motivated him to publish the *Commentaries*, underlies most of Kadens's examples. She notes that in the case of *Perrin v. Blake* (1772), Blackstone preferred the exact words of a testator's will over his expressed oral intent; that in an assault case, Blackstone "quoted Bracton and Coke regarding the nature of the fear demanded . . ."; that on occasion he quoted directly from the *Commentaries*; that he frequently lighted on "authoritative medieval texts"; and that in one case, he sought not legal precedents, but print evidence from "the book of rates attached to the Statute of Tunnage and Poundage," deciding in the end that there was not enough "authority in print" to make a just decision.[67] It seems clear that although Blackstone valued precedent—as he indicates not only in most of these examples, but also in *Onslow*—it was precedent preserved in print that he relied on.

Examining *Onslow v. Horne* reveals it as an extraordinarily condensed representation of anxieties related to oral, manuscript, and print cultures, all in the context of public embarrassment and disfluent, disruptive speech. That these anxieties were contained under the umbrella of a libel case is itself suggestive, for libel is in its essence interruptive of social norms. As Blackstone put it, libel has a tendency "to disturb the public peace," causing breaches in social relations and potentially leading to violence (IV:150). More commonly, libel causes embarrassment through loss of reputation (as in *Onslow*), a dynamic uncomfortably close to Blackstone's own issues with embarrassment and reputation. Here, Blackstone's "diffidence" reverberates with the embarrassment of the libeled plaintiff, while Blackstone's disfluent assertions, his efforts to assert the primacy of text, interrupt the eloquent efforts of counsel to subordinate text to oral interpretation.

The case itself was highly politicized, almost guaranteeing that it would become at least a minor media event, exposing Blackstone to scrutiny beyond the confines of Westminster Hall. Horne was a well-known political agitator who took on many political battles over his long life.[68] By the late 1760s, he had developed a reputation for providing "counsel to every man who thought himself capable of being made an object of public commiseration."[69] Apparently this was the role he took on for a Mr. Burns, whom he believed to have been cheated by George Onslow, MP for Surrey. In the April 1770 case that Blackstone presided over, Horne was accused of libeling Onslow in a letter published in the *Public Advertiser*.[70] As a libel case, *Onslow* was bound to bring at least some issues of speech, writing, and print into play, but the case is notable for the range of expressive forms it brought to the bench and for its repetitive, recursive motion between orality and print culture: first, a speech by Horne, overheard and repeated by witnesses who may or may not have been reliable; second, two letters in manuscript, which may or may not have been written by Horne, one of which remained available while the second was accidentally destroyed by the printer; third, those letters reprinted in the *Public Advertiser*, purportedly as written and yet with at least one error; fourth, other letters written by those implicated in Horne's letters, now read into the record and reprinted in the "transcript" of the case; fifth, a letter written by Onslow, the plaintiff; sixth, Horne's letters reprinted in the record, incorporating several misprints, including the word "11th" for "11"; seventh, testimony by various witnesses as to the provenance of these letters; and finally, the "transcript" of the case itself, entitled,

The Whole Proceedings in the Cause on the Action Brought by The Rt.Hon. GEO. ONSLOW, Esq. Against The Rev. Mr. HORNE . . . for a DEFAMATORY LIBEL, Before the Right Honourable Sir WILLIAM BLACKSTONE, Knt. . . . Taken in Short-hand (by Permission of the Judge). By JOSEPH GURNEY.

Much of the case "transcript" purports to record concerns about the status of these documents, their reliability, their meaning, and the accuracy of their transcriptions, concerns that will ironically reappear here in my discussion of the potential inaccuracies of the very trial "transcript" we rely on for analysis.

Kadens calls on this case as a rare opportunity "to listen to Blackstone as he struggled spontaneously with a legal problem."[71] And if Joseph Gurney's transcription is accurate, the case also offers a rare opportunity to analyze Blackstone's "performance" on the bench. That accuracy is almost impossible to judge; court reporting during this period was an uneven business.[72] In fact, a comparative examination of other records demonstrates the unlikelihood of Gurney's claims to accuracy. Almost everyone in Gurney's world speaks rather eloquently; even an uneducated victim of rape is well-spoken in *The Trial of Frederick Calvert, Esq; Baron of Baltimore* (1768).[73] Applying a similar comparative method to what we might call part two of the *Onslow* case, we find that when these facts were revisited in August 1770, Mansfield presided and it appears that someone other than Gurney, listed as "anonymous" on the title page, transcribed the case. One is surprised to see here that Mr. Serjeant Leigh, so eloquently well-spoken the first time around, has suddenly taken to blurting out run-on, ungrammatical sentences.[74] Given the vagaries of eighteenth-century legal transcription, what can be learned then from a "record" of the case? While we can know little of the actual facts, of what really was said and how it was said, we can learn much about how Blackstone was represented to the larger world, by examining the record, such as it is, for what it has to tell us about representation rather than about the "real." Was Blackstone *really* embarrassed or literally (a weighted word in this context) stuttering or searching for words? It is difficult to tell. Certainly, he sounds hesitant when the issue of the two-letter mistake first arises: to Leigh's confident "it is not necessary that it should have *th* over it," he replies, "In common understanding it is not necessary."[75] It is only after ten lines of back and forth between the lawyers that he finally says he does "really think" the variance is fatal.[76] From this point on in the Gurney transcript, his assertions become more forceful and assertive and begin to elicit impatient responses from his interlocutors. To read this transcript at a bit of a slant, for its performative value, is to notice the impatience Blackstone evoked in others and to recognize the ways Blackstone's style interrupted the oratorical smoothness of on-the-bench performances.

This case was complex, mired in the interpretive issues that plague the oral–literate continuum, involving the identity and intent of the letter writer; the differences between accusing someone of taking bribes and asking someone in a public forum whether or not he had taken a bribe; the question of whether or not letters actually ever "speak for themselves"; the importance of stories; and even the question of whether certain rhetorical ploys were honest or more typical of the notorious "Jonathan Wild."[77] But in the end, Blackstone's decision to non-suit the case was predicated on a simple rule of libel law that required a print libel to be reprinted in the pleadings with minute accuracy. The mistake here was indeed minute, so minute that in print it could barely be seen. It consisted of the substitution of "July 11th" for "July 11," a difference of "two insignificant letters," as the plaintiff's junior counsel put it.[78] While this mistake did not result in any interpretive confusion, it was a sticking point for Blackstone as well as an interruptive moment in a case that had largely consisted of lengthy, eloquent speeches until the last few pages. Here, Blackstone is legally correct as well as quick to correct others. But one sees a shift to short queries, interrogatories, exhortations, and expressions of disbelief in all the speakers just as the issue of the "letter" or the literal adherence to it is raised. The number of times Blackstone references text and textuality is itself striking:

- "We are not to conclude . . . what he writes must be strictly grammatical: he might mean to write July *eleven*. Dates are written differently. Some put the figures before the name of the month, some after; and in describing the year, the Scotch write, that such a thing happened in *the* 1770, not in 1770, as we do."[79]
- "You ought to prove it *literatim* in the words, letters, and figures; it strikes me as being so."[80]
- "Your argument would have done better, if in the record they had wrote it *eleven* in letters; for 11 in figures, and *eleven* in letters, certainly read both alike. But they have wrote the figures, and put the *th* over it; which alters the reading and the grammar."[81]
- "Your solution then is, that these are two different marks to signify the same word; one mark is used in the printed letter, another in the record; in

the letter two units, in the record two units and *th*; but the word so signi-fied is still the same."[82]

- "If I admit the variation of a single letter, I don't know where to stop."[83]
- "It must appear to be literally and numerically the same. . . . You ought to have copied it exactly."[84]
- "Had it been a record of the crown-office, it would have been sent down more correct."[85]
- "I . . . should be glad if you could draw me a line, to get rid of so minute a nicety; but I take the law to be so settled."[86]
- "If you can draw me any rational line, at which I can stop, consistently with the rules of law, I would not consent to non-suit a plaintiff."[87]

Blackstone's responses are both repetitive and as interruptive as the line he wishes someone would draw, making much of an issue that On-slow's lawyers thought insignificant. The interruptive theme repeats at the level of the sentence: with hardly any clause going over ten words, every sentence is sprinkled with semicolons and comma breaks. Repeat-ing his point again and again underscores the poignancy of his plaintive "if I admit the variation of a single letter, I don't know where to stop"— indeed, he seems not to know when to stop. And although it is difficult to interpret either his tone or the tone of those who respond, the ten-dency of his remarks is oppositional, an interruptive force in what might otherwise have been the smooth and collegial operations of the court.

Ironically, Blackstone's interruptive moments induce interruptive re-sponses in others: the possibly irritated responses of the generally genial and long-winded Cox and Leigh, including Cox's "it is only two letters; it must amount to a word; it is two insignificant letters," almost call out for exclamation marks. But Blackstone sticks to his point, revealing what Kadens rightly argues is a didactic loyalty to precedent, but also to text. His rejection of "the variation of a single letter" corresponds to his re-jection of any departure from what he understands to be the law. The almost sacred nature of text in a libeled letter, reflected in the principle of exactitude that he adheres to, points directly to the *Commentaries* and to his insistence on the importance of the system he had "methodised" over any expedience that lawyers might wish for. His purpose, though expressed through discordance, is to seek a larger harmony, as he points out when he says, "I'm afraid that would not do. That would let in a hundred altercations."[88] (Note that he is interested in reducing *altercations* as well as alterations.) In the midst of an altercation against altercations and alterations, then, Blackstone points towards the idealized harmonies of the law as represented in print, and in the book. While Kadens sees this as a negative ("Whereas the other judges . . . accepted the limits of the ideal, [Blackstone] . . . did not accept that law in practice did not fit into his neat theories"), one might just as easily read it as pushback, as loyalty to principle, to a system that Blackstone had spent many years perfecting and one that many had praised for its beauty.[89] At least some commentators approved of his position. Some time after the trial, we find, buried among reviews of novels and plays, a review of the eight-volume "Proceedings" of the Onslow case in *The Monthly Review or Literary Journal*. The reviewer comes out in favor of Blackstone's position, arguing that "with respect to the exactness required by the law . . . this rigid formality seems to be very right."[90] By over-expressing interruptive opposition and calling attention to the importance of the word, even to the very letter of the law, Blackstone urged observers towards the perfections of the *Commentaries*.

Blackstone's Dying Words: Be Firm in Your Opinion

Ephemerality is the greatest enemy of law in any society.
—Bernard J. Hibbitts, "Coming to Our Senses: Communication and Legal Expression in Performance Cultures,"
Emory Law Journal 41, no. 4 (1992): 960

In an anecdote recorded in 1792, Blackstone was reportedly asked on his deathbed his opinion on a decision involving penitentiary house management. As the story goes, he responded in favor of firmness, leading the biographer to remark, "Mr. Justice Blackstone's dying words, *be firm in your opinion*, seem to me the most important direction for our conduct."[91] These words may as well have been directed to the English legal system as to any one person, for they mandate a consistency that Blackstone associated with the book, one that he had attempted to make concrete in the *Commentaries*. Thus, to condemn Blackstone as a poor speaker, whether embarrassed or irascible or inflexible, does not tell the whole story, or at least does not reveal in full what he valued in his own time. Blackstone's terse last words reflect a lifetime of adherence to principle, not so much to abstract principle, but to the principle of the text. For how could one be "firm in your opinion" if opinions were based only in memory or shifted with every shift of eloquent expression? Seen in hindsight and filtered through these words, Blackstone's frequent and disfluent insistence on the text over the word suggests the oratorical over-expression of anti-oratorical fervor that in itself elaborates a performance.

Let me explain: Jessie Allen has noted the occasional twenty-first-century use of what she calls a "naturalistic drama": "so unstudied . . . [but] much more heavily masked than a formal legal ritual, whose artifice is readily apparent."[92] As Allen suggests, an "unstudied" performance can sometimes be the most effective of all. But Blackstone over-expresses this anti-performative, unstudied style, over-performing a "naturalistic drama," his diffidence and halting expression so marked as to become the subject of spectatorial comment and critique. His anti-performances thus become what Allen calls "disruptive revelations," moments in which the theatricality of his environment is revealed, when performance has revealed its own artifice.[93] If skilled enough, such disruptive revelations can bolster the illusion performances are meant to create. And yet, this over-expression of failures of expression can seem spectacular in itself. As Julie Fawcett argues, performative over-expression can employ "gestures, or words that deliberately draw attention to themselves: misspelled words or ungrammatical sentences, pages blotted with too much ink, or a deformed body that . . . is undeniable and yet impossible for the spectator to categorize or make conventional."[94] In Blackstone's case, over-expressive performances of the natural, refusals of convention, ugly gaps, and disagreements all drew attention to Blackstone's own "naturalness"—even sparking comments about his possible physical disabilities—while avoiding accusations of falsity.

Blackstone's problem evokes thoughts of what Joseph Roach has referred to as an anxiety of authenticity, an "anxiety generated by the process of substitution."[95] In Roach's schema, actors are "surrogated doubles," performing as surrogates for the "thing," person, idea, or, in Blackstone's case, book that is represented. Their self-representation hovers in a space between "body politic and body natural."[96] In Blackstone's case, this surrogated double is actually a sort of quintuple surrogate: Blackstone on or off the bench stands in for the *Commentaries* and the *Commentaries* stands in for the law of England, while the law of England stands in for natural justice and finally for the harmonic justice that Blackstone idealized. Much mediated and attenuated, then, the relationship between Blackstone's body and the abstraction he called justice is both represented and protected by his hesitant, pedantic elaboration. Like Pope, who contrasted his deformed body to his perfectly formed poetry, Blackstone contrasts his less than fluent speech to the perfections of writing and thus to the new dominance of print as its own sort of performance, one that made the *Commentaries* not only a bestseller, but the primary conduit for the transmission of English legal principles to Britain's colonies.[97] Turning to either Austin's theory of the performative or Samuel Johnson's definition of performance, as "to execute, to do, . . . to achieve an undertaking, to accomplish, completion of something designed," we can reinterpret Blackstone's performance as a lecturer, barrister, and on the bench as successful.[98] His disfluency marked his dissension from the usual way of doing things, from everyday practice at Westminster Hall, and led observers away from performance and towards the sophisticated print texts that were to become the normative expression of the English common law. Meanwhile, this strategy, if we can call it that, undid the distinction between the natural and the artificial, even as it underscored both the authority of the book and the machinations of juridical oratory. In some ways, it celebrated the book as *more* authentic, more reliable than any performance on the bench. Thus, Blackstone's mode of affective embodiment both communicated and accomplished the decline of one system and the rise of another.

Books, as Milton asserted, have a "potencie of life" and contain "the precious life-blood of a master spirit."[99] As we have seen, Blackstone rejected traditionally understood theatricality and performance in favor of anti-performance or what might be called the performance of the book. Instead of performing oratorically, he performed the necessity of the book as a method of access to law—and implicitly of access to justice. While oratory could not, at least in his hands, reflect the harmonies of the English common law, in the book, he could artfully present his material to manage and mitigate disharmony and disfluency.[100] This was not a matter of misrepresenting his sources so much as of careful organization and the use of various literary devices to substitute for the metaphorical "filler phrases" that he found so difficult to utter in public. As Christopher Ricks has pointed out in his study of Keats and embarrassment, art "helps us to deal with embarrassment, not by abolishing or ignoring it, but by recognizing, refining, and putting it to good human purposes."[101] Blackstone's diffident public self-representations, so frustrating to his audiences, paradoxically promoted the book, encouraging a readership that lasted for generations and made the *Commentaries* an iconic cultural monument, a representative of what Northrup Frye termed "the authority of tradition."[102] As such, it is similar to other iconic texts like the Declaration of Independence, a text which Fliegelmann points out is now so "radically cut off from its original rhetorical context by the mystique of print that it is made to seem permanent and immutable."[103] The *Commentaries*, like the Declaration, had the potential for permanence, for influence that went beyond that of any single physical object, precisely because as a print production, it could be easily replicated, distributed, and preserved. As its endlessly proliferating copies were annotated, discussed, read again and again, never read at all but carried about, and collected purely for their historical value, they achieved monumental status, and became absorbed into Anglo-American legal culture. Books like the *Commentaries* could be as performative as performances themselves, staging certain ideas and habits of thought through their remembered existence even when not physically present. As such, the *Commentaries* need not even be present to perform its mission; mere citation, even when cited by those who have never read it, operates as a sign of Blackstone's long-standing influence and of the victory of print over performance that has dominated the modern period.

4

Terror, Torture, and the Tender Heart of the Law

The law is mad.

—Jacques Derrida, "The Law of Genre," *Critical Inquiry* 7,

no. 1 (1980): 81

Derrida tells us that we cannot constitute law or justice without the irrational, violent, inexplicable other, its extravagance and wildness, coming into play.[1] Embedded in each "rational" legal decision is a bit, or maybe quite a lot, of irrationality that cannot be contained within the rational.[2] No matter how hard Blackstone tried to perfect the *Commentaries*, no matter his devotion to harmony and balance, his work was still subject to "contrarieties," moments where rationality did not hold, harmony was disrupted, and unruly emotions seemed to control the text. As we saw in the last chapter, such disruptions punctuated Blackstone's legal career, as Blackstone struggled to reconcile the exigencies of the body, of stutters both metaphoric and actual, with the seamless, harmonic understanding of law he had idealized. But they also occur within the *Commentaries* as instances that suddenly jar us with their lack of rationality, moments that are signaled textually by an odd repetitive, stuttering ineffectuality, or a crazy juxtaposition of reasoned, historical thinking with veiled references to unthinkable violence.

In that light, we must ask how the tender emotions of the heart could possibly be related to the English law of ritualistic torture. Although the English famously claimed not to indulge in judicial torture, the practice of *peine forte et dure*—"pressing" resistant defendants to death—persisted well into the eighteenth century. And English law, it turns out, was never so "tender" as when it considered the question of whether to torture a defendant who had refused the court's jurisdiction.[3] Blackstone's *Commentaries* foregrounds these paired emotions of terror and tenderness in its discussion of *peine forte et dure* by relying on gothic conventions—what we think of as literary conventions, but also emotive conventions—both to legitimize the practice and to distance it from "modern" Enlightenment English law. In this chapter, I locate *peine forte et dure* in the larger context of the literary gothic to unpack a powerful, if contradictory, nexus for generic, historical, and emotional commentary, one that reveals the clash between pre-Enlightenment practices of torture and the Enlightenment reaction to them.[4] For in his discussion of criminal law, Blackstone offers an opening for the study of the use of both terror and tenderness as juridical technologies meant to manage resistance.[5]

"We Inherit an Old Gothic Castle," or Do We?

I begin with Blackstone's famous description of a gothic castle, an image or a "figure"—not so much of speech as of emotion—that Sara Ahmed might refer to as "sticky."[6] For Ahmed, the question of what "sticks" is also a question about "how we become invested in social norms," while the "stickiness" of such figures is "dependent on past histories of association that often 'work' through concealment."[7] In volume III of the *Commentaries*, Blackstone introduces this sticky image thus:

> We inherit an old Gothic castle erected in the days of chivalry, but fitted up for a modern inhabitant. The moated ramparts, the embattled towers, and the trophied halls, are magnificent and venerable, but useless. The inferior apartments, now converted into rooms of convenience, are cheerful and commodious, though their approaches are winding and difficult. (III:268)

References to this passage have become almost a cliché among legal historians and literary critics: most scholars treat the renovation metaphor as an attempt to grapple with England's legal history.[8] And, of course, this approach makes sense and can aptly be mapped onto my discussion of melancholia and English legal history in chapter 2: architecture offers material traces of what has been memorialized and thus is a powerful metaphor for imagining—and managing—the past. Here, though, I explore Blackstone's castle imagery for its ability to layer intimations of the literary gothic—with its metaphors, suspense, anxiety, terror, and also concern with tyranny and rebellion—onto well-worn historical gothic references. This reading suggests that the gothic castle offers a complex key to Blackstone's shaping of the relationship between law, justice, and emotion, a key that exceeds any single interpretation or emotional reaction. What happens if we ask not so much what this passage means in general terms, but instead what it *does* in its immediate context in volume III of the *Commentaries*?

Blackstone introduces the castle not at the beginning of the *Commentaries*, not even at the beginning of a particular volume, but at the very end of chapter 17, volume III, after his final comment on a "private" wrong, in the chapter entitled "Of Injuries Proceeding from, or Affecting the Crown."[9] Perhaps the most striking (and most gothic) sentence in the opening paragraphs of this section is this: "That the King can do no wrong, is a necessary and fundamental principle of the English constitution" (III:254).[10] Blackstone follows this aphoristic comment with an earnest discussion of the unlikeliness of a king ever committing a personal wrong against a commoner—this unlikeliness operating as a justification for the law's failure to take up such matters. But any comfort we commoners might take from these assertions is quickly undone. As if uncomfortable himself, Blackstone ends this short discussion by turning to preoccupations with the complexity of the law, its "great variety, which is apt at our first acquaintance to breed a confusion of ideas, and a kind of distraction in the memory" (III:265). "This intricacy"—involving, among other things, legal fictions or "terms of art"—Blackstone believes essential to the preservation of English law (III:266). As we might predict if we've been reading William Reddy on how emotions work, reasoned discourse is no match for the cognitive overload signaled by "intricacy," "confusion," and "distraction."[11] Reddy argues that emotion is activated when incoming stimuli exceeds attention's ability to translate it into thought or action. For Reddy, emotion takes loosely connected thoughts and consolidates them in ways that urge us on to pursue our goals. Adopting Reddy's logic, then, we are not surprised that Blackstone switches discursive modes here, abandoning a confused attempt at rational exposition for the emotionally evocative description of his imaginary castle. When we enter the castle, we leave the world of rational argument to enter a world of familiar but also unfamiliar images, each of which evokes feelings.

What an overdetermined set of images! The gothic castle of Blackstone's imagination attempts to reduce gothic mystification by bringing it into the light, offering us a comforting, domesticated version of what was once a terrifying or at least awe-inspiring architectural structure. Yet the castle metaphor's location in the text reminds us that once we are under the king's absolute dominion, we risk entering the world typical of gothic novels, a world in which the irrationality of kings trumps the law and makes nothing of peasants. No matter how cheerfully we might confront the "rooms of convenience," they can only be reached through the "winding and difficult" corridors that readers were beginning to recognize from gothic fiction and poetry to be terrifying places where almost anything could happen. Indeed, we end the passage not in one of these "cheerful and commodious" rooms, but in a "winding and difficult" corridor. Here we see a prime example of the way the Gothic castle serves as an inadequate map of the law: as David Punter and Glennis Byron suggest, the "castle has to do with the map, and with the failure of the map; it figures loss of direction, the impossibility of imposing one's own sense of place on an alien world."[12]

That Blackstone would draw on the literary gothic as he produced the *Commentaries* in the later part of the 1760s would hardly surprise a literary historian. This volume of the *Commentaries* was issued right on the heels of Horace Walpole's 1764 *Castle of Otranto*, which is often hailed as the first gothic novel.[13] In *Castle of Otranto*, Walpole established the ancient Gothic castle with its "intricate cloisters," "subterranean regions," "rusty hinges," and "long labyrinth of darkness" not as the locus of liberty and communal harmony that Blackstone associated with the ancient Goths, but as one of the central tropes for despotic rule.[14] Of course, there are no true "firsts" in literary history. As Robert Miles points out, "the origins of gothic lie, not in Horace Walpole's mind, but in the aesthetic that preceded his novel," an aesthetic that included a range of repeated motifs found in various texts throughout the period.[15] In fact, Blackstone's use of what literary critics think of as gothic imagery dated back to his teenage years where he worked some gothic imagery into his early poetry. In "The Lawyer's Farewel," Blackstone's poet-lawyer reluctantly drags himself away from poetry, "As, by some tyrant's stern command, / A wretch forsakes his native land."[16] Exiled from poetry, the young poet-lawyer is forced to enter a nightmarish scene where law is associated with an anxiety-laden labyrinth of smoke, "midnight conflagrations" "in frighted streets" where "orgies hold" and "fell murder walks her lonely round."[17] Here, law solves no problems, but is instead a "mystic, dark, discordant lore."[18] As we have seen earlier, the poem ends with the contemplation of death: "Thus may I calmly meet my end, / Thus to the grave in peace descend."[19] To contemporary critics familiar with gothic motifs, the gothic conventions will seem obvious. Blackstone's legal environment is characterized not only by a tyrannical master and an adolescent adventurer who must be disciplined, but also by obscurity, mysteries, indistinguishable noises, illegibility ("mystic, dark, discordant lore"), a metaphoric live burial followed by imagined death, and unspeakable tortures that appear obscured and apparitional in "nocturnal landscapes and dreams." (I am, of course, borrowing from Eve Sedgwick's famous description of the gothic in her first book, *The Coherence of Gothic Conventions*.)[20] In Blackstone's poem, patriarchy, filial obedience, authority, and power play prominent roles while "affect exceeds reason" as in a gothic novel; law is associated with formlessness and with the impossibility of ever arriving at a rational, legible clarity.[21]

Blackstone pursued this theme of gothic obscurity and darkness in other references in the 1740s and 1750s. In a letter written in the 1740s, he compared eighteenth-century law to a building built two centuries ago, now "altered and mangled by various contradictory Statutes . . . according to whim, or prejudice, or private convenience of the builders . . . the original remains a huge irregular pile, with many noble apartments, though awkwardly put together and some of them of no visible use . . . a new labyrinth."[22] Guiding young lawyers through this mangled labyrinth became Blackstone's concern in the 1750s when he began developing the law lectures for the Vinerian Chair. In his introduction, "On the Study of the Law," later included with volume I of the *Commentaries*, he embarks on a darkening narrative passage that starts with the hopes of (our typically gothic) "raw and inexperienced youth, in the most dangerous season of life"; emphasizes a "tedious lonely process"; and ends with the image of legal education as a peculiar kind of torture that has led "so many" to "confuse themselves at first setting out, and continue ever dark and puzzled during the remainder of their lives!" (I:31)[23] One might see the *Commentaries* as Blackstone's response to this problem: he wanted to save the common law's victims from the dark through bringing law itself into the light.

Getting stuck in the "winding and difficult corridor" of the gothic rather than surfacing in the "cheerful room" of Enlightenment progress was inconsistent both with Blackstone's own goals and with how he was viewed by his contemporaries. William Meredith commented in 1770 that the law, "til you brought it from Darkness into Light, had been as carefully secreted from common understanding, as the Mysteries of Religion ever were."[24] Edward Gibbon used the gothic language of horror when he praised Blackstone for having "cleared" jurisprudence "of the pedantry and obscurity which rendered it the unknown horror of all men of taste."[25] And *The Barrister* noted that the *Commentaries* "brought darkness to light, and reduced to system & method a farrago of legal knowledge."[26] Darkness versus light, obscurity versus clarity, confusion versus solutions: these critiques suggest that Blackstone left the dark past behind for a well-lit present. However, they also point to the function of the *Commentaries* as, in a sense, a gothic text aligned with what scholars of the gothic call the "explained supernatural," a version of the gothic that presents the reader with obscure mysteries dealing with the despotic origins of the majestic power of the law, and suggests that such mysteries could be solved, domesticated, and made safe through careful exposition. The *Commentaries* thus became both gothic tale and gothic antidote as Blackstone drew on Enlightenment historiography and rational organizational principles to bring English law out of the past and into the modern world. Few could read the final words of the fourth volume of the *Commentaries* without thrilling to Blackstone's project: he had presented his readers with a problem of gothic obscurity—both historical and literary—led them through dark passages and past frighteningly obscure and dimly lit forms, but, in the end, come out into the light. "I have endeavoured to delineate some rude outlines of a plan for the history of our laws and liberties; from their first rise, and gradual progress, among our British and Saxon ancestors, til their total eclipse at the Norman conquest; from which they have gradually emerged, and risen to the perfection which they now enjoy." Along the way, as he put it, "we have taken occasion to admire at every turn the noble monuments of antient simplicity, and the more curious refinements of modern art . . . defects, chiefly arising from the decays of time or the rage of unskilful improvements in later ages." "To sustain, to repair, to beautify this noble pile," has been his life's work (IV:436).

"To sustain," "to repair," "to beautify": worthy goals, but were they as self-evidently worthwhile as Blackstone held them to be? Certainly, Mary Wollstonecraft, who reconfigured the gothic castle as a madhouse in *Maria*, didn't think so. Responding to Blackstone as much as to Edmund Burke, she advocated abandonment rather than reform: "Why was it a duty to repair an ancient castle, built in barbarous ages, of Gothic materials? Why were they obliged to rake amongst heterogeneous ruins; or rebuild old walls, whose foundations could scarcely be explored, when a simple structure might be raised on the foundation of experience, the only valuable inheritance our forefathers can bequeath?"[27] As Robert Miles points out, for Wollstonecraft, Gothic structures offered only "the twin pillars of monarchy and patriarchy," and resulted in a "disparity of wealth, false benevolence, licentious sensibility, exaggerated filial obedience [and] craven attitudes towards power."[28] Jeremy Bentham also sneered at the castle metaphor as representative of Blackstone's purposefully obscure legal fictions, associating it not with an ancient and venerable tradition, but with "habits of dark and secret rapine."[29] As Dale Townshend points out, Bentham calls out Blackstone, arguing that he could only have turned the law into a gothic castle "through a radical process of rhetorical alchemy" that in Bentham's eyes represented an immoral imposition of a false and damaging ideology.[30]

Meanwhile, in architectural circles, "renovation" was under attack as architects attempted to straddle practical challenges (to ensure the safety of ancient buildings), political distrust (modernization could be seen as undermining traditional English values), and aesthetic critiques (mixing styles aroused some venomous responses).[31] A writer with deep and broad architectural interests, Blackstone must have been alert to the fact that by the 1760s, architects and their critics were engaged in an impassioned dispute over how gothic renovations should be managed. Indeed, he contributed to the conversation.[32] Suffice to say that Blackstone published on architecture (1747), had a Gothic spire designed for St. Peter's Church in Wallingford (1767), and befriended Sir Roger Newdigate, who had remade his conventional mansion into a Gothic-influenced structure that rivaled Walpole's Strawberry Hill. He must have been alert as well to the issues plaguing the Gothic Westminster Hall, badly in need of renovations, home of most of Blackstone's public legal endeavors, and, of course, the seat of English legal tradition. The

Hall, subject of renovation-related disputes throughout the century, was noisy, cold, and prone to flooding. In the *Builder's Magazine* of 1788, John Carter denounced those who had added "deformity and extravagance" to Westminster Hall's original gothic structure, while later he denounced "improvement" as "the most threatening of renovations" with particular reference to the Hall: "To take down Westminster-hall would be such an outrageous attack on the love, duty, and veneration, which Britons feel for former greatness, that it is almost the thought of a lunatic to suppose such a thing to be possible."[33]

Thus, "repair" and "beautify" were not neutral terms when applied to Gothic architecture or to its symbolic corollary, Gothic institutions and traditions. The overdetermined symbolic use of the old Gothic tradition and what was seen as a new gothic literary style signifies perhaps anxieties about law's origins, perhaps intensified efforts to promote loyalty to the idea of a specifically English law. In any case, when Blackstone pressed these images into service, his goals transcended legal education. Instead, Blackstone aspired to do what psychologists call "binding"; he wished to create an affective bond to the common law, historically construed, but reimagined for present conditions.[34] Drawing on the historical Gothic but also the literary gothic prompted a particular kind of emotional investment in readers, as the reader balanced reverence for English law's historical past with anxiety about its future. Group identity can be built through both positive and negative emotions, through both "the shared tangible reservoirs of images associated with positive emotion" and shared trauma.[35] The evocation of the gothic castle offered a way of containing this emotional nexus; its materialized structure sheltered a number of necessary but inapposite concepts, metaphors, and above all, emotives, all designed to engage readers, to develop their loyalty to the "paradise of law" that some thought England to be. As a reference to a particular kind of narrative, the gothic castle also made certain promises to the reader; most importantly, it promised that, as in gothic novels such as Walpole's *Castle of Otranto*, in the end all would be resolved, tyrannical practices would be eliminated, and the English legal heritage would be passed on to its rightful owners.

"Where Torture Is Unknown": *Peine Forte et Dure* as English Torture

The Castle of Otranto is, like all gothic novels, full of dark passages and scary dungeons. And like most of the gothic novels that followed, it displaces its rather English-sounding characters in both time and place—in this case to medieval Naples. The novel is often held out as the first English gothic: it established certain motifs, including those of the spooky castle and dark passage. As early as the first chapter, the heroine—a young lady threatened with marriage by the aptly named, elderly but lascivious Manfred, prince of the castle—flees into a "subterranean passage" of the novel's old castle where "an awful silence reigned."[36] Then a sudden and unexplained "gust of wind" blows out her lamp and leaves her in darkness.[37] Perhaps more striking than this common gothic trope is the use of animated, gigantic objects to create both bewilderment *and* darkness and obscurity. We are not five pages into *Castle of Otranto* when a surprisingly mobile "enormous helmet" crashes through the castle, crushing the young heir Conrad and leaving his father, Prince Manfred, bereft. The helmet is soon identified as an animated version of a black marble helmet from the nearby church, now super-sized and dangerous. Manfred blames "a young peasant" who happens to be in the wrong place at the wrong time for this "necromancy" and sentences him to starvation through imprisonment under the now quieted helmet, an odd choice for a prison, but one that serves well as it is "a hundred times more large than any casque ever made for human being, and shaded with a proportional quantity of black feathers."[38] The local populace responds enthusiastically to what the narrator tells us is a "preposterous" punishment: "The generality were charmed with their lord's decision, which, to their apprehensions, carried great appearance of justice; as the magician was to be punished by the very instrument with which he had offended: nor were they struck with the least compunction at the probability of the youth being starved."[39] Terror enforced by darkness; young men, at best, banished, at worst, sentenced to die by irrational tyrants; silence; obscurity; the sudden movements of supposedly inanimate objects, artifacts of the past that take on a huge significance in the present; starvation; autocratic pronouncements; the sensation of being buried alive—none of these strike us as characteristics related to a "great appearance of justice," but they are all part of the new order in which the young peasant finds himself.[40] In fact, the novel eventually rejects them: by the end of the book, the tyrannical Manfred's humor shifts from autocratic irrationality to remorseful humility, and the "young peasant" Theodor is discovered to be the rightful heir to the castle.

Blackstone's *Commentaries* is, of course, not a gothic novel. Nor would I ever argue that Blackstone was directly influenced by Walpole.[41] Yet both men were as shaped by the Gothic historical tradition as they were by new gothic literary devices.[42] Walpole reportedly nailed a copy of the Magna Carta to the wall of his bedroom, while Blackstone's interest played out in serious historical study, evidenced by the edition of the Magna Carta he produced, an edition that Prest refers to as "a major piece of pioneering scholarship, as the first critical, systematic attempt to sort out the sequence and distinguish clearly between the different texts of the great charter."[43] Historical gothic and literary gothic slip and slide into each other's arenas; when the literary gothic appears in the *Commentaries*, it seems a resurfacing of the underside of Enlightenment thought, of a repressed critique of the order and reason we associate with Enlightenment law. In that sense, the *Commentaries* and *Castle of Otranto* seem intertextually paired, especially in their efforts to grapple with punishment, a central problem in *Otranto* where, as we have seen, a tyrannical prince metes out draconian punishments at the slightest provocation. As in *Castle of Otranto*, moments of violence in the *Commentaries* represent fissures in the Enlightenment project: volume IV on criminal law contains many indications that Blackstone wished to divorce English law from the violence of what he saw as pre-Enlightenment practices, partly to associate the English common law with modernity, with the emerging bond between humanitarianism and what counted as civilized to the Western world. But he may have also wished to avoid what eventually became a postmodern critique of law, the idea that the founding moment of the law is not one of rational agreement, but of despotic violence.

Threatening this lofty goal were the many practices in mid-eighteenth-century English criminal law that could not be jostled into an Enlightenment frame, that did not easily lend themselves to modern "Enlightened" ideals related to justice. In fact, volume IV begins and ends with Blackstone's apologetic efforts to balance and counterbalance conflicting ideologies. As early as page three, English criminal law practices are set against European practices and judged both less advanced than other branches of English law and more advanced than European practices. Noting that "the criminal law is in every country of Europe more rude and imperfect than the civil," Blackstone praises English criminal law as better than European. Yet he follows this up with an apologia: "Even with us in England, where our crown-law is with justice supposed to be more nearly advanced to perfection; where crimes are more accurately defined, and penalties less uncertain and arbitrary; where all our accusations are public, and our trials in the face of the world; *where torture is unknown.* . . . Even here we shall occasionally find room to remark some particulars, that seem to want *revision and amendment*" (IV:3, emphasis added). Blackstone erases torture from Englishness here, but "revision and amendment," like "repair and beautify," take the place of aggressive efforts to reform or rebuild what should have been considered a teardown. Blackstone offers excuses rather than reform for England's oppressive system of punishments for criminal acts, as critics of his conservativism have often noted. For example, in this first chapter of volume IV, although he deplores the imposition of the death penalty for minor crimes, he does not fully delineate the extreme penalties convicted criminals received for what today would result in, at worst, a jail sentence, leaving out the brandings, mutilations, and executions, all of which were detailed in the press of his time and have been well covered in the legal history literature.[44] Instead, he attempts to soften what was an ugly situation by suggesting that very few defendants accused of minor crimes (to allow fish to escape a fish pond; to cut down a cherry tree; to be in the company for one month with "Egyptians") actually received such severe punishments (IV:4). And he assures us that English law should be based on what we have come to think of as Enlightenment principles, citing "Baron Montesquieu, Beccaria, & etc" as support for the following ideals: "It should be founded upon principles that are permanent, uniform, and universal; and always conformable to the dictates of truth and justice, the feelings of humanity, and the indelible rights of mankind" (IV:3).

When we turn to the final chapter of the volume, we find this rhetorical move repeated: Blackstone again excuses the harsh requirements of the law by suggesting that they seldom occur in practice. Summarizing the law on capital crimes, he notes that generally the law requires "being hanged by the neck till dead," but "in very atrocious crimes other circumstances of terror, pain, or disgrace are superadded," including "embowelling alive, beheading, and quartering; and in murder, a public dissection" (IV:370). Fortunately, "the humanity of the English nation" has tempered such treatment in practice, "by a tacit consent" mitigating measures that "savour of torture or cruelty" (IV:370). As examples, he points out that those about to be drawn and quartered are usually allowed a "sledge" and that few cases of emboweling or burning to death occur without the defendant being "previously deprived of sensation by strangling" (IV:370). Mutilation, dismemberment, slitting of the nostrils, or branding occur "only very rarely." In short, "disgusting as this catalogue may seem," English law is much more lenient than "that shocking apparatus of death and torment" seen in Europe (IV:370).[45] Moreover, it is "one of the glories of our English law" that punishments are mandated by law rather than left to the discretion of judges; otherwise "men would be slaves to their magistrates" (IV:371). Blackstone does not attempt to resolve the problems of selective prosecution this kind of system (harsh penalties leavened by judicial mitigation) tends to foster.[46]

In short, volume IV both begins and ends with a denunciation of not only torture, but all sorts of brutal punishments: it begins with claims that English law rejects torture ("where torture is unknown") and ends with the idea that England has reduced the effects of brutal punishments through "mitigation." This framing seems straightforward enough as Blackstone walks us through the various offenses ("Of offenses against persons," "Of offenses against habitations," etc.). No "winding and difficult passage" here; we are in the world of the "convenient" and the "commodious." But when we get to "Of Arraignments, and Its Incidents," what might seem like a purely administrative section takes a strange turn: we find ourselves in one of Blackstone's "winding and difficult" approaches as he creates what we might call, following Daniel Tiffany, a "spectacle of obscurity," one that implies a "weighty and occupied and consequential epistemological space."[47] "To arraign," Blackstone tells us, "is nothing else but to call the prisoner to the bar of the court, to answer the matter charged upon him in the indictment" (IV:317).[48] Fair enough, but quickly we discover that this is a procedure regulated not by reason, but by ritual: for instance, when the defendant is "brought to the bar, he is called upon by name to hold up his hand: which, though it may seem a trifling circumstance" (and indeed, it does) "yet is of this importance, that by the holding up of his hand . . . he owns himself to be of that name by which he is called" (IV:318). (Interpellation anyone?) A refusal in that instance is easily smoothed over, for a prisoner can simply admit to his name rather than hold up his hand. Such is not the case at the next stage of arraignment. At that point, the prisoner must either "stand mute" or "confess the fact" of his arraignment by pleading guilty or not guilty to the indictment (IV:319).

A serious problem arises if the prisoner "be found to be obstinately mute, (which a prisoner hath been held to be, *that hath cut out his own tongue*)" (IV:320, emphasis added).[49] At this moment we know we are entering not uncharted territory, but the territory of the gothic: self-mutilation, the cutting out of one's own tongue, transports us from the age of reason to a gothic world alien to Blackstone's larger intentions. Within a sentence or two, we are told that should a prisoner insist on this "obstinate" muteness, he "shall, for his obstinacy receive the terrible sentence of penance, or *peine forte et dure*" (IV:318).[50] Confronted with this, the English-speaking reader cannot be blamed for wishing that some explanation of this "terrible sentence" be offered. This is one of the few times that Blackstone uses untranslated Law French; he had himself termed it a "barbarous dialect" and "an evident and shameful badge . . . of tyranny and foreign servitude," while suggesting that in combination with "the terrors of a Gothic black letter" it had caused many law students to give up on their studies (IV:317).[51] (Walpole claimed in his first edition of *Castle of Otranto* that his novel had been originally written "in the black letter.")[52] To the mystified reader, Blackstone here begins to seem more like the unreliable narrator of the gothic novel than a legal scholar. Instead of offering a translation, Blackstone elaborates a full paragraph of qualifications, noting that before this "terrible sentence" is pronounced, the prisoner shall be warned three times (this begins to feel more like a fairy tale than a legal hearing); given a "convenient" respite so he can consider his actions (we see that word "convenience" again); have the sentence read to him; and have benefit of clergy (IV:320). Such elaborated procedures and warnings suggest the seriousness of a prisoner's opposition without explaining its consequences. The mystery only deepens as the passage ends abruptly with this disturbing sentence: "*Tender* has the modern law been of inflicting this dreadful punishment: but if no other means will prevail, and the prisoner . . . continues stubbornly mute, the judgment is then given against him . . . A judgment, which the law has purposely ordained to be exquisitely severe, that by that very means it might rarely be put into execution" (IV:320, emphasis added).

What is this "exquisitely severe" and "rare" judgment? Continuing, we find only an abrupt transition to "a practice of a different nature," "the rack," and a lengthy discussion and condemnation of its use in "French and other foreign nations" (IV:320–21).[53] While Blackstone's point is to distinguish English from European practices of judicial torture, to the naïve reader, this departure from linear narrative feels like a digression rather than an explanation. Like a character in a gothic novel, we are kept in the dark, offered only dire hints about the meaning of *peine forte et dure*, while surprisingly transported to a European context more appropriate to gothic fiction than to English law. This refusal to get to the point while simultaneously displacing "severe" practices onto European nations bears comparison to gothic conventions. As David Punter points out, "Gothic is . . . proliferative . . . : in its trajectory away from right reason and from the rule of law it does not choose to purify itself . . . it tells stories within stories, it repeats itself, it forgets where it left off . . . it loses its place."[54] In any case (and we will return to these "European" passages later in our discussion), Blackstone ignores *peine forte et dure* for two very long pages—only to reveal eventually that it is even more horrifying than we might have imagined in the absence of explanation. It requires the prisoner be

> put into a low, dark chamber; and there be laid on his back, on the bare floor, naked, unless where decency forbids; that there be placed upon his body as great a weight of iron as he can bear and more; that he shall have no sustenance, save only, on the first day, three morsels of the worst bread; and, on the second day, three draughts of standing water, that shall be nearest to the prison door; and in this situation this shall be alternately his daily diet, *till he dies*, as the judgment now runs, though formerly it was, *till he answered*. (IV:322)

In short, because the defendant has refused to admit to the jurisdiction of the court by obstinately standing mute, his body will be pressed under heavy weights—either pressed until he agrees to accept jurisdiction, expressing his consent to the court's authority, or pressed until he dies.

Blackstone goes on to trace the fuzzy historical origins of this practice, noting that originally under Edward I, such persons were only "foient mys en la prisone fort et dure" or, as Blackstone translates it, ordered "into hard and strong prison" (IV:322). More than a full page of text is devoted to an unsatisfying historical exegesis before Blackstone opens another paragraph by announcing that this practice should be abolished by the legislature because of "the uncertainty of its original, the doubts that may be conceived of its legality, and the repugnance of its theory . . . to the humanity of the laws of England" (IV:323). We then leave this dark topic to return to the light: what follows is a well-organized, methodical, highly technical chapter, chapter 26, on pleas—the plea of sanctuary, the declinatory plea, the plea to the jurisdiction, in abatement, in bar, of a former acquittal. Thus, it is a surprise when on the last page of the chapter, a chapter full of abstract language, of the *science* of the law, we return to *peine forte et dure*, this time offered as the remedy for the obstinate and mute defendant without explanation or apology (IV:335). This second reference, rather carelessly tossed out at the end of the penultimate paragraph of chapter 26, is presented as the standard solution to a prisoner who, "adjudged to stand mute[,] . . . perseveres in his obstinacy" (IV:335). Perhaps not wishing to leave the words *peine forte et dure* as the last words of this chapter on pleas, Blackstone appends a final paragraph that operates as a sort of happy ending and offers a stark contrast to the brutality he has just tacitly approved. Should the prisoner plead appropriately, Blackstone tells us, "the clerk answers in the humane language of the law, which always hopes that the party's innocence rather than his guilt may appear, 'God send thee a good deliverance'" (IV:335). The chapter ends almost like a chapter in a domestic rather than a gothic novel, as the final sentence offers a bright emphasis on "convenience" that reminds us of Blackstone's original description of the Gothic castle with its winding passages and "convenient" rooms: "And then they proceed, as soon as conveniently may be, to the trial; the manner of which will be considered at large in the next chapter" (IV:335). At the end of chapter 26, we have left the gothic and re-entered domestic space; we've come home.

What are we to make of this chopped up, obscurely presented, confusing invocation of what can only be construed as torture?[55] That these fragmented and contradictory references to the practice "slot into each other only like a badly tessellated pavement; between the slabs of description and history the weeds of uncertainty sprout through" locates us firmly in the gothic literary tradition.[56] For although Blackstone tells us that inquisitorial tortures, such as the rack, have been "used as an engine of state, not of law," and that it has long been held that "no such proceeding was allowable by the laws of England" in order to achieve a confession, what is *peine dure et forte* but a form of torture designed to induce the prisoner to confess that he is subject to the law? (IV:321) A little etymology mixed with a little history may help here, or may confuse us more. *Peine*—from the Latin *Poena*, a penalty, fine, or blood money. *Peine*—pain, effort, sorrow. So perhaps penalty, and then, *forte et dure*, perhaps strong and hard? But how did English law take the idea that one might be penalized "strong and hard" and develop the practice of ritualized pressing leading to death that Blackstone describes?[57] J. H. Baker explains that the practice originated in an insistence that prisoners recognize the common law: as early as the thirteenth century, if prisoners refused to state how they wished to plead, they were returned to prison "as one who refused the common law."[58] But the gradual evolution of the practices associated with *peine forte et dure* resulted from a translation or perhaps a transcription mistake. In 1275, Parliament "expressly provided that [the punishment] should be a *prison forte et dure*," meaning a strong and hard imprisonment, but over time "by a grisly misunderstanding the *prison* of the statute was read as *peine*, and by the 1300s the 'hard penance' usually involved pressing the accused to death under heavy weights."[59] Is it fair to point out the irony in the contrast between the careful attention given to the procedure itself ("a low dark chamber . . . three morsels of the worst bread . . . three draughts of standing water, that shall be nearest to the prison door") and the lax attention given to translation and transcription? Or, for that matter, to the way this narrative regarding writing intersects with the gothic convention of the obscure and barely legible text?[60] As in the gothic, human agency intersects here with non-human, non-living forces that nevertheless seem to be animated. When language takes on a life of its own, apparently without human intervention, we are in the realm of the uncanny, of the gothic. In any case, Blackstone glides over the problem, noting that "prisone" somehow became "*peine*," and fantasizing that this could have been a "species of mercy," as it was clearly better to crush a prisoner with heavy stones than to let him slowly starve to death in prison (IV:323). As Ronald Paulson has pointed out, the gothic moment tends to involve "cases of justification followed by horrible excess."[61]

If this was a "mistake," then it was a terrible one. For as Andrea McKenzie demonstrates in her fine *Law and History Review* essay, *peine forte et dure* took on a life of its own in the 1720s and 1730s, becoming everyman's way of proving manliness and independence in an era when men felt the new formality of legal regulation and policing to be oppressive and their resistance to these pressures to be heroic.[62] While I will detail only one of the many cases McKenzie brings to bear on this question, suffice to say that men sentenced to the *peine forte et dure* could live as long as nine days and often *did* live for several days in screaming agony before the stones did their work, "not either to die or live, the torment being lingering."[63] Some held out until death, but McKenzie reports on one Burnworth who in the 1720s "continued for the space of one hour and three minutes, under the weight of three hundred, three quarters, and two pounds," meanwhile "endeavouring to beat out his brains against the floor" before finally being persuaded to enter a plea.[64] These eighteenth-century prisoners suffered over trivialities. While in past centuries men of property may have willingly chosen to be pressed rather than give up their estates by pleading, the debates of the eighteenth century tended to be about a few shirts, a "periwig," or a gold watch, with prisoners obstinately standing mute as to their pleas, but not as to their demands that their goods be returned.

Records of *peine forte et dure* as practiced in the eighteenth century provide a deep, wide repository of evidence for studying the history of emotion, and particularly legal emotions. Nathaniel Hawes's case, its details preserved in a number of varying accounts over a hundred years, offers only one of many condensed and yet comprehensive set of texts for analyzing its operations.[65] Hawes's story is one of almost carnivalesque resistance, of a world turned upside down and in opposition to law.[66] As a member of the notorious Jonathan Wild's gang, Hawes developed a reputation for rebellious high living as a youth, rejecting life as an apprentice to an upholsterer and choosing instead to rob his employer. "No honor among thieves" must have been his motto, as his repeated ploy was to turn in others for receiving his stolen goods. In the popular criminal literature of the time, he was described as "bold," a "downright *Don Quixote*," and a consummate escape artist.[67] A hilarious account of an escape from "New-Prison" recounted in *The Lives of the Most Remarkable Criminals* has Hawes proclaiming, "There's nothing I won't undertake for Liberty," and plotting with a fellow prisoner, a woman referred to as "this Politician in Petticoats," to persuade a jailer to give them a poker for the fire.[68] This incident makes much of the manipulation and management of emotion: Hawes and his friend feign dejection, sitting "with the same Air as if the Rope already had been about them at Tyburn," thus engaging the sympathies of their jailers who indeed give them a poker for their fire.[69] Using the poker and some other tools, including "four yards of strong Cord" hidden in his new female friend's apparently voluminous clothes, they chip away at the jail's mortar and escape.[70] Their almost novelistic gallantry is noted: Hawes supposedly helps his female confederate out before leaving himself.[71]

Accounts of Hawes's life hover somewhere between the admiring and the judgmental. Was he "naturally vivacious, sprightly, and daring," or a coward, ready to turn in his associates for any advantage?[72] All accounts note his adolescent rebelliousness and reckless behavior, his flaunting disregard for the law, while some cite him for heroism. When finally brought before the court for the robbery that would lead to a death sentence, Hawes refused to submit, saying that he would not plead to the indictment unless the "good Suit of Cloaths" that had been taken from him was returned. He added, "No one shall say that I was hanged in a dirty shirt and ragged coat."[73] The court reportedly responded by upbraiding him for his "brutish obstinacy" in the face of English law's reputation for being "more tender of the Lives of its subjects than any other in the world."[74] Was it an excess of this "tender" feeling that led the court to attempt to persuade Hawes to plead by tying his thumbs so tightly that two strings broke? In any case, Hawes refused, stating "he had lived with the Character of the boldest Fellow of his profession and he was resolved to die with it, and leave his memory to be admired by all the Gentlemen of the Road in succeeding Ages."[75] At least one report characterizes Hawes's response as insulting to the court, citing Hawes' rebellious speech, "That, instead of Justice, he was likely to receive injustice: but therefore doubted not that they would, some time or other, undergo a heavier sentence than could be inflicted on him."[76] Far from being "obstinately mute," then, Hawes was, if anything, loquacious. But he was no match for *peine forte et dure*. After what must have been a long seven minutes under a 250-pound weight, he submitted to the court's jurisdiction, having had the very force of the law pressed into his body. Reports differ as to Hawes's docility following *peine forte et dure*; some suggest that he became an exemplary prisoner thereafter, and others state that it was the death sentence and expectation of being hanged that transformed him from rebel into penitent. But post–*peine forte et dure* Hawes is represented as a chastened figure, in so much pain from "the Bruises he received thereby on the Chest" that he had difficulty praying and spoke only to warn others against thwarting the law.[77]

A 1797 account of Hawes's life and death makes light of the issue of "impression" by using all caps to refer to the IMPRESSION Hawes had of himself as a "hero" in the same sentence in which it describes the 250-pound weight used in his torture.[78] It might as well have referred to the fact that Hawes was reportedly *unimpressed* by the court, concerned more with his peers' opinions of his behavior than with what the authorities might advise. Through Hawes we can better understand the functions of *peine forte et dure* and why it persisted despite the persistent calls that it be abolished. A prisoner who refuses bodily, emotionally, and cognitively to submit to the court's authority and thus exposes the social contract in all its fragility, one who exercises his individuality against law's desire to categorize and dispose of "cases," takes on an outsized importance and cannot be ignored, especially during times when the law feels itself under threat. As J. Jeremy Wisnewski points out, torture works by "obliterating agency by turning agency against itself."[79] Thus, *peine forte et dure* takes advantage of one of the most important tools torture has at its disposal: the infliction of pain to force the internalization of consent. To transform Hawes from self-fashioned hero, a "regular Don Quixote," to repentant legal subject, he must appear to choose the law, to accept its great weight and incorporate it into his worldview. By being made to choose, he was forced to exert agency in the infliction of his own bodily pain. This dynamic is commonplace in theories of torture: the worst tortures break the victim's spirit because the victim is made to feel that he has chosen the pain inflicted upon him and then, in the end, has chosen to obey the torturer.[80] *Peine forte et dure* translated the symbolic weight of the law into a physical weight brought against the actual body of the prisoner, making of his body "the anchoring point for a manifestation of power."[81] To mark the defendant as this "anchoring point," it relied in part on the estrangement of the victim from his community, on the symbolic casting out of the victim, here to a "pressing room," in gothic novels to dungeons or underneath giant helmets.[82] Thus, Blackstone is able to argue (in a somewhat tortured fashion) that "torture is unknown in England" because by refusing to plead, the victim of *peine forte et dure* has placed himself outside of the law, outside of its jurisdiction, meanwhile being physically removed from official jurisprudential space to the "pressing room" at Newgate. And yet, *peine forte et dure*, despite these distancing tactics, remains in another sense under the law. The "pressing room," not even mentioned by the court in Hawes's case, works as one of the gothic's "Chinese boxes," interior to the law, boxed up inside it, only pretending to exteriority.[83] While in the pressing room, Hawes is isolated from the larger community, confined to a small room in a dark, dank prison, but literally pressed by the law to take up less space, his body metaphoric for the value the jurisprudential community has placed on his views. As Ahmed notes, "Fear works to contain bodies within social space through the way it shrinks the body."[84] As part of the ritual, the prisoner loses the individuality signified by his clothes, his body exposed, "naked, unless where decency forbids," as if to further mark "the asymmetry of power, knowledge, and prerogative" endemic to torture and of heightened import here, given that Hawes had triggered these acts by insisting on the return of these items.[85]

Peine forte et dure forces a prisoner to express consent: by oppressing, it forces an expression. It also creates an impression, not only on the body of the prisoner, but also on his psyche. As Ahmed points out, "we need to remember the 'press' in an impression. It allows us to associate the experience of having an emotion with the very affect of one surface upon another, an affect that leaves its mark or trace."[86] *Peine forte et dure* creates a visible, legible trace of psychic trauma, of the forces of the law on the body. And that visible impression communicates the power of the juridical to the larger public. In this sense, Hawes's pain was not solitary, but instead created impressions on others as well, on all who heard about or read about his case. It thus served a binding function, drawing others into an allegiance to the rule of law. *Peine forte et dure* also offers a demonstration of the uncanny power of language, the way a "mistake" can take on a power of its own and give words the authority to control human behavior. This sort of uncanny, the animation of inanimate objects, reminds us of gothic fiction's relationship to objects, and particularly of *Castle of Otranto*, where, as we have seen, mysterious totems of the past suddenly become animated and take on the power to kill. Like the giant mobile helmet in *Castle of Otranto*, Blackstone's *peine forte et dure* offers an imposing symbol of ancient tyranny, somehow unloosed from its moorings and set free to cause havoc, characterized by the oppression of rebellious youth by erratic tyrants, unspeakable tortures located in dark, gloomy, distant cells, punishments that do not fit crimes (except, perhaps, in expressing tyrannical power symbolically), and objects that become animated in unexpected fashion. One can see how much affect exceeds reason here when one thinks about how easy the solution to a prisoner standing mute could have been: simply assume that a failure to respond is a not guilty plea and try the prisoner, an easy solution and one the English eventually adopted.

As in Blackstone's much earlier poem and his later warnings to law students, the law here is "mystic, dark, discordant" and "dark and puzzled."[87] The gothic inference heightens the sense of being subject to a higher power, even while reminding English readers of their past, a past when instead of cold reason, they were governed by folk tales, superstitions, and rituals, a past that returns to haunt the law even as late as 1772, when *peine forte et dure* was finally abolished. Gothic stories are meant to impart moral lessons, usually lessons in which unworthy rulers exact a terrible price for youthful rebellion and yet, in the end, everyone ascends to the light. They play with obscuring and then revealing secrets; their role is to provoke unease, and as Bridget Marshall points out, much of the unease they provoke relates to justice.[88] The hereditary secret as well as secret abuse are both specialities of the gothic, and also of Blackstone's account of *peine forte et dure*, where the "secret" of *peine forte et dure*'s indefensible origins becomes the "secret" of the mystification necessarily resulting from adherence to legal history divined from ancient law.[89] The very cloudiness of *peine fort et dure*'s origins suggests the fictionality of the origins of law itself and might explain the law's perverse insistence on its continued use. For to admit that a familiar and oft-used practice was founded in legal misunderstandings and translation errors *and then use that admission to justify change* could mean calling many other common law practices into question.

One of the "secrets" that all accounts of *peine forte et dure* skirt is the secret of pain.[90] Blackstone's account is not cohesive; scattered and interruptive, it skirts not only the "facts," but also the real issues of pain, noise, and the physical signs of trauma, blood, drool, and vomit that must have accompanied *peine forte et dure*. Those who chronicled Nathaniel Hawes's experiences mention only the later effects of *peine forte et dure* on Hawes's body and mind, never attempting to directly describe the agony he must have felt. By focusing on the rituals that surround the infliction of pain and on the results of pain (capitulation), but stinting descriptions of pain itself, these accounts hint at a gothic unspeakable, at what Sedgwick refers to as "the difficulty the story has in getting itself told."[91] But these accounts also suggest that the extreme pain of torture is unnarratable, unspeakable, and, as Elaine Scarry has so compellingly argued, resistant to language.[92] Scarry tells us that the "difficulty of expressing pain" intersects with both the "political and perceptual complications that arise as a result of that difficulty" and the "nature of expressibility . . . or of human creation."[93] While her position has been critiqued as reifying pain, as treating it as an irreducible fact rather than an interpretation, Scarry's work nevertheless offers some productive ways to think about *peine forte et dure*. That we cannot or will not fully express the meaning of pain in ways that another can understand speaks to the problems of expressibility generally, to the inefficacy of words to represent the human condition. In Blackstone's work, *peine forte et dure* becomes a metaphor for the unspeakable, and for the ways English law generally and Blackstone specifically could not fully encompass law's not always rational or explicable origins and present practices.

Given the stakes, Blackstone's seeming indifference to the historical origins (or lack of origins) of this practice, and his admonition almost as an aside that the practice should be prohibited by the legislature at some unknown point in the future, seem cold, horrifyingly so. And yet, perhaps both the practice and Blackstone's accounting of it make more sense than we might think. Freud, as Adam Phillips tells us, associated fear with the past: "Fear returns us to what we already know; it is a symptom of knowledge, knowledge of and from the past."[94] Sartre associated fear with the future, with the unknown.[95] *Peine forte et dure* encompasses both versions of fear: in Phillips's terms, it is a fear of a future set in the past.[96] It represents a fear of an old system where elite subjects could not be assumed to consent to the king's rule as well as a new order where the lower classes cling to their self-fashioned identities and refuse the subjectivity thrust upon them by the law. To the extent we can shift uneasily back and forth between the world of the symbol and the world of the real, we can see the symbolic valence of this practice in response to a prisoner's refusal of the jurisdiction of the court. Such refusals increased in the first half of the eighteenth century, as McKenzie demonstrates, but even more importantly, resistance to law itself increased, or was at least newly viewed as a social problem, a problem Henry Fielding addressed in his famous *An Inquiry into the Causes of the Late Increase of Robbers*, published in 1751. That Jonathan Wild and his colleagues became wildly popular figures only underscored the appeal of disorder and instability and the need for the law to respond. In fact, a commonplace in theories of torture is that torture crops up in response to particularly unstable features of a government that might otherwise appear to be powerfully situated. When faced with what must have seemed to an eighteenth-century justice the irrational behavior of a prisoner, the court resorted to what was at least thought to be the ancient practice of *peine forte et dure*. When faced with incommensurability, with paradoxical problems, with the absence of reason, Blackstone similarly turned to conventional practices, here gothic conventions.

Against the unheimlich gothic environment of the "pressing room," a place outside of the law and yet regulated and thus under the umbrella of the law, Blackstone offers English law's "tenderness." The pressing room becomes a gothic space of confusion and obscurity, a space where, as Robert Miles puts it, the self becomes "fragmented" and is "dispossessed in its own house, in a condition of rupture, disjunction, fragmentation."[97] Where then does the "tenderness of the law" come in? Much recent work on fear and domestic space suggests that fear of the other, of the violence without, pushes us to choose domestic space and call it "community," creating a simple dichotomous relation. But Blackstone's operation is a bit more complex. In the *Commentaries*, the law's tenderness creates both spaces, the inner home of the law, patriarchal but predictable and thus relatively safe, and the outer space of torture, of no-law (which is nevertheless defined by, maintained by, and operated by the law). Under *peine forte et dure*, the defendant enters a public space of law, resists it, is banished to be tortured in a separate, dark, dangerous space distanced from the actual operations of law, and then, should he choose, is returned to the now-safer-seeming space of juridical authority. What better way to emphasize the value of Enlightenment law than to contrast it to its other, even while maintaining control of the other and thus demonstrating a truly awe-inspiring power to manipulate our world?

"So Tender Is the Law": An Opening for Critique?

With Scarry as my role model, I want to return to Blackstone's rendering of the horrors of *peine forte et dure*, the ways it both silences its victims and forces them to express their compliance with authority, as I attempt to recover something creative, something that is attempting to be born. Scarry tells us that "to witness the moment when pain causes a reversion to the pre-language of cries and groans is to witness the destruction of language; but conversely to be present when a person moves up out of that pre-language and projects the facts of sentience into speech is almost to have been permitted to be present at the birth of language itself."[98] Both Scarry and Joanna Bourke document pain sufferers' inability to easily express their pain. But Bourke goes a step further than Scarry, suggesting that, following Wittgenstein, there must be "inter-subjective" words for pain; to be known as pain, pain must be named. And naming occurs in the context of social interaction, of communication.[99] Torture, however, "deliberately sets the victim out of those human communities within which . . . pain is communicable."[100] In Blackstone's description of *peine forte et dure*, speech is absent. The prisoner has initiated the process by refusing to speak after speaking all too much, and then is reduced through pain to a speechless body, at best able to speak only authorized, pre-scripted words. Like but unlike the prisoners, Blackstone initially refuses the words that would detail the punishment, offering unannotated Law French and vague and terrifying descriptors—"exquisitely severe," "terrible sentence," "dreadful punishment"—before finally providing us with details (IV:320). Even in the most florid accounts of *peine forte et dure*, the pain of the sufferer is described only symptomatically (he beat his head against the floor, he was unable to speak), while in more self-contained accounts, the entire *peine forte et dure* episode is glossed over, dismissed in less than a sentence. Blackstone deals with severity, terror, and dread through escape: he flees from pain just as gothic authors abandoned their characters in dank cells, and he embarks on gothically long departures from the topic. Yet his repetitive returns to *peine forte et dure* suggest that we take a closer look at what conceptually may be struggling to emerge.

In his description of English *peine forte et dure*, Blackstone emphasizes the law's insistence on affording the defendant a full explanation of what's to come if he "obstinately" refuses to plead. Before ordering *peine forte et dure*, the court must explain the penalty three times, offer a "convenient respite of a few hours," and read the sentence "distinctly . . . that he may know his danger" (IV:320). These measures both result from and trigger awareness of what Blackstone calls the law's "tenderness." As Blackstone explains, "Thus tender has the modern law been of inflicting this dreadful punishment" (IV:320). What could the law's tenderness possibly mean in a context in which pain has been ordered, inflicted, and yet erased? And how could naming this emotion help us change our orientation towards its object?[101] Ahmed notes that "naming emotions involves different orientations towards the object they construct."[102] For Blackstone to name the law's emotion as tenderness changes our orientation towards the law, but also suggests a particular understanding of the law's orientation towards the defendant.[103] In the legal context, "tenderness," of course, has a related word: "tender," to offer, to propose acceptance, to convey. Blackstone often uses it in that sense.[104] In other usages, Blackstone seems to be implying that "tenderness" could mean wise discretion, in that judges who enforce rules with extreme exactitude lack "a decent degree of tenderness" (III:409). Less commonly, he draws on "tenderness" to mean "cautious": in volume II, the courts are "tender of extending or multiplying acts of bankruptcy by any construction" (II:479). But he also uses it to refer to youth, as in "of tender years" or "tender age" or "tender in age" (II:70, 83, 88).[105] And he recognizes "the most tender affections" as feelings one has for one's family (II:11). In this context, when Blackstone refers to the king's death, the word "tender" in the expression "so tender is the law of supposing even a possibility of his death" (I:242) seems to move both beyond cautiousness into the realm of compassion and beyond cognition into the realm of the body.

This more emotive use of tenderness was supported by the culture at large. "Tenderness" is the word that Samuel Johnson defines as "the susceptibility of impressions" and the "susceptibility of the softer passions," and even "the anxiety for the good of another."[106] Adam Smith argued for tenderness as a special quality associated with extraordinary virtue: "Virtue is excellence, something uncommonly great and beautiful, which rises far above what is vulgar and ordinary. The amiable virtues consist in that degree of sensibility which surprises by its exquisite and unexpected delicacy and *tenderness*."[107] Fielding too had praised the "tender-hearted and compassionate disposition" as "the only human passion that is in itself simply and absolutely good," although he warned against indulging it when the prosecution of robbers was at stake.[108] And given that the law's tenderness in this section of the *Commentaries* consists of warnings and threats of violence, while being associated with pain and trauma as much as with fear, the word could have evoked several related meanings included in Johnson's *Dictionary*: "easily injured; easily pained; soon sore."[109] It almost seems as if the law's "tenderness" prefigures what the defendant is about to go through.

Other examples in the legal literature position the tenderness of the law in relation to compassion; they appear in the context of rights, particularly where the liberty of the defendant is at issue. For instance, in John Rayner's 1765 "A Digest of the Law Concerning Libels," we find a particularly interesting incident that embeds the law's tenderness in a field of emotional responses. Rayner tells us that in cases of prosecution for spoken "scandal," the law exercises a more lenient standard than it does for written scandal: "The *law through compassion*, admits the Truth of the Charge to be pleaded as a Justification, yet *this Tenderness of the Law* is not to be extended to written Scandal, in which the Author acts with more Coolness; and Deliberation gives the Scandal a more durable Stamp, and propagates it wider and further; whereas in words, Men often in an Heat and Passion say things which they are afterwards ashamed of."[110] In other words, the law not only exhibits tenderness (or compassion), but also does so by measuring the emotions of offenders and offering leniency when emotions are high. In an account of "The Trial of Earl Ferrers" (Ferrers was the last peer to be hanged in England, in 1760), the Westminster Hall justice reportedly urged the jurors to remember that "the greatest or meanest subject of this kingdom (such is *the tenderness of our law*) cannot be convicted capitally, but by a charge made by twelve good and lawful men, and a verdict found by the same number."[111] In a similar usage in the capital punishment context, William Paley in 1791 argued that it is the "tenderness of the law" that spares defendants capital punishment "as far as the necessity of restraint and intimidation permits."[112] Does Blackstone's reference to "tenderness" in his portrayal of *peine forte et dure* suggest a tenderness related to the rights of the defendant, to the protection of the idea of liberty, even a compassion that wants to be sure the defendant understands the full power of the law and the repercussions if he does not submit to it? If so, "tenderness" becomes the one positive, emotive, non-analytical, irrational word in these passages, the one word that points us to a law that Blackstone repeatedly defines as "humane." In choosing this word, we might even argue that Blackstone implies a personified "Law" that seems to be feeling the prisoner's pain, to be responding sympathetically even as it exercises its power to terrorize through the infliction of pain and bodily injury.

Blackstone uses the word "tenderness" not once but twice in describing the rights of the prisoner in regard to *peine forte et dure*. The second usage occurs in one of the passage's oddest moments, when Blackstone seemingly drops the discussion of *peine forte et dure* without explanation to turn to "a practice of a different nature"—the use of the rack in France and Europe (IV:320). In an effort to distinguish the English practice of *peine forte et dure* from the "rack for torture," Blackstone instead draws too close a comparison.[113] Shifting the scene to Europe "distances, relocates, reterritorializes these scenes," as Punter points out in reference to the gothic novel, even while "it ceaselessly incarnates precisely the material which it claims to be banishing, and in doing so provides us with a kind of secret history of what goes on beneath the veneer of culture."[114] Instead of presenting tenderness as the law's natural reaction to a prisoner's potential distress, its motivation for making sure a prisoner understands his options, Blackstone finds it "astonishing" that the French should claim that they use the inquisitorial rack "from a tenderness to the lives of men . . . because the laws cannot endure that any man should die upon the evidence of a false, or even a single, witness; and therefore contrived this method that innocence should manifest itself by a stout denial, or guilt by a plain confession. Thus rating a man's virtue by the hardiness of his constitution, and his guilt by the sensibility of his nerves!" (IV:321) Tenderness in this foreign context thus signals the emergence of a contradiction and a new understanding of the law's responsibility. The contradiction is clear: English tenderness expressed around the practice of *peine forte et dure* appears as an almost parental concern for the defendant's rights, indicative of the highest virtue, while French tenderness is incomprehensibly astounding and irrational. Herein lies Blackstone's critique of his own culture's "tenderness," a recognition that tenderness and the purposeful infliction of pain are in open conflict. Unpacking this tenderness allows us to see the space Blackstone creates, perhaps reluctantly, perhaps without even knowing it, for a critique of not only *peine forte et dure*, but of all governmental inflictions of pain, a space that we should attend to if we are to lay claim to the best in the Enlightenment heritage even as we legitimate torture with exceptionalist rhetoric.

The Gothic, the Real, and the Real-ish: Guantanamo Bay

When literary critics speak of the gothic, they speak of a genre, of fiction, not of the "real," the real workings of law or illegality, and especially not of the real bodies of real people. But Sedgwick—referring to the porousness of the boundaries between gothic fiction and the "real" of historical imprisonment, oppression, and even torture—reminds us that "no nightmare is ever as terrifying as is waking up from even some innocuous dream *to find it true*."[115] She thus suggests that incidents that strike us now as "gothic"—such as imprisonment in dungeons, subjugation of adolescents by tyrannical fathers, the suppression of mysterious and horrifying secrets, the misinterpretation of illegible writings, or the disappearance of the one written document that could offer clarity—occur in the world of the real as well as in fiction.[116] The story of Comte de Mirabeau offers an apt example of a sort of Mobius strip where real and fictional discourses intersect around Blackstone's *Commentaries*. Mirabeau, the victim of his father's rage, was imprisoned in the dungeons of a chateau in France, where he became enamored of the *Commentaries*. On his release, he published *Essai sur le despotism*, condemning arbitrary imprisonment, and then was again locked up from 1777 to 1780.

As John Emerson tells it, "Not having access to writing paper, Mirabeau tore out blank pages from the books he was allowed to borrow and read, wrote in tiny writing and sewed the resulting text into his clothing."[117] In these notes, Mirabeau cited Blackstone as "the scholarly and judicious" thinker who advocated for *habeas corpus* and trial by jury.[118] The gothic, of course, is replete with images of secret and secreted texts, written in barely legible script or script about to become so, but also with what Sedgwick loosely refers to as "writing on flesh," which can occur through "marking on the surface with a liquid, by staining through the surface, or, finally by impressing in the surface."[119] As Sedgwick points out, "the depth of the inscription . . . does not show that the graphic character is . . . intrinsic in the bearer. . . . Its depth merely shows the mutilation caused by the attrition of experience."[120] This gothic image of the French Mirabeau adopting Blackstonian principles as a result of his imprisonment, sewing his Blackstonian argument for liberty into his clothes, and of Blackstone's words literally pressed next to Mirabeau's flesh, words molding to the body in order to be smuggled out of a dungeon, is wonderfully suggestive in light of *peine forte et dure* with its gothic pressing, pressure, and impressions. Even if it is not quite literally true (for at least some of his "incarceration" Mirabeau was simply exiled to a small town and at other times he was at liberty if he remained out of the major cities; there is also some evidence that his father incarcerated him primarily to protect him from creditors), it provides an example of gothic images that hover disturbingly between the "real" and the fictional, images that highlight certain aspects of Enlightenment law. By contrasting the gothic dungeon to Blackstone's *Commentaries* as an emblem of liberty, but also in mirroring Blackstone's own beliefs about French oppression versus English Enlightenment, the story emphasizes Blackstone's "reasonableness," subordinates French law to English law, and conflates ideas of freedom and liberty with Blackstone's text. Perhaps most importantly, it raises the issue of the relationship between the oppressed body and Blackstone's text, in that Mirabeau's liberation becomes associated with his physicalized adoption of Blackstone's words. By recording an event that involved pressing the very words of the *Commentaries* against the flesh of the imprisoned Mirabeau, the incident suggests that oppressed subjects could almost physically absorb Enlightenment law into their very bodies.

Like others writing from the Law and Humanities perspective and also in sympathy with the gothic tendency to disrupt boundaries, specifically disciplinary and historical boundaries, I want to bring Blackstone's text to bear on contemporary events, particularly on recent and ongoing US discussions of torture in the so-called "War on Terror." Is it possible to rehabilitate Blackstone, if only a bit, by teasing out a new application of Blackstonian tenderness for international law? Like Ahmed, I want to ask, "How are emotions bound up with stories of justice and injustice? How do emotions work through texts . . . to open up the possibility of restoration, repair, healing and recovery?"[121] I do not need to detail the situation at Guantanamo Bay after all that has been in the press, but I do want to mention one press report.[122] In April 2005, *60 Minutes* covered the story of the FBI agents who refused to engage in interrogations at Guantanamo Bay because they found them, among other things, "inconsistent with American values."[123] And, of course, "American values," at least those values of "life, liberty and the pursuit of happiness" espoused by Jefferson and his compatriots, are largely Enlightenment values, given the influence of French, Scottish, and English Enlightenment figures on the American colonies. Over the years since this story came out, much evidence of torture has accrued, and in June 2015, the testimony by Majid Khan, prisoner at Guantanamo Bay, was released, providing even more evidence that the tortures carried out at Guantanamo Bay were not only inconsistent with what we like to think of as American values, but staggeringly barbaric. It is interesting to examine the language surrounding the release of this information: a CIA source told the *Telegraph*, "They got medieval . . . and far more so than people realise."[124] Guantanamo Bay's ongoing story has been addressed by political scientists, rights activists, and, of course, the military; here I want to map the Guantanamo Bay atrocities onto my analysis of "gothic Blackstone" to suggest how the dynamic relationship between gothic representation and the "real" revealed both in the literary gothic and in the *Commentaries* continues to control how we pursue and construe torture. As with Blackstone's description of the English practice of *peine forte et dure*, many accounts of the events at Guantanamo Bay have elided descriptions of torture, renaming it or adopting the jargon of "enhanced interrogation" and "military necessity" for their power to obfuscate, or simply refusing to discuss it, as in the CIA's omission of the issue of rectal feeding in its 2013 report.[125] The rationale for this terminology was similar to Blackstone's argument: US law does not tolerate torture; therefore, these practices either did not exist or must be distinguished from torture. The activities at Guantanamo Bay have been couched in the language of the gothic, as references to torture as "medieval," expressions such as "a dark and surreal world," and the description of Guantanamo Bay as "a constitutional black hole" and a "dungeon" demonstrate.[126] Locating torture in a "black hole" or "black sites" displaces the torture practices of the United States to areas unknown, dark, and marked as other, such as Cuba, Thailand, Poland, Lithuania, Romania, Afghanistan, and perhaps other unadmitted locales. Such displacement, as much for jurisdictional reasons as for secrecy (or "national security," as some would have it) operates much as it did in the gothic novel, or in Blackstone's *Commentaries*, to indicate that "it can't happen here": torture happens elsewhere and what is not-here we can claim to be not-us.[127] Other similarities abound, as torture does not change much across historical periods or cultures: black sites have engaged in *peine forte et dure*–like rites, chaining defendants to the floor, depriving them of food and/or force-feeding them, leaving them naked before their clothed captors, using common objects (chairs, tables, "pieces of material culture to annihilate the culture within one," as Wisnewski puts it), and manipulating victims into "choosing" their own punishments.[128] Most importantly, the fact that the United States continues to torture long past the point where any information could be gained demonstrates that, as with *peine forte et dure*, we torture not so much to gain information as to gain compliance, particularly emotional compliance, to control "others" who do not answer in the affirmative when we assert our jurisdiction. (That we also seem to torture purely for reasons of sadism is beyond the scope of this chapter.) One difference between US torture and *peine forte et dure*, of course, is that the United States has not adhered to Blackstone's "tenderness doctrine," a doctrine that we should expand beyond the mere recital of rights to an overt recognition of the "tender" condition of certain individuals, ones that are especially disadvantaged by their status, situation, or background.[129]

As Gavin Miller points out, to admit to tenderness, to choose it as a value, has become taboo in modern culture.[130] We are, though, beginning to develop arguments for a new "tenderness doctrine" that would protect those at Guantanamo Bay. Such arguments bring the concepts of "tender," "tender years," and "tenderness" together with the physical implications of tenderness to allow us to reconsider the value of a tenderness doctrine for our time. They are related both to the "vulnerability" thesis propagated by Martha Fineman and the "capabilities" approach favored by Amartya Sens and Martha Nussbaum.[131] Such a tenderness doctrine might suggest that we take Blackstone's claims for the law's tenderness seriously, and begin to ask how, in fact, the law became tender and how might it become more so? Given our resistance to applying tender emotions to legal situations, some might argue against a new tenderness doctrine as relativistic: What would prevent jurists from defining tenderness subjectively? But tenderness could be construed as an objectively defined response to an objectively defined condition. Tenderness in the physical sense is itself related to pain but is not pain. Where pain is subjective, felt by the patient, tenderness is a diagnostic category, noted when a physician palpates an area and the patient reacts. This recognition of tenderness in another leads physicians to act, whether or not they feel sympathy, empathy, or possibly even sensations of pain themselves. In the emotional realm, tenderness involves the sympathetic or empathetic response to another's situation of vulnerability (those children "of tender years" treated tenderly by the law). Is there a sense in which English law became tender at the thought of *peine forte et dure* as it sensed the defendant's imagined future pain? Was it perhaps vibrating in an attenuated sympathetic response to that pain? The communicability of pain has been extensively documented; people often wince when they see another suffer a blow.[132] Scarry describes incidents in which the torturers lay claim to their victim's pain, albeit in a self-serving fashion meant to reduce their personal responsibility for suffering, and, of course, we all know the expression "too painful to watch," an indication that pain can be transferred from the individual experiencing it directly to others in the vicinity.[133] McKenzie notes that in 1658, those inflicting *peine forte et dure* found it a "horrid Spectacle"; others were so desperate to end the victim's suffering that they threw themselves on his body to bring on a faster death.[134] Bourke provides much evidence of the eighteenth-century awareness of the communicability of suffering.[135] If we are capable of imagining the law as tenderhearted, then perhaps we can also imagine it as tenderly responding to the pain of its subjects or even as feeling tender (warm, gentle, but also pained) itself. And thus we can reread the "tenderness of the law" in Blackstone as a moment of empathy, a moment even going beyond empathy to action, in an effort to expand the protection (or the "home") of the law to those most vulnerable.

What can be recuperated from this for today? Affective economies involve the circulation of emotion to create feelings; if we wish to change both the economies and the feelings, we must circulate emotional language differently.[136] I would like us to explore unifying three understandings of tenderness: first, the tenderness that Blackstone and his peers associated with compassion; second, the tenderness referred to in the "tender years" doctrine; third, the tenderness of bodily pain resulting from seeing or "feeling" the injury of another. The first form of tenderness imagines tenderness as "a key component in translating the ability to share the feelings of others into action in their interests,"[137] while the second form goes beyond patriarchal power to include the impulse towards caregiving; the third offers a "trigger" that should initiate a particularly specific sort of judicial review. As Kalawski suggests, "tenderness can be regarded as the impulse toward tender—that is, caregiving—behavior; or else as the acute act of recognition of an object as a fit object for such behavior."[138] Can we imagine a legal system that adheres to a tenderness doctrine, not patriarchal, not simply invested in full disclosure of consequences, but one that recognizes vulnerability as a trigger for certain protections beyond those afforded by equal rights or the prohibition of cruel and unusual punishment? In short, I am arguing for tenderness as an umbrella term for an expanded understanding of moral cognition that takes into account its complexity and yet has legal applicability. Such a tenderness doctrine would engage the entire human "integrative system of neural interconnectedness for human morality— one that sustains contributions from intuitive and controlled emotion processing, imaginative processes, semantic and motivational facets of moral cognition, as well as interactions with a social knowledge base."[139] We could ask then that the law should treat defendants *as if* law itself could be imagined to exhibit tenderness, as if the pain of the defendant could be felt, although perhaps in only the slightest, most tremulous way, by the law itself. And in asking the law to take on the pain of the defendant, we could ask it as well to make alleviating that pain its priority, to create a new understanding of rights, based not on equality or deservedness or national identity, but in the body and in that body's vulnerability, a human trait that, as Fineman points out, is a "universal, inevitable, enduring aspect of the human condition that must be *at the heart* of our concept of social and state responsibility,"[140] and thus, at what we could imagine as the tender heart of the law.

5

Blackstone's Long Tail

The (Un)Happiness of Harmonic Justice

In a conversation that draws upon her work on "the cultures of affect," Lauren Berlant asks, "What if people were to take the opportunity to reimagine state/society relations . . . in which consumer forms of collectivity were not the main way people secure or fantasize securing everyday happiness?" What we need, she says, is better fantasies: "New misrecognitions of the relation of the materialized real to a projection but now a projection that reorients us to a different better mode of the reproduction of life . . . a different structure of feeling associated with the good life."[1]

Berlant's work on happiness intersects with and takes a critical view of what has been called the "happiness industry," or in cultural and literary studies, the "happiness turn."[2] This turn towards the study of happiness has its corollary in legal studies.[3] But even the most thought-provoking recent work on law and happiness has tended to neglect the historical foundations of their dynamic connection. John Bronsteen, Christopher Buccafusco, and Jonathan S. Masur's claim in *Happiness and the Law*, for instance, that happiness and law "seem to have little to do with each other" would astonish anyone who is familiar with the history of emotions.[4] As Darrin McMahon remarks in his history of happiness, happiness was seen as a political, legal, and social concern in the eighteenth century when "Enlightenment visionaries dreamed of bringing happiness to entire societies and even to humanity as a whole."[5] This eighteenth-century "happiness turn" invites us to turn ourselves to Blackstone's understanding of the relationship between happiness and law. Blackstone was instrumental in consolidating and communicating eighteenth-century commonplaces about the relationship between law and happiness. He explored his fantasy about the relationship of happiness to justice in his early poetry, then mapped these ideas onto the

English common law in the *Commentaries*. Though Blackstone wrote at the height of the first great modern age of consumerism, he fantasized about a different form of happiness, a structure of feeling that oriented happiness around harmonic justice.[6] Like Berlant, he wanted better "projections," better fantasies of a collective good life or of how good government might make us happier.

Most legal historians tend to associate Blackstone with the origins of our contemporary free market approach to happiness. In this view, liberty, economics, and happiness are intertwined, or as *Black's Law Dictionary* puts it, "The constitutional right of men to pursue their 'happiness' means the right to pursue any lawful business or vocation, in any manner not inconsistent with the equal rights of others, which may increase their prosperity or develop their faculties, so as to give to them their highest enjoyment."[7] In the United States, this understanding of the relationship between happiness and liberty has been construed largely in free market terms. Restraints on the market tend to be interpreted as restraints on liberty, while other social and cultural limits on liberty, such as limits on access to education, are set aside.[8] This restricted understanding of happiness reduces the pursuit of happiness to the pursuit of income, and thus to the pursuit of purchasing power—ergo, consumer happiness. In part, we owe this free market, production- and consumption-based understanding of happiness to the eighteenth-century development of consumer culture. As production increased and costs of products decreased, average people, who in previous generations might have owned no more than one set of clothes, began to acquire possessions. They also began to have greater access to entertainment, especially in big cities like London. Thus, happiness became less associated with the afterlife and more associated with the ability to attain and consume goods and services.[9] But Blackstone actually promulgated a far more complicated, even at times contradictory, approach to happiness than this model suggests. He blended classical and eighteenth-century ideas, drawing on multiple conceptions of happiness to prompt a multifaceted, multilayered happiness response in his readers, one that incorporated personal, hedonic reactions as well as a larger moral response. For Blackstone, as for many moral and political philosophers of his era, happiness was a political concept, the aim of government and the purpose of law, but it was also a way of encouraging readers to become attached to the *Commentaries*, to English law, and to Englishness itself. When the *Commentaries* represents English law as just, as balanced, in harmony with its own past and with the world, readers respond by feeling happy and thus become attached to the common law.

As argued throughout this book, the encounter with justice was, for Blackstone, a central emotional and aesthetic experience, available to anyone, and evidenced in emotions as various as desire, melancholia, embarrassment, terror, and happiness. The first hint of the connection between happiness and justice appears in his early poem, "The Lawyer's Farewel," where Blackstone offers us his poet-lawyer, an unhappy young man who finds relief only when he finds justice. On finding justice, the narrator exhorts us to

> Observe how parts with parts unite
> In one harmonious rule of right;
> See countless wheels distinctly tend
> By various laws to one great end;
> While mighty Alfred's piercing soul
> Pervades and regulates the whole.

Here we are urged to "observe" Blackstone's version of harmonic justice, one in which a just world consists of a great harmonic organization in which all sectors of society, all goods and benefits and duties are in balance with each other. In this idealized understanding of justice, the world revolves and evolves "to one great end," which for Blackstone was an English end, grounded in a careful balance of power and influence, one Blackstone represented as capable of producing what twenty-first-century theorists of happiness have recently been calling "the good life" or more simply, happiness.

While the poem offers only a negative understanding of happiness (the poet-lawyer is unhappy; his happiness on observing harmonic justice is assumed), the *Commentaries* offers a more sustained, carefully articulated discussion of the relationship between happiness and justice. Blackstone begins to articulate this in the "Introduction to the Study of Law," where he asks how we determine just results. Must we have a detailed knowledge of the law or a highly evolved intellect that allows us to reason our way to justice? Answering his own question, Blackstone offers a remarkably democratic, if a bit condescending, take on justice. If the only way to understand justice is through "the due exertion of right reason," or what he also calls "metaphysical disquisitions," most average humans would spend their time in "mental indolence" with "ignorance its inseparable companion" (I:40). Only the highly educated would be able to recognize justice. Fortunately, Blackstone tells us, God has given everyone the ability to recognize justice affectively rather than cognitively:

> [The creator] has so intimately connected, so inseparably interwoven the laws of eternal justice with the happiness of each individual, that the latter cannot be attained but by observing the former; and, if the former be punctually obeyed, it cannot but induce the latter. In consequence of which [God] . . . has graciously reduced the rule of obedience to this one paternal precept, that man should "pursue his own happiness." (I:40-41)[10]

In other words, we know justice because when we "observe" it, we feel happy.[11] The double use of "observe," first in the poem and later in this crucial passage from the *Commentaries*, suggests that happiness will result not only from observing justice in the sense of *doing* it, but also through aesthetic observation of its wondrously complex, harmonically organized workings. Choosing "observing" to designate our apprehension of English law suggests more than the usual utilitarian argument that the law must be enacted for humankind to be happy. Instead, this spectatorial view will lead to a happy recognition of the ways English judgment reflects not only English justice, but universal "natural" justice, because observing justice as reflected in the English common law—in the sense of obeying and enforcing it, but also in the sense of seeing it, *knowing* it—will make us happy. This is why "the creator" has not confused us with "a multitude of abstracted rules," but has instead "graciously reduced the rule of obedience to this one paternal precept, 'that man should pursue his own happiness.'" Of course, this was a philosophical commonplace by the time Blackstone wrote the *Commentaries*. As McMahon puts it, Locke had presented "happiness as a natural and wholesome part of a divinely orchestrated world in which human beings are led along by pleasant sensations, ending, if they get it right, in God."[12] Blackstone's contribution is to assert that such a pursuit "naturally" results in observing (seeing, but also doing) justice. He embeds ideas of harmonic justice ("the divinely orchestrated world") in the history and practice of the common law and thus connects the common law of England to natural law. For Blackstone, pursuing one's own happiness "is the foundation of what we call ethics, or natural law," which turns out to mean that if an "action tends to man's real happiness," then it participates in natural law, or the law that the "Creator" has given us (I:40–41). Blackstone's understanding of justice thus participates in the natural law tradition, a tradition emphasizing harmony, one that, as Erik Angner has argued, offers "the historical backdrop against which the modern science of happiness emerged."[13] But Blackstone's allegiance to natural law is uneven and, as was typical of the period, expansive. The "natural" in his view included man's rational faculties, and he believed that these rational faculties had yielded an English legal system that mimicked the harmonies we might think to find only in nature. It was those harmonies that he equated with justice.[14]

What does Blackstone mean by "real happiness"? Real happiness is a personal, affective response, but although he recognizes the value of individual affective happiness, his focus on observation evokes not only Adam Smith with his impartial spectator, but also the classical Greek understanding of happiness.[15] As Carli N. Conklin has pointed out, for Blackstone, happiness was at least in part "Eudaimonia: it evokes a sense of well-being or a state of flourishing that is the result of living a fit or virtuous life, one that was in harmony with the law of nature as it pertains to man."[16] Discussions of Greek Eudaimonia have been resurrected recently in Vivasvan Soni's *Mourning Happiness*, in which Soni advocates for a better understanding of an almost inconceivable classical version of happiness, Solon's version of Greek Eudaimonia, a form (and form is crucial here) of happiness that involves a communal judgment.[17] This judgment takes into account a life in its entirety, can only occur after death, and accepts human limits, including the limit represented by death. In Soni's view, only by recovering this formal understanding of happiness can we recover a positive conception of happiness suitable for political use. Soni's conception of happiness presents, as he says, "an empty question," but one that implies that a life that can be construed as well-lived when seen in the aggregate.[18] Communal observation of a completed life is what allows us to judge whether it was "happy." Though Soni is silent on the issue of whether the judgment of happiness leads to an affective feeling of happiness in those who are judging, one can imagine this communal judgment resulting in at least a sense of communal satisfaction. To observe a well-lived life might be a cause of happiness in itself.[19]

Soni argues that in privatizing happiness, in conceiving of it as an internal emotional state, we have lost Eudaimonia. In fact, Eudaimonia in the Solonic sense of communal judgment after death now seems so foreign to our contemporary understanding of happiness that we are loath to use the word "happiness" to refer to it. When did this happen? In Soni's account, the shift occurred sometime in the eighteenth century. He attributes our modern, hedonic understanding of happiness to what he calls the trial narrative, a previously unrecognized genre that arose in England during the eighteenth century, exemplified by novels such as *Pamela* with plots that repeatedly defer happiness, reducing it to an ephemeral, meaningless pleasure always on the horizon, never realized.[20] Trial narratives personalize happiness, even as they defer it, Soni argues, and thus preclude its larger political value. While it is tempting to map Soni's trial narratives onto legal trials or what lawyers call "trial procedure" and onto the account Blackstone gives of this area of the law, such a critical move would lead both to a reductive reading of Soni's argument and to an overly simplistic reading of Blackstone's understanding of happiness. For Blackstone, the legal trial, though important symbolically as demonstrating the English commitment to human rights, offers a way of determining or administering law, not law's central narrative. The *Commentaries*, of course, encompasses much more than trial procedure, which is not even mentioned in the first two volumes, and covered in depth only in volume IV. Thus, we cannot map Soni's "trial narrative" onto Blackstone's account of the trial without losing a great deal. But Soni's work is still relevant to an understanding of Blackstone's representation of happiness, if instead we draw on Soni's *story* about the history of happiness to better understand the *Commentaries* as offering a similar narrative in multiple contexts.

The story of the history of happiness, as Soni tells it, is really a story about a halting recursive movement from Solon's Eudaimonia towards individualized affective happiness. It starts with Solon's idea that we can only judge happiness communally, after a man has completed his life. The eighteenth century "killed" this idea of happiness, in part by suggesting that our lives are lived as trials in which we defer happiness until we have demonstrated a level of virtue or endurance that can be rewarded by happiness. At that always-deferred point, happiness becomes unnarratable, as it signifies the *end* of the narrative. Characters like Pamela can claim happiness (I am so happy), but they cannot narrate it because happiness is the end (in every sense of end), not the story itself. It is assumed rather than narrated. Given Soni's account, we might expect to find only our contemporary *Pamela*-influenced version of happiness in the *Commentaries*. Happiness should be deferred, our desires should create our trials, and should we find satisfaction, it will be unnarratable. And, indeed, we do find this version of happiness in Blackstone's *Commentaries*, as I will demonstrate. But Blackstone was deeply invested in classical conceptions of justice: Eudaimonia, both in the generalized sense and in the Solonic sense, is an active force in the *Commentaries* where it coexists with our modern hedonic understanding of happiness. In other words, for Blackstone, and here I paraphrase Sara Ahmed, happiness is felt both "in here" and "out there"; it is both an internal sensation one might have in response to "observing justice," and a "thing" called justice that can be attained, observed, and judged in the aggregate.[21] Blackstone represents the common law then as a narrative in which the law has undergone numerous trials and emerged the better for them, *and simultaneously* as a totality that can be observed and judged to be "happy" in the Greek sense of well-conceived, well-lived, or harmonic. Thus, Soni's narrative of the transition from Greek happiness to modern happiness, with its crucial eighteenth-century turning point, is flattened out in the *Commentaries*, yet still provides a useful heuristic. To pursue this heuristic, though, we must recognize that both older Greek conceptions of happiness and the newer affective model coexist here, sometimes in concert and sometimes in opposition to each other.

Blackstone weaves the language and philosophy of political happiness into the four volumes of the *Commentaries* through direct reference, but also through structural and stylistic choices. Blackstone not only tells readers what sorts of things should make them feel happy, he provides the experience of inhabiting an affective-aesthetic system that when judged as a whole can be judged for its happiness. Thus, he reinforced the general conversation that held that the primary function of a legal system is to foster happiness, and he positioned that conversation in the most influential law book to be published in the colonies. The rest of this chapter will focus on Blackstone's systematic treatment of happiness in its relationship to the common law, and then shift to what we might call the unintended consequences of this treatment: its impact in America on our understanding of civil rights, one that I illustrate through a reading of one of the most influential novels of the twentieth century, *To Kill a Mockingbird*.

The Pursuit of Happiness: Following a Word Around

To borrow from Sara Ahmed, I want to "follow the word *happiness* around," both in Blackstone's *Commentaries* and in its Blackstonian afterlife in America.[22] But I also want to follow the *form* of happiness around, to assert that Blackstone's understanding of justice-as-happiness relied on harmonic forms as much as it did on affective reactions. For here word and form work together as Blackstone embeds multiple invocations of "happiness," "hap," and "happens" into a formal structure meant to embody harmonic justice as a happiness-producing form.

As most students of happiness have pointed out, the word "happiness" is connected to contingency and unpredictability, to fortune, both good and bad. In English, "happiness" comes from the Old Norse word "happ," which is also related, as McMahon points out, to "what happens in the world."[23] Happiness includes connotations of chance (happenchance, perhaps), of inevitability (things happened), and of both good and bad fortune (haply, hapless). Happiness can also be an aesthetic term, or at least it could in the eighteenth century when Johnson recorded one of its meanings as "fortuitous elegance, unstudied grace."[24] And, of course, today, happiness can also mean, as it did in Johnson's time, "a state in which the desires are satisfied."[25] In the *Commentaries*, Blackstone draws on all of these meanings, weaving them together to suggest that English law has suffered many trials and overcome them, thus leading to its current happy state, but also that English law has always been and always will be a completed artifact, like a complete life, capable of being analyzed in its totality and judged for its happiness. Observing this state of affairs makes us happy; thus, man's affective response to justice plays a central role in Blackstone's schema. In other words, in Blackstone, as in Ahmed, "happiness can be what we want, a way of getting what we want, and a sign that we have got what we want."[26] This distributed model of happiness crosses subject and object, fields and endeavors, and eventually continents and oceans.

To pursue happiness, we need to pursue "haps" in all their locutions. A lot "has happened" in the *Commentaries*. In fact, this phrase appears so frequently and is so naturalized that it fades into the background. But to read the *Commentaries* carefully is to realize that what "has happened" troubles the dichotomy Soni has posited between the classical form of happiness and the debased, modern, affective form. Some happenings follow the pattern of what Soni calls the trial narrative; these happenings have threatened the common law directly, forcing it to overcome obstacles if it is to survive. Blackstone's account of the Norman Conquest and its impact on the ancient Saxon customs that he sees as the basis of English common law, for instance, takes the form of a trial narrative. As I discussed in chapter 2, the common law faced a challenge or obstacle that it had to overcome to survive and thrive. In another example of the use of Soni's trial narrative, Blackstone tells us of "an accident" that "happened" to make a single copy of Justinian's pandects available at a time when the common law was known only through its oral history (I:17–18). What a mishap! According to Blackstone, the common law risked being wiped out by the spread of civil law, becoming "entirely despised" except by a few practitioners (I:21). Fortunately, a "peculiar incident which *happened* at a very critical time," the establishment of the Court of Common Pleas at Westminster, saved the common law by encouraging centralization. Soon, the common law was "raised to the pitch of perfection" through the establishment of the Inns of Court and the serious study of English common law (I:22–23, emphasis added). As in Soni's trial narrative, the common law has undergone a trial and overcome it, leaving law at an unnarratable point, as Blackstone says, at the "pitch of perfection." This is the characteristic "structure of modern happiness," according to Soni.[27] There is nothing to judge after desires are met because "desire, work and life represent times of trial amenable to narrativization, while consummation, leisure, and the afterlife signify times of happiness that resist narrativization."[28] To the extent that the common law adheres to this paradigm, it is imagined as having only two possibilities: strife during which happiness must be gained, and a post-trial "quasi-narcotic leisure" in which happiness is passively enjoyed.[29]

If this was all that happened in the *Commentaries*, we could stop here and argue that the *Commentaries* simply offers another example of the privatization of happiness. Blackstone's law is personified; it becomes a Pamela, subjected to trials, overcoming them, and being rewarded in an unnarratable happy ending. But, of course, Blackstone does not stop narrating; instead, he creates space for the observation of the common law, a celebratory observation that imagines the common law as a static, finished object, subject to judgment. Here we find what Adam Potkay calls the "vestigial sense of happiness as a communal and thus more or less objective assessment of a life," in this case of the life of the law.[30] This tendency in the *Commentaries* to, as Soni puts it, "linger over the infinite details of a life in order to make a judgment of happiness" implies the sort of concern about a life that Soni attributes to Solonic understandings of happiness, and it contains an aesthetic as well as an emotive element that has had amazing endurance in jurisprudence.[31] It reappears, for instance, in ghostly form in John Rawls's *Theory of Justice*, where we find happiness associated not only with "achievement in action," but also with the contemplation of a fulfilled plan. As Rawls expresses it, "we can think of a person as being happy when he is in the way of a successful execution (more or less) of a rational plan of life drawn up under (more or less) favorable conditions. . . . Someone is happy when his plans are going well, his more important aspirations being fulfilled, and he feels sure that his good fortune will endure."[32] "Achievement in action," though, is only one Rawlsian route to happiness: "The actual fulfillment of the plan itself may have, as compositions, paintings, and poems often do, a certain completeness which though marred by circumstance and human failing is evident from the whole. . . . Happiness is not one aim among others that we aspire to, but the fulfillment of the whole design itself."[33] In the *Commentaries*, as in Rawls's *Theory of Justice*, happiness is both affective and formal, meaning partaking of form: it can be immediate, related to the fulfillment of an aspiration to be just. And it can be a reaction to "the whole design itself," to seeing the common law in the same way we see "compositions, paintings, and poems," as harmonic, complete, and perfect. Justice then is an aesthetic and formal as well as a social and affective concept. We can turn to Mark Canuel's work for a more explicit detailing of the relationship between a satisfying aesthetic and justice. He details the various theorists who have embraced the argument for harmonic symmetry and offers a clever reading of the word "fair": "To be 'fair' is to be both beautiful and equitable—thus 'fair' constitutes 'a two-part cognitive event' linking beautiful or fair objects to just or fair social arrangements."[34] Blackstone relies on this relation: to be in harmony is to be beautiful; to be beautiful is to be just, as we can see in examining two related phenomena in the *Commentaries*: descriptions of what happens out in the world (the hap) and descriptions of the law's reactions to those happenings.

In the *Commentaries*, we find that much happens, will happen, or has happened out in the world. In fact, one could argue that Blackstone's primary function is to put the world's contingencies in conversation with the English common law. Blackstone tends to introduce these happenings rather casually, even though they often represent devastating loss to people or to their property. For instance, destruction to property could have "happened by lightning, tempest, the king's enemies, or other inevitable accident," and thus would not be construed as "waste" by someone holding a life estate in a property (III:129). Someone may "happen" to find their stolen goods and reclaim them (III:4). Treason may "happen" (IV:75); "foreign pirates or robbers . . . may happen to invade" (IV:83); a parent may "happen" to kill his child when offering correction (IV:182); someone may "happen" to set fire to a house (IV:222). Certain offenders "not of good fame . . . may happen" to put the public at risk (those not of good fame include "pilferers or robbers; such as sleep in the day, and wake on the night; common drunkards," and many other undesirables) (IV:253). Blackstone's use of "happens" to avoid attributions of agency can begin to seem absurd. It may "happen," for instance, both in foreign countries and in England during the suspension of habeas corpus, that "persons apprehended under suspicion have suffered a long imprisonment merely because they were forgotten" (III:138). His description of King James's abdication muses on what might have occurred if this abdication had not "happened" (I:208). To be fair to Blackstone, he is not always blasé about these sorts of happenings. Although killings may "happen," "the death of a man, however it happens, will leave some stain behind it" (IV:187).

The *Commentaries* generally manages to represent the law as a good match for these devastating happenings: random "happenings" trigger a second kind of happening, one in which the law, already existent, becomes operative. Blackstone offers a number of striking examples of this, not surprising given that the English common law was developed as a reflective response to the various contingencies or "haps" that tend to throw human life out of kilter. His goal was to demonstrate the common law's ability to embrace what happens, to absorb contingencies, while maintaining that sense of harmonic balance that he associated with justice. So, for instance, "a reception or reprisal," a form of legal remedy, "happens when any one hath deprived another of his property" and the injured party locates the property and reacquires it (III:4). The injury of "discontinuance happens when someone who has an estate tail makes a larger estate than he is entitled to" (III:171). A "subtraction . . . happens" when someone owing a duty fails to perform it (III:185). A "disturbance of franchise happens" when someone with a right to a franchise is prohibited from its lawful exercise (III:236). These legal events "happen," meaning that they are automatically activated by certain circumstances, seemingly without human agency. And thus, the law—at least as Blackstone represents it—maintains a separate existence from the world, meanwhile interacting seamlessly with the world's haps, responding to each unexpected hap, with a preexisting happening of its own and bringing all back to the harmonic balance that Blackstone idealized in both the poem and the *Commentaries*. Overall, we are left with the impression that the world and the law interact in a seamless harmonic interchange while human agency plays a negligible role. Blackstone's vision then is one of harmonic justice, of everything, world and law, working together to create a harmonic whole. This is the vision of justice that Blackstone imagines will make us happy: when we observe harmonic justice as a formal, operative device, we feel happy.

To reinforce this vision, Blackstone situates the diction of happiness within a larger didactic discourse involving overt instruction regarding what should make us feel happy. To give only one small, personalized example, Blackstone offers himself as a model: he pronounces himself "happy" when he can balance rules with the presentation of evidence meant to illustrate them (I:13). If we turn to his rationale for the criminal law, we can see both this personal response and larger principles of balance and proportion at work. Blackstone tells us that "it is but reasonable that among crimes of different natures those should be most severely punished, which are the most destructive of the public safety and happiness" (IV:16). But what does he find to be "most destructive of the public safety and happiness"? As it turns out, these "most destructive" crimes are crimes that tend to rend the social fabric by disturbing the harmony created by hierarchical relations. For instance, a servant robbing his master or a child killing his father should be punished more severely than a servant robbing a stranger. Speaking more generally, crimes should fit their punishments, while uniform and predictable prosecutions are more effective than "excessive severity" (IV:17). To the extent the English common law creates distinctions between crimes, punishing more severe crimes with greater punishments, we can "glory" in it (IV:18). Blackstone also provides negative examples, admitted imperfections in the law that create unhappiness. Thus, we must recognize a "melancholy truth": because the English common law punishes a wide variety of different crimes with "instant death," the law will be circumvented by lenient victims, juries, and judges and ignored by hardened criminals. In short, criminal punishments should be calibrated to their offenses, and to the greater good and "happiness" of the community. This entire section must have made Blackstone happy, for he follows almost every "rule" or larger principle with individual examples to support it.

To shift to more totalizing examples takes us to some of Blackstone's most magisterial pronouncements about the common law. For Blackstone, "the happiness of our Constitution" lay in its harmonious balance of powers (I:132). Here he uses happiness both in the sense that Johnson used it when he defined happiness aesthetically as "fortuitous elegance, unstudied grace" *and* as an affective term.[35] An important elaboration of this concept appears in the first volume in the section on "Of the Nature of Laws in General." After laying out the value of "three species of government," democracies, aristocracies, and monarchies, Blackstone concludes that the "British constitution" combines the best of these "happily for us of this island" (I:50). This happy condition is the result of the balance created by "three distinct powers": the king who can execute laws, the lords who can invent them, and the House of Commons who can "direct the end of a law." Each branch of government balances out the others, canceling out "any innovation which it shall think inexpedient or dangerous" (I:51). This is the only form of government, Blackstone tells us, where "we be so certain of finding the three great qualities of government so well and so happily united" (I:51).

On a formal level, the *Commentaries* attempts a harmony meant to mimic and thus represent on the page the harmony of justice and of the English common law.[36] From the length of the volumes to the symmetry of their titles (all four volumes of the *Commentaries* are about the same length; two volumes on "Rights" counterbalance two volumes on "Wrongs"), Blackstone attempts a symmetrical appearance even when the actual substance of a section is not really supportive of symmetry.[37] What one might call Blackstone's Palladian structure reinforces the idea that the work as a whole exhibits a "clear" and harmonious understanding of England's "body of laws."[38] Volume divisions and chapter headings, some of which seemed strange or illogical to his critics, seem to have been chosen more to create a sense of balance than for their descriptive power. See, for instance, the opening passages of volume I, where Blackstone lays out his organization in terms of "division," "distribution," and "parts." Not surprisingly, critics have often complained that the title of the second volume, "Of the Rights of Things," seems nonsensical to those who associate rights only with human beings. But given Blackstone's search for harmony and balance, setting "Of the Rights of Things" against volume I, "Of the Rights of Persons," makes *harmonic* sense in terms of balance and rhythm.

On the micro level of content, no matter how complex the subject matter, Blackstone attempts to consolidate, summarize, and harmonize it. For instance, he takes the complex state of the law of corporations and reduces it thus: "The general duties of all bodies politic, considered in their corporate capacity, may . . . be reduced to this single one; that of acting up to the end of design" (I:467).[39] "Acting up to the end of design," as Blackstone puts it, means placing the emphasis on proportionality, on the harmony of laws with each other and with the law of the past. Blackstone applies the concept across numerous conceptual fields, from the basic division of "the objects of the laws" (I:117) that provides the organizing principle of the *Commentaries* to the purposes of nobility ("it is this ascending and contracting proportion that adds stability to any government" [I:153]).[40] This emphasis on proportional balance goes deeper than discursive reference, though. Throughout the *Commentaries*, Blackstone relies on a rhetoric of gain and loss, which results in perfect balance: if there are too many statutes, that's related to the perfecting of the common law system; if there are too many delays, that's because deliberations offer a better result (III:422–23); if Westminster Hall seems to exert too much authority over the ecclesiastical courts, that's to "rescu[e] their jurisdiction from . . . contempt" (III:103); if legal fictions have proliferated "to breed a confusion of ideas," this "arises principally from the excellence of our English laws" (III:26). As Blackstone says in the context of real property, "gain and loss are terms of relation, and of a reciprocal nature" (II:200).

This structural approach—neo-classical in its emphasis on proportion and ratios—repeats throughout the text, where Blackstone uses measured periodic sentences to create some of his most magisterial, stylistically elegant passages.[41] Take, for instance, his commentary on the balanced duties of subject and monarch, a passage I quote at length because it displays the formal relationship between style and content:

> It will be our especial duty . . . to reverence the crown, and yet guard against corrupt and servile influence from those who are intrusted with its authority; to be loyal, yet free; obedient, and yet independent: and, above every thing, to hope that we may long, very long, continue to be governed by a sovereign who, in all those public acts that have personally proceeded from himself, hath manifested the highest veneration for the free constitution of Britain; hath already in more than one instance remarkably strengthened its outworks; and will therefore never harbour a thought, or adopt a persuasion, in any the remotest degree detrimental to public liberty. (I:326)

To reverence and yet guard; to be loyal, yet free; obedient, yet independent: Blackstone here draws on the balances and counterbalances we associate with the couplet, freely using the caesura to both join and divide ideas, then eases into the more generous frame of the periodic sentence to finish his thought, but also to contain the possibility of disruption ("never harbour a thought . . . detrimental to public liberty") in a larger frame in which differences are harmonized. The passage, like so many in the *Commentaries*, reinforces the idea of an underlying harmonic order, as Blackstone resorts again and again to a weighing process in which differences are subsumed under similarities and conflict is reframed in service to a larger sense of harmony. It is poetic in the same way that the couplets of his early poem are poetic: it incorporates dissonant ideas into a larger frame that promises a measured, balanced, final appraisal. The last chapter of the *Commentaries* offers a compressed version of this dynamic. There Blackstone starts by laying out the "discordant" origins of English law in the oral tradition, an oral tradition further made chaotic by "the great variety of nations, that successively broke in upon, and destroyed both the British inhabitants and constitution, the Romans, the Picts, and after them, the various clans of Saxons and Danes, must necessarily have caused great confusion and uncertainty in the laws" (IV:401–2). This confusion involved what must have seemed like an overabundance of "foreign" sources, the rich vocal mix of dialects and languages that had gone into English law and into Englishness itself, what Michael Meehan calls "a series of vocal intrusions—by the Normans, with their 'dialect' and 'fanciful niceties,'" by the civil law, by Latin, and by "that badge of slavery, that '"barbarous dialect"' Norman French.[42] Here is the conundrum: without the discordant noise of the oral, without the combined contributions of a variety of peoples from the past, the common law had no authority or foundation, as it could not be imagined as resulting from the ongoing consent of a diverse people, one united in the ideas of liberty and balance that Blackstone so admired. English law, in particular, presumed the consent of the people and grounded its authority in this consent. Thus, harmonizing or, some might say, harnessing the discord that characterizes diverse communities in close proximity was crucial to its genesis and continued existence. But not to worry, Blackstone soon reconciles these differences, noting that though Romans, Picts, Saxons, and Danes had once flooded England, "they were very soon incorporated and blended together . . . so that it is morally impossible to trace out, with any degree of accuracy, *when* the several mutations of the common law were made" (IV:401–2).[43] Emphasizing the "moral" impossibility of tracing difference, Blackstone reduces English law's oral, multivocal languages to one harmonious chorus in the *Commentaries*, quieting the cacophony of voices that undergirded it, meanwhile replacing them with a supple, almost melodic surface text. Morality, harmony, and Blackstone's magisterial style all map onto the common law here to create a moral, legal, juridical aesthetic that calms whatever anxiety might result from unrestrained difference, and thus reassures us and makes us feel happy.

Blackstone ends the *Commentaries* with more on this theme, covering (or perhaps as some of his critics would say, covering up) centuries of conflict in one short section, all to the end of showing the eventual unity of the law, its return to first principles and to harmonic balance. By this point, we have read four volumes of the *Commentaries*, ranging from the laws respecting familial relations, to laws governing kings and parliaments, to laws covering the lowest criminals. At the end of volume IV, Blackstone sums it all up, asking us to observe the whole as one unified entity. Here he displays a love of "a constitution, so wisely contrived, so strongly raised, and so highly finished, it is hard to speak with that praise, which is justly and severely its due" (IV:436). Harmony and proportion play their roles as Blackstone neatly wraps everything up on the final page: "It hath been the endeavour of these commentaries . . . to examine its solid foundations, to mark out its extensive plan, to explain the use and distribution of its parts, and from the harmonious concurrence of those several parts to demonstrate the elegant proportion of the whole" (IV:436).

Examining the final sentence of the *Commentaries* brings home the depth and breadth of the aesthetic refinements that helped Blackstone derive harmony from what had seemed a chaotic mess to others, but also raises a question that we should, perhaps, have been asking earlier. As Blackstone puts it, "The protection of THE LIBERTY OF BRITAIN is a duty which they owe to themselves, who enjoy it; to their ancestors, who transmitted it down; and to their posterity, who will claim at their hands this, the best birthright, and noblest inheritance of mankind" (IV:436). What are we to make of the all-caps LIBERTY OF BRITAIN? Having read four volumes of Blackstone without encountering any similar typography, we might be excused for being startled by this intrusion. The phrase stands out as an advertisement for the common law and for Britain. But Blackstone contains this moment by gradually incorporating it into the balance and harmony that typify the phrases that follow. LIBERTY is subordinated to "posterity" with its "best birthright" and "noblest inheritance." LIBERTY is elaborated on, but also weighed down with the words "duty," "birthright," and "mankind," associated with each other through alliteration, consonance, and assonance, through internal rhymes and hard ending sounds. LIBERTY, in Blackstone's harmonious world, thus becomes a duty that has been "transmitted" by a hoard of diverse ancestors through an equally discordant but unmentioned cache of customs, case law precedents, and half-remembered maxims until it is domesticated and calmed by an invoked shared responsibility across historical eras. Even the sounds of the word LIBERTY are harmonized, quieted, and calmed, as LIBERTY is translated from a noisy "it" with its sharp "t" to a smoother, more harmonious "this" with its softened "th" and sibilant end sound. The discordant noise of the past, future, and present are all united in a balanced periodic sentence that harmonizes liberty with duty, and draws together "ancestors" with those who can only anticipate the noise of the future, "descendants."[44] Thus, within this short section, we see Blackstone's aesthetics in concentrated form: he draws on stylistic devices as much as reason to reconcile difference, balancing, for instance, past against future, rights (that bring enjoyment) against duty (to protect that very liberty), the common man against the "noblest," "birthright" against "inheritance." Balanced oppositions are all subsumed in the end in "mankind," a word that has taken the insular and self-interested concept of "Britain" and universalized it.

Throughout the *Commentaries*, Blackstone fosters his readers' attachment to the English common law through this complex aesthetic and emotional management of a matrix of interrelated contradictory and yet balanced elements, through insisting on that harmonious balance that makes us "happy." This is, of course, how "Justice" works in the poem he wrote as a teenager. In the *Commentaries*, as in the poem, he asks us to "observe how parts with parts unite / In one harmonious rule of right." In this sense, the *Commentaries* are as aspirational and inspirational as the poem; they both offer us a vision of justice that is supposed to make us happy. This is harmonic justice in action, the observation of which results in "real" happiness, a form of happiness that seems to contain both the personal, affective, responsive understanding of happiness and the Solonic understanding of happiness (after the fact, we judge). This doubled, distributed model of happiness makes much of the deeply satisfying feeling we associate with balance and harmony, with making sense of things—in short, in feeling that everything is right (both correct and morally synchronized) with the world. Thus, Blackstone's readership becomes a communal judge of justice, observing justice, testing it to see if it makes us happy, and pronouncing it good when it evokes "real" happiness. To accomplish this, the *Commentaries* takes up what was actually a rather chaotic and poorly understood set of cases, customs, and maxims, remaking it to suggest a transparent and legible harmonic order in which "parts with parts" have united to form "one rule of right."

The Harm in Harmonic Justice: Liberty, Slavery, and the "Machine"

"Happiness," Soni tells us, "is nothing but the name for what is at stake in existence."[45] If this is the case, we must ask what is at stake in aligning happiness with harmonic justice. What does Blackstone's version of happiness do? Are we happy now that we have observed justice through reading the *Commentaries*? Do we have the sense of satisfaction that Blackstone thought we should when we "observe justice"? Blackstone's readers often expressed happiness on completing the *Commentaries*—and not only because they had endured a lengthy reading experience. Their comments reveal an affective response to having seen "the fulfillment of the whole design itself," as Rawls puts it.[46] The American lawyer James Kent, who became the first professor of law at Columbia College and later produced the *Commentaries on American Law*, praised "the excellence of [Blackstone's] arrangement, the variety of his learning, the justness of his taste and the purity and elegance of his style."[47] Even twenty-first-century readers are often surprised by how readable Blackstone is, how much more interesting than they had been led to believe, how readily a reading of Blackstone lends itself to a better understanding of contemporary issues.[48]

But lest we celebrate "the excellence of this arrangement" too quickly, we should return to some of the passages I've relied upon above and examine the issue of "liberty" that Blackstone managed so adroitly in the final sentence of the *Commentaries*. Ahmed suggests that "real happiness" may be a bit more difficult to parse than Blackstone allows: "Ordinary attachments to the very idea of the good life are also sites of ambivalence involving the confusion rather than the separation of good and bad feelings. Reading happiness would then become a matter of reading the grammar of this ambivalence."[49] Harbingers of ambivalence, of the surfacing of a counter-narrative, have already appeared in the selections I have called upon above. If to preserve harmony, we must "never harbor a thought detrimental to public liberty," we might wonder what we are to do with such thoughts. Does public liberty not include the possibility of thoughts detrimental to it? Even more doubtful is the directive to "be loyal, yet free." Isn't loyalty an emotion that binds rather than frees us? A brief rhapsody about harmonic justice in volume I may alert us to the sheer effort it takes to sustain the perfect form that harmonic justice demands. Explaining how the English government works, Blackstone waxes Newtonian: "Every branch of our civil polity supports and is supported, regulates and is regulated, by the rest. . . . Like three distinct powers in mechanics, they jointly impel the machine of government in a direction different from what either, acting by themselves, would have done; but at the same time in a direction partaking of each, and formed out of all, a direction which constitutes the true line of the liberty and happiness of the community" (I:151). This passage encapsulates one of the fundamental contradictions in liberal thought: How can a machine-like devotion to harmonic justice offer what Blackstone calls the "true line" to both liberty *and* happiness?[50] It is tempting to invoke Samuel Johnson's multiple definitions of machine here in an effort to make sense of this passage. As we might expect, "machine" had taken on most of its modern meaning by the 1760s. Johnson offers as a first definition "any complicated piece of workmanship." But it still retained a poetic use as well, familiar to anyone who has read the great epic poems: *machine* could refer to the "supernatural agency in poems," machinery to "that part which the deities, angels, or demons, act in a poem," as Johnson points out.[51] Perhaps the "machine of government" speaks to the magical, enchanted understanding of justice that Blackstone often seems to invoke. But is this reading too tempting? Does Blackstone's reference to the "powers of mechanics," an explicit reference to (as Johnson defined it) "the geometry of motion, a mathematical science which shows the effects of powers or moving forces, so far as they are applied to engines," lead us to the enchantment of "supernatural agency," or rather to the regulatory powers of natural science? Its meaning is ambiguous. Regulation, "regulated," "the machine": here the harmonic justice Blackstone associates with happiness seems the result not of some wonderfully supernatural power, but of some very hard work indeed. In this model of happiness, some branches (some people?) may be "impelled" in a direction they might not have chosen for themselves. How then might the "machine" of justice offer the "true line of liberty and happiness"?

Liberty both brackets and infuses Blackstone's detailing of English law. In the first pages of the introduction, he announces that "liberty is the very end and scope of the [English] constitution" (I:6). He foregrounds liberty structurally as well, by starting the series with "the rights of persons" and treating "the absolute rights of individuals" in the first chapter. Overall, he mentions liberty over sixty times in the first volume alone and over three hundred and fifty times total across the four volumes of the *Commentaries*. And, as discussed above, he ends the *Commentaries* by emphasizing liberty: "The protection of THE LIBERTY OF BRITAIN is a duty . . . the best birthright, and noblest inheritance of mankind" (IV:436). Within the *Commentaries*, Blackstone references liberty far more often than he references happiness. It is fundamental to his claim for the exceptional nature of the English common law. Liberty defines the English character and English nation in that only through fighting to liberate themselves from oppression have the English established themselves as an independent nation. The English citizen differentiates himself from the French through ancient traditions that included, for instance, habeas corpus and the right to be free from unreasonable seizures. Thus, this national emphasis on liberty is embodied in every English person under the English common law.

This emphasis on liberty as an English attribute and virtue suggests that slavery should have been abhorrent to English sensibilities. And, in fact, Blackstone was hailed not only by Adam Ferguson and James Beattie, but also by some twenty-first-century historians for bringing Montesquieu's arguments against slavery to a larger audience.[52] As Simon Gikandi has pointed out, Blackstone's ideas about slavery were "the fulcrum around which his authoritative commentaries on liberty revolved."[53] Let us then turn to Blackstone's comments about slavery and test them for consistency. Does slavery, which, alongside war, was seen by Enlightenment thinkers as the greatest threat to happiness, represent the limit case for harmonic justice?[54] One especially stirring attack on slavery appears in volume I under the "Rights of Persons," where Blackstone offers a two-page assault on Justinian's rationale supporting institutional slavery: "Pure and proper slavery does not, nay cannot, subsist in England . . . and indeed it is repugnant to reason, and the principles of natural law, that such a state should subsist anywhere" (I:411). English law "abhors, and will not endure the existence of slavery within this nation," he continues. In particular, Blackstone argues that a man cannot sell his liberty to another: "Every sale implies a price . . . an equivalent given to the seller in lieu of what he transfers to the buyer, but what equivalent can be given for life and liberty?" (I:412) Thus, "a slave or negro, the instant he lands in England, becomes a freeman; that is, the law will protect him in the enjoyment of his person, his liberty, and his property" (I:412). Based on this statement of the law, Granville Sharpe was so encouraged that he attempted to hire Blackstone to represent an escaped slave he was trying to help.

With Granville Sharp, we might think that Blackstone was a strict abolitionist, adhering to what historians of slavery call "immediacy."[55] Unfortunately, this impression is quickly dispelled once we read on, for within the same paragraph Blackstone begins to equivocate: "Yet, with regard to any right which the master may have acquired, by contract or the like, to the perpetual service of John or Thomas, this will remain exactly in the same state as before: for this is no more than the same state of subjection for life, which every apprentice submits to for the space of seven years, or sometimes for a longer term" (I:412–13). It does not require a twenty-first-century education to recognize that "a state of subjection for life" is difficult to distinguish from slavery. In fact, some of Blackstone's near contemporaries pointed this out.[56] By 1766, Blackstone had amended his first seemingly unequivocal statement to make it consistent with this later explication, adding the rather unconvincing phrase "and so far becomes a freeman; though the master's right to his service may probably still continue." Equivocation on equivocation: the words "may probably" emphasize uncertainty rather than purpose.

Blackstone's equivocation only begins to suggest the various pressures and pressure groups he was attempting to conciliate. In trying to somehow make slavery "fit" models of harmonic justice, English jurists were struggling with a lengthy history of what George Van Cleve has called "near slavery," a term meant to indicate English familiarity with a number of different concepts of involuntary service, including indentured servitude and forced conscription into military units.[57] As Ruth Paley has pointed out in her discussion of the Somerset case, "forms of 'near slavery' were both familiar and even welcome as ways of retaining control over the lives of working men and women."[58] Of course, "near slavery" did not come close to replicating the slave system that developed in the Caribbean or the American South. For instance, it did not imagine that the children of "near slaves" were born into slavery. But when Blackstone navigated this arena in the 1760s, he must have been thinking about how to balance his abhorrence for the African slave trade with his recognition of the efficacy of numerous forms of English servitude. While freeing African slaves who happened to step onto English soil would cause little commercial disruption in England, complete destabilization of these categories would have thrown relations between masters and servants into disarray. Blackstone was not the only jurist who believed gradual change preferable to revolutionary change. Mansfield, for instance, commented in the Somerset case that "setting 14,000 or 15,000 men at once loose by a solemn opinion, is very disagreeable in the effects it threatens."[59] In fact, Blackstone's treatment of feudal slavery may reveal his gradualism to be more consistent with his contemporaries' ideas of English liberty than opposed to it. As Teresa Michals points out, "the slave's slow transformation into a more formally autonomous individual" was used "to signal the reliberation of society itself back to a state of quasi-contractual 'freedom.'"[60] Through such reasoning, gradualism offered a watered-down version of liberty consistent with harmonic justice and thus also offered the linchpin that connects the happiness of harmonic justice with the celebration of liberty.

But gradualism, though it preserved some sense of harmonic balance, forced those who remained without liberty to make do with hope rather than happiness. For them, the association of happiness with harmony could start to feel more like tyranny than liberation. As Olivier Abel has argued, the happiness we might feel when we encounter harmonic justice "requires totality" and can only exist "upon condition of all the other happinesses."[61] Such efforts might require, as Ahmed points out, that "certain bodies 'go along with it,'" even bodies that might not feel particularly happy.[62] To the extent that happiness is understood as involving harmonic balance, it resists change and justifies oppression. This is Blackstone's conundrum: the happiness associated with harmonic justice requires all to be in balance; it requires that disequilibrium be eliminated almost before it occurs, or at least that it be absorbed into an already preconceived system. Such a system cannot be reconciled with the contingencies liberty introduces. Wholesale happiness is only possible if we have blinded ourselves to the ways this "whole design" has subsumed liberty, a central precept in the common law and one Blackstone relied upon as he celebrated the unique qualities of English justice. Instead, happiness as harmonic justice imagines a reified object, a completed narrative that lies at our feet, dead and thus subject to our observation, commentary, and judgment. The minute we start judging, the minute we are happy when confronted with harmonic justice, we have closed down possibilities. The common law—to the extent it is modeled on ideas of harmonic justice—has become a thing, as reified as the bodies of the dead, their lives scrutinized for "happiness" in Solon's world. If this is happiness, then it cannot help but become a site of ambivalence involving not only both good and bad feelings, but both good and bad outcomes.

Blackstone's Long Tail and *To Kill a Mockingbird*

That the *Commentaries* resides on the knife edge of the transformation that Soni describes has had consequences that have extended far beyond England's borders. As Robert A. Ferguson argues in his formative work on the relationship between law and literature in early America, "All of our formative documents—the Declaration of Independence, the Constitution, the Federalist Papers, and the seminal decisions of the Supreme Court under John Marshall—were drafted by attorneys steeped in Sir William Blackstone's *Commentaries*. . . . [It] ranks second only to the Bible as a literary and intellectual influence on the history of American institutions."[63] This impact can be traced through publication records (1,500 sets of the *Commentaries* were available prior to 1776, and the first American edition came out in 1771),[64] Ngram statistics (the number of references to Blackstone between 1800 and 2000 was greater in America than England), United States Supreme Court references,[65] and in the many anecdotes involving American legal practitioners who relied on the *Commentaries*.[66] Blackstone's work was the chosen text for law students at William & Mary, the first law school in the colonies and the school where John Marshall studied; one can still observe the Blackstone stained glass window there. Of course, not every emotional or intellectual idea in the *Commentaries* influenced American law and culture. It would be hard to imagine US citizens becoming melancholic over the loss of the origins of the common law, for example. But one of the central cultural ideas that Blackstone helped transport to America was that of justice as a happiness-creator and of the law as central to communal happiness.

The story of Blackstone's reception in America is a complex one that has not been fully told. Was his work rejected or admired by the colonists? Did John Marshall own only two books growing up, Blackstone and a collection of Pope's poetry? Did Abraham Lincoln buy a barrel of goods from a man going west, only to find a copy of the *Commentaries* in it, thus launching his career as a lawyer? Every American legal historian seems to have a story about someone throwing a copy of the *Commentaries* into his saddlebags and heading west to start a law practice. Whether or not these stories are true, they point to the larger truth of Blackstone's influence in America. The prevalence of cheap copies and eventually of American annotated editions, the use of Blackstone as the first textbook at the first American law school at William & Mary, the fact that, as Grant Gilmore tells us, "for more than a hundred years, thousands upon thousands of lawyers and influential laymen on both sides of the Atlantic read the *Commentaries* and believed them": all of these factors influenced American legal culture.[67] This influence was not simply or perhaps not even most importantly an influence of particulars. It was rather an ideological influence: reading Blackstone influenced how lawyers and judges understood the world of law and politics. To the extent that American lawyers absorbed his work, Blackstone contributed to and reinforced the general discourse that associated law with civic happiness. John Adams believed that "the happiness of society" was the aim of government[68]; George Mason was only one of many to include the right to happiness in his state's Declaration of Rights; James Madison focused on happiness as a political good.[69] In short, Blackstone's ideas resonated with the Founders, finding a ready American audience educated in the great Enlightenment ideas that Blackstone brought to the law, and in need of images of certainty and comfort in the face of colonial revolution and the instability of a new republic struggling to unify areas with disparate geographies, ideals, and allegiances.

What then of the afterlife of the *Commentaries*? While a full history of Blackstone's influence on American law and letters lies beyond the scope of this book, we can trace Blackstone's influence by asking what a Blackstonian reading of one of our most canonical Law and Humanities texts might teach us. How might treating *To Kill a Mockingbird* as a descendent of Blackstone's *Commentaries* add to our understanding of the novel? Written by Harper Lee and published in 1960, when the United States was in the midst of the civil rights movement, it has been one of the most read books in American culture, so frequently taught in US middle and high schools as to be read by (or at least assigned to) almost every student in the country. When I query my college students as to whether they have read it, fourteen out of every fifteen say yes, with many reporting multiple readings in different grades. ("Seventh grade, ninth grade, and then again in the eleventh," reported one student with a sigh.) A Book of the Month Club survey in 1991 reported that *To Kill a Mockingbird* was second only to the Bible as one of the top three books that was "most often cited as making a difference" in people's lives.[70] Sales figures are estimated in the thirty to forty million range; the book still sells more than 750,000 copies a year. And the novel's influence goes beyond the United States. In 2006, British librarians ranked it number one of books people should read before they die, right above the Bible.[71] In 2014, Lee was reported to be earning over $3 million in royalties based on sales of the novel.

On Amazon, where it is astonishingly highly ranked (#5 in literary fiction and #8 in American fiction), the novel is represented as a "prize-winning masterwork of honor and injustice in the deep South—and the heroism of one man in the face of blind and violent hatred . . . a crusading local lawyer risks everything to defend a black man unjustly accused of a terrible crime."[72] In public school education in the United States, it has almost always been presented as "timeless, classic literature," meanwhile weakly historicized as an intervention meant to support the civil rights movement of the 1960s.[73] While it is difficult to understand how a novel in which a black man is falsely accused, found guilty in a travesty of a trial, and shot dead while being held in prison during his appeal could become a symbol of the fight for racial justice, the critical reception has mirrored the popular reception and, until recently, been almost entirely admiring.[74] This reaction is not limited to literary critics and high school English teachers: the legal community as well has adopted Atticus Finch as a role model.[75] Recent readings of the novel, however, have interrupted this lovefest, historicizing the novel more carefully, recognizing its gender and class biases, and questioning its reinforcement of the American tolerance for racial inequality.[76]

To bring Blackstone to the critical party is not as antic as it might seem. *To Kill a Mockingbird* invokes Blackstone in ways that complicate the generally celebratory reception the novel has received. In the novel, Calpurnia, a black servant, descendent of slaves, works in Atticus Finch's house and raises his children, Jem and Scout. When asked, she explains how she learned to read and how she taught her son to read. Here is the passage, narrated by Scout:

> "Did you teach him out of a primer, like us?" I asked.
>
> "No, I made him get a page of the Bible every day, and there was a book Miss Buford taught me out of—bet you don't know where I got it," she said. . . .
>
> "What was the book, Cal?" I asked.
>
> "Blackstone's *Commentaries*." . . .
>
> "They were the only books I had. Your granddaddy said Mr. Blackstone wrote fine English."
>
> "That's why you don't talk like the rest of 'em," said Jem.
>
> "The rest of who?"
>
> "Rest of the colored folks."[77]

To Kill a Mockingbird thus places the Bible and Blackstone's *Commentaries* on the same plane, while treating both as superior substitutes for the "primer" the white children have encountered in school. Much is made of the fact that Blackstone wrote "fine English" and thus trained Calpurnia so she "don't talk like the rest of 'em." (Ironically, Calpurnia "don't" even talk like Jem, the educated son of the town's white lawyer; at least when she's with white people, she speaks "fine English" herself, reverting to what American linguists call Black English only when in the black community church.) The novel treats the *Commentaries* as offering entry into the civility of the white world and leaves us with the message that Blackstone's aesthetic in the form of "fine English" is something worth knowing.

Blackstone does not stand only for "fine English" though. *Mockingbird* makes much of southern history and the traditionalist racist force it exerts on small-town Maycomb. But in activating Blackstone as a text used to teach illiterates to read and thus with the potential to lift the virtually enslaved Southern blacks of the 1930s out of their servitude, Lee plays a cruel trick. She seems to be offering her readers an alternative, more optimistic history, a history that reaches back behind and geographically away from southern Mississippi and towards English ideas of liberty. Blackstone's triumphing of liberty offers any number of passages that might have drawn Calpurnia to the text and thus made it a book to wave in the face of the societal apologists and racists that populated *To Kill a Mockingbird*. In the most generous reading, his vision was optimistic: he was attached to the idea that he could make liberty the foundation of a set of laws that circumscribed liberty, that he could make sense of the disorderly consequences of a liberty-focused justice by embedding liberty in order. But as I have discussed, this version of justice only works when every person finds the right place in the natural "harmonic" order. Thus, an allegiance to harmonic justice is less than ideal for Calpurnia. The novel's pursuit of "fine English," of a "fine" understanding of an English justice ideal, undermines Calpurnia (and the reader) by offering a fictional model of "fine English" aligned with Blackstonian ideals, embodied in the Finch family with its revisionist history, its reading, its books, and its stability. Although a somewhat denucleated nuclear family (Calpurnia has taken the place of the lost white mother), the Finches are governed by a Blackstonian balance of rationally worked out liberties and constraints, as well as by reasoned discourse embedded in an affective, affectionate regard for others. Through them, the novel offers not so much an optimistic understanding of justice, but, to return to Lauren Berlant, a cruelly optimistic one.[78]

The aesthetic appreciation Calpurnia seems to take in Blackstone alerts us to the *Commentaries*'s actual relationship to the novel's themes and to the way Blackstone's ideas about the common law came to structure American culture's understanding of race relations. As discussed in brief above, Blackstone could map harmonic justice onto the common law only if he could also represent the common law as committed to gradualism, not simply in regard to slavery, but in regard to all historical change. Harmonic justice is static; history is not completely static, but the slower the changes, the less revolutionary they are, and the more possible it is to map history onto harmonic justice. Revolutionary ideas such as the call for immediate abolition are discordant, or, if we prefer the metaphor of the machine, they jam the machine. An almost glacially slow approach to change is one of Lee's major themes in *Mockingbird*; Maycomb is stuck in time, changing, if at all, at a very slow pace. The novel begins with a comic twist on historical slippage as the children try to trace the origins of Jem's broken arm, first to the evil deeds of the Ewells, then to Dill's arrival, but finally all the way back to Andrew Jackson and even to the Battle of Hastings.[79] After three pages of narration meant to bring us to the present of the novel, we are told that "Maycomb was an old town, a tired old town," where people move slowly and days seem longer than twenty-four hours. Lee hammers home this point and associates it with the law as early as page five when she remarks that "the courthouse sagged in the square." Later, she describes the courthouse as "early Victorian with a big nineteenth-century clock tower . . . housing a rusty unreliable instrument, indicating a people determined to preserve every physical scrap of the past."[80] The slow pace of change becomes crucial to the defense of the town's racism. When an African American man, Tom Robinson, is tried on false rape charges and found guilty, this counts as progress because jury deliberations took more than a few minutes. As Miss Maudie says, "We're making a step—it's just a baby-step but it's a step."[81] Like Blackstone's "villeins," Maycomb's African Americans are meant to be content with baby steps, with infinitely slow progress that can always be harmonized with the past.

If harmonic justice with its united "parts with parts" and "countless wheels" structures happiness, then happiness here is bound up not only with racial but also with class and gender injustice. While a full discussion of the class and gender injustice recapitulated in the novel is outside the scope of this chapter, a glance at the hierarchical structuring of Maycomb County society makes it seem almost as stratified as Blackstone's England. As Jessie Allen points out in her essay "Blackstone in the Twenty-First Century," Blackstone's "method of representing civil society is strikingly categorical and status bound."[82] Everyone in the English nation can be categorized under one heading or another: duke, earls, and barons take their places above the commonality, but the "commonality" is also divided into degrees (I:391). "Tradesmen, artificers, and labourers" must be categorized by "their estate, degree, or mystery" in legal actions (I:394). No one is without a place. Even the most casual reader of *Mockingbird* will note the categorization at work in Lee's fictional world: Atticus's first case involves two volatile clients who have killed a blacksmith in an argument over a horse. Scout remarks, "They were Haverfords, a name synonymous in Maycomb County with jackass."[83] As the novel proceeds to introduce its different types, we learn that Cunninghams are poor but honest and proud, Ewells are poor, dishonest, and feckless, that virtually everyone in the novel has been neatly pigeonholed and defined by class, gender, or race. This sort of structuring of difference has been seen as a flaw in Lee's work; characters are all good (Jem is a gem, for instance), or all bad (Ewell is pure evil), and the good and evil characters form pairs meant to show contrast. Types are defined by gender as well as class. Much of the novel is concerned with teaching children to take their place in the structured world of class and gender: Scout must be taught to wear dresses; Jem must be taught to control his temper; disobedient children are thought to cause disruptions in the natural order.[84] Those who don't fit or can't be made to fit (Dill and Miss Caroline, for instance) are invariably from out of town. This is a society where everyone fulfills his or her function, where what Gregory Jay has termed "the systematic machinery of socio-political power" is on display.[85] Disruptions may jam the machine a bit, but it soon returns to working order. Snowstorms are followed by fire, quickly doused by the local volunteer brigade; rabid dogs are shot; black men who have the nerve to feel sympathy for poor white women are tried, convicted, and then shot like rabid dogs.

Where is happiness to be found in such a world? Despite the numerous crises that drive the plot of *Mockingbird*, happiness, not crisis, is the governing principle in the novel. To return to Berlant's discussion of cruel optimism, sometimes "crisis" is simply a rhetorical way of making something appear to be an event when actually it's a "structural or predictable condition."[86] Following the word "happiness" around in *Mockingbird* is to realize that the inhabitants of the novel are happy when they are pursuing their regular activities—in other words, when they are not disrupted by difference. Children can be happy in their innocence (a mixed-race child "skips happily"; Dill has a "happy" laugh); adults can be happy when pursuing conventional activities ("happy picnickers" become sullen when confronted with what they see as a racial uprising during the trial). Most ominously, Aunt Alexandra's racist group of "ladies" are seen to be "chattering happily," until the moment Tom Robinson's death is announced. (They then take a short break for sadness before returning to their chat.) One of the odder moments in *Mockingbird* occurs after Calpurnia has taken the children to visit her church and they see the churchyard, where they observe what Lee calls a "happy cemetery." Here the African American community celebrates the dead by decorating their graves as Lee offers us an image of aestheticized Solonic happiness that also speaks of making do, of collaborating with the system. This is happiness: the observation of a balanced aesthetic of the wheels turning in unison in this carefully constructed machine.

The machine-like nature of this form of happiness becomes even more apparent when we shift from happiness to what happens. The most prominent use of "happens" occurs during the trial scene where "what happened?," "what happened next?," and "tell us what happened" are frequent locutions. One might almost think that the end result of the trial has not been predetermined, that "hap" is going to exert its sway. But careful readers will have noted an earlier exchange between Atticus and his brother, a moment immediately preceded by Scout's effort to explain how justice works to Uncle Jack. Lee signals to us that this is going to be a didactic moment about justice by having Scout start with issues of fairness. "You ain't fair," Scout says to Uncle Jack, continuing on to explain the importance of listening to both sides before coming to judgment. After a reconciliation of sorts, Scout leaves and overhears Atticus discussing her with Uncle Jack. Explaining that Scout needs to learn to control her emotions, Atticus shifts to discussing the upcoming trial of Tom Robinson. After carefully outlining his prediction that Tom will receive an unfair trial, be convicted on the basis of known lies, and only possibly be vindicated in an appeal, Atticus sums it up by saying, "You know what's going to happen."[87] He may be referring to the trial; he may be referring to the town's racist rage, but one thing is clear: in this world, what's going to happen has already happened. Disruption will be absorbed into process and liberty will be controlled by the machine of justice.

If being "fair," in the sense of hearing both sides, doesn't lead to justice, where do we find justice in *Mockingbird*? One might think we find it in empathy, a word represented in the novel only metaphorically as "walking in another man's shoes," which becomes Atticus's mantra when faced with unjust circumstances. This "lesson" has been one of the central moral truths that *Mockingbird* has been celebrated for. But where is empathy located in the novel? Atticus preaches it to his children, suggesting that Walter Cunningham and Scout should have put themselves in Miss Caroline's shoes rather than tormenting her (this is ironic, as Walter has explicitly been described as having no shoes). Later Atticus credits his rescue from the Cunningham mob to Scout's ability to make the elder Cunningham walk in Atticus's shoes. But the novel's emphasis on empathy takes an odd turn during Tom Robinson's trial, for it is Robinson's expression of empathy for Mayella Ewell that turns the jury against him. From the moment Tom explains that he did chores for Mayella because he felt sorry for her, his fate is sealed. The novel suggests that empathy can be owned only by white people; it is a sign of white privilege. Empathy then is subordinated to harmonic justice; it may provide some lubrication for its machinery, but can never supersede its commitment to hierarchy.

At the end of Blackstone's early poem "The Lawyer's Farewel," the poet-lawyer, seemingly defeated by the difficulties of law practice, its discord and strife, finds peace through retirement. As Howard Mumford Jones once explained, this motif commonly accompanied theories of happiness, amounting to what Jones calls a "spectator theory of felicity," in which happiness can only be achieved through withdrawal from life's strife.[88] "Thus it was," Jones intones, "that the classical doctrine of happiness as resignation to the course of things was domesticated in America."[89] But as I have discussed in chapter 1, even Blackstone's poetic retirement was interrupted by memories of discord, of the "harpy tribe" and the "orphan's cry." How different then seems the final scene of *Mockingbird*, a paradigmatic scene of warm family life, of calm after the storm, a scene that lulls most readers into a happy feeling of closure and completion. Here we find Atticus and Scout, finally alone together, with Scout in a dreamy state, listening to Atticus read her a story about an innocent boy who finds justice. "Atticus, he was real nice," she says, drifting off into sleep. "Most people are, Scout, when you finally see them," replies Atticus.[90] The reader too is tempted to drift off in a happy daze, enchanted by this warm, familial resolution to what has been a hectic last third of the novel. But who is there to be "seen" by this point in the novel? Calpurnia, central to the nucleated Finch family group, has been edged out by Aunt Alexandra, who arrives right before the trial, establishing her place by immediately ordering Calpurnia to take her heavy suitcase to her room in chapter 13. By chapter 16, Aunt Alexandra is instructing Atticus not to talk about race in front of Calpurnia, or, as she puts it, "in front of them," effectively othering a person who has raised the Finch children. And by chapter 24, after Tom Robinson's death, Aunt Alexandra, shocked and saddened, sits in Calpurnia's chair. One might want to read this as a "walking in her shoes" moment, but instead it marks the end of Calpurnia's influence; she fades away as if she has never existed. The last nine chapters of the novel might as well be signposted "whites only," as Tom Robinson is dead and Calpurnia is never mentioned again. Even the poor whites are eliminated: Aunt Alexandra has explained that, shoes or no shoes, young Walter Cunningham can never be friend to Scout. If any of these characters were ever objects of empathy, they have now been distanced from the center. And as the objects of empathy have receded, the prominence of empathy as a theme in the novel has faded as well, to become only a notch in the rhetorical frame of white-splaining that reduces everything to harmony. In short, the better we "see" this novel, the less nice it seems. To achieve harmony with its wheels within wheels, turning in unison, the novel has sacrificed both the black and the poor white populations: Calpurnia and her world hover at the far margins, while Tom Robinson commits "suicide by cop," attempting escape from prison under circumstances that assure not only his death, but his own responsibility for that death. Bob Ewell's death will never be investigated; his daughter is left to her own devices, uneducated and unloved. Harmonic justice comes at a very high cost: in the original Blackstonian model, the "contrarieties" that vexed Blackstone's ideals were minimized and contained through an elaborate system of checks and balances, not to mention fine rhetoric. In Lee's world, these "contrarieties," represented by poor whites and hapless black victims, are simply killed off or relegated to a silent world of impoverished struggle. As Berlant might argue, justice for the marginalized has become "too expensive," as full liberation lies beyond what the novel can imagine and retirement, or sleep, is all that's left for us to long for.[91]

Where then might we find justice? For that, we need to look not for harmonic balance, but for something quite different, for deformity, for deviations from form that alert us to what else might be going on. To locate this in *Mockingbird*, we might first look at family life: this is a novel of depopulation, as Maycomb appears to be a town populated only by denucleated families. There is only one example of a heteronormative family and that is not a happy one.[92] The Finches have lost a mother; Dill has lost a father; Miss Maudie lives alone; Dolphus Raymond's bride has committed a particularly brutal suicide on discovering that her bridegroom has a black family on the side; that the Ewells are missing a mother has led to child abuse and incest. The Radley family is intact, at least at the start of the novel, but it remains so only by virtue of keeping Boo a prisoner, cruelly marking him as a beaten-down "ghost" who only wanders at night. Even that emblematic figure of childhood, the snowman, deviates from our expectations, becoming a "morphodite" in Scout's words, turning white to black, male to female, and finally melting away. Departures from form are also figured through the human body as the novel begins, peaks, and ends with representations of deformity. The first paragraph of the first chapter starts with a description of Jem's broken arm, which has resulted in a permanent and serious disability ("his left arm was somewhat shorter than his right; when he stood or walked, the back of his hand was at right angles to his body, his thumb parallel to his thigh").[93] The climactic moment in Tom Robinson's trial turns on the fact that his ruined left arm would have made it impossible for him to have caused Mayella's injuries. And the novel ends full circle, with the wounded Jem lying unconscious in the room next door while Atticus reads Scout and the reader to sleep. We might then look for moments out of balance—where ratios don't align and harmony has not been achieved—as symptomatic of the harm in harmonic justice. The out-of-place family, the not-to-normative standards body, these equate with a refusal to succumb to formal conventions, but they also stand out or maybe up to assert claims for liberty. They signal to us that rather than allowing liberty to be subsumed in floods of soothing words, we should perhaps examine it more closely, reading it as an absolute value that resists our desire for harmonic balance and for happiness when all seems (but is not actually) right with the world. In the sense then of the negative photographic image, Blackstone's emotional aesthetic has value only if we see it slant. We need to replace foreground for background, focus on what doesn't fit, on what is "deformed." We must prioritize what jams the machine over its efficient operations, and follow that jamming action to disrupt the workings and availability of happiness. Such a conclusion suggests neither Soni's prescription for happiness, nor Rawls's prescription for justice. We should not wait until after its (symbolic) death to judge whether the life of justice is good; we should not view "the whole design itself" and, finding it good, reward it with our happy feelings. Instead, we should see such claims of happiness as symptomatic, a "sign of an insoluble problem" that we must nevertheless endeavor to solve.[94] To do so we must focus on the places where the design breaks down, the pattern is marred, where discord rather than harmony reigns. This would result in a different aesthetic of justice, in an aesthetic of what's broken, of the fragment, and in a different approach to justice, one that focuses on emotions as signs meant to organize our understanding of rights.

Coda

Excessive Subjectivity Is the New Subjectivity (Speculations)

Or I might better say excessive subjectivity *should be* the new legal subjectivity. Recent news brought word of an unfortunate defendant in a Texas court who seems to have become agitated during the proceedings.[1] When the defendant, Terry Lee Morris—a mentally ill, disabled alleged child molester who "rambled" and "smelled bad"—refused to concede to the court's jurisdiction, the judge responded by electrocuting him—not to death, but into submission—using a stun belt that had been wrapped around the defendant's legs. Meagan Flynn reported in the *Washington Post* that "the judge shocked Morris three times, sending thousands of volts coursing through his body" even as Morris begged him to stop "torturing" him.[2] Morris was so traumatized that he opted not to attend the rest of the trial, after which he was sentenced to sixty years in prison. On an appeal based on the defendant's failure to receive a fair trial, the appellate court pointed out that the type of stun belt worn by the defendant "contains enough amperage to immobilize a person. The wearer is generally knocked to the ground and shakes uncontrollably. . . . An electrical jolt of this magnitude causes temporary debilitating pain and may cause some wearers to suffer seizures."[3] The defendant was ordered a new trial.

What is one to do with an agitated or "disruptive" defendant? As the appellate court said in the Morris case, it is a judge's "heavy burden" to "take the chaos before him, impose order, and uphold the dignity of the justice system."[4] Terry Lee Morris represented this chaos: his behaviors flew in the face of any ideas we might have about judicial decorum, that distant heir of harmonic justice with its symmetrical forms and "wheels within wheels." He seems to have had problems with boundaries, both in the popular psychology sense and in the sense that he lived a life out of bounds: his offense involved obscene cellphone pictures exchanged with the teenage daughter of his girlfriend; he "rambled" in court; he testified to taking numerous psychotropic prescription drugs; he claimed to be agoraphobic. Morris was not violent, but was simply attempting to represent himself and be assigned a new judge, not surprising given both the judge's and his attorney's attitudes towards him. One of the attorneys present characterized his behavior as "smarting off" to the judge. But his agitation seemed to infect everyone around him. His own attorney (whom he had tried to fire) told the jury that he "smelled bad." And his trial judge (whom he had tried to recuse) made no secret of his intentions: when Morris repeated his wish to recuse the judge, the judge responded with the very indecorous orders "Hit him" and "Hit him again." Morris represents the way such agitated defendants disrupt the modern form harmonic justice has taken. They interrupt decorum, the formal, outward sign of justice observed, of processes proceeding in an orderly fashion, and authority respected. Dignity, orderliness, good form, correctness: the words we associate with decorum offer signposts indicating that a modern form of harmonic justice still exerts formal pressure on our legal system.

Agitation—one outward sign of what has been called "excessive subjectivity"—jams the wheels of the harmonic justice machine and thus demands our attention. This is not the first time I have broached this topic: we saw it in chapter 4 where recalcitrant defendants were pressed into submission under the authority of the English law. We can also detect its presence in Mary Wollstonecraft's critique of the structure that Blackstone had spent a lifetime repairing and bringing up to date. Blackstone had imagined the law as a gothic castle in need of repairs and himself as the eager renovator, as I pointed out in chapter 2. In response, Wollstonecraft asked, why bother? As I mentioned in chapter 4, instead, she laid out the case for a tear-down, arguing, "Why were they obliged to rake amongst heterogeneous ruins; or rebuild old walls . . . when a simple structure might be raised on the foundation of experience, the only valuable inheritance our forefathers can bequeath?"[5] Not much agitation here, just a straightforward argument. But she followed up on this thought in *Maria* where she conflated an ancient, crumbling gothic castle, meant to represent a moribund, masculinized legal system, with a madhouse full of agitated, rambling prisoners, and imprisoned her agitated heroine there.

In other work, I have argued that Wollstonecraft's construction of the agitated, resistant figure inhabiting an agitated, resistant text in *Maria* could provide the model for a new form of legal subjectivity, full of content rather than empty, defining itself rather than being defined by the law.[6] As Jamie Boyle notes, legal subjectivity is about "who gets to be a subject. . . . What qualities or attributes about them are included in the box of subjectivity and what attributes are excluded?"[7] To follow Boyle further is to recognize that the supposedly empty vessel of the "legal subject" is "actually full. . . . The legal subject's biases, motivations, and assumptions are the same ones honored in the dominant culture."[8] Full, but not overly full, not overflowing. As Boyle makes clear, our understanding of legal subjectivity, our *recognition* of it, depends on the legal subject's ability to reflect the law back to itself: to the extent that the law recognizes certain emotions, they are permissible; to the extent that certain emotions go outside the bounds of what is recognized, they are outlawed, banished from the law, forced out or treated as invisible. But legal subjectivity is not static; it can change. Recent work on legal subjectivity has begun to attempt to expand its boundaries to include animals and the environment; if legal subjectivity can include humans without the capacity to reason, why not include animals? If it can include corporations, why not the environment? If it is defined by status, then why not include "vulnerability" as a status?[9]

What if we turn harmonic justice on its head, valuing it not for what it does include, those harmonic wheels within wheels, always turning in unison, but rather for what it reveals about exclusion, for its dependence (or maybe co-dependence) on the very agitation that we saw in Wollstonecraft and now see in Terry Lee Morris. Agitation is itself agitated: it could be viewed as both a physical, autonomic, and pre-conditioned condition *and* an emotional practice shaped by social and cultural forces that may or may not be consciously directed. In being *both* rather than *either*, it traverses the boundary between the natural and the cultural, between the personal, physical body and the politicized and socialized body. It is, in its essence, movement that disrupts its frame. That we cannot locate its restless presence with any precision seems inherent in its nature. Is it in our bodies or out in the world? It's worth noting that in political spheres, agitation refers to a resistant form of political discourse as well as to the stirring up of radical unrest. Wollstonecraft used "agitation" as both verb and noun—as something that she might actively do and as something she might experience as acting upon her and within her—invoking both usages in a sort of Mobius strip of cause and effect. As an in-between, sort-of feeling, something unspecified but physicalized and impossible to ignore, something moving from individual bodies out into the public sphere and back again, it resists harmonious resonances and instead vibrates unevenly and uneasily, disturbing the "peace" or happiness we might feel when we observe justice. It is the emotional but also physical, embodied sign of what we might begin to think of as a new and important form of legal subjectivity: excessive subjectivity.

Dominik Finkelde's recent work on the philosophical understanding of excessive subjectivity is helpful here. Finkelde asks how it is that we can have political change, given that our actions are always in the process of being folded back into the existing order. He points to certain historical figures as representing "excessive subjects," in that they were change agents: Martin Luther, Rosa Parks, Jesus, and Paul are his figures of choice. Their embodied excessivity is what makes change happen: excessive subjects "again and again shake" ethical life "to its core as if emerging out of the ethical life's own blind spot."[10] Excessive subjectivity is a formal operation because it can only be recognized when it occurs within an oppositional structure that allows us to see this "shaking" action. And this concept of "shaking" evokes our discussion of agitation, that emotion that shakes everyone around it. What if we add the Terry Lee Morris's of the world to Finkelde's list of excessive subjects? Morris's agitation, his refusal to step down or back, to stop "rambling," to contain his bodily odors, his emotional expressions, his vocalizations, all intersect with Finkelde's concept of the excessive subject devoted to "spontaneity, rule-breaking," the subject who articulates himself "without always having consciousness as the clear agent of this articulation."[11] In this sense, then, Morris's agitation speaks coherently even when he could not. The legal subject who has to be shocked into submission, like the defendant subjected to *peine fort et dure*, may seem incoherent or at least indecorous, but is trying to tell us something about a system that has broken down, an ethical system in need of being shaken to its core.

To fully appreciate agitation and reframe it as a legal emotion, we need to turn briefly back to chapter 5 where I discussed the law's "tenderness" in reference to sympathy and empathy. Here I want to think a little harder about sympathy, that feeling state that may in some ways seem like agitation's opposite. David Hume's understanding of sympathy suggests we read it as aligned with harmonic justice: "As in strings equally wound up, the motion of one communicates it to the rest: so all the affections readily pass from one person to another and beget corresponding movements in every human creature."[12] Without sympathy, that generalized receptivity to the emotions of others, we would have no moral feelings, no way of imagining how others feel or what they are experiencing. Blackstone does not discuss sympathy much if at all; he doesn't need to. He counted on sympathy as the field in which other emotions could operate, assuming what Adam Smith had argued, that "whatever is the passion which arises from any object in the person principally concerned, an analogous emotion springs up, at the thought of his situation, in the breast of every spectator."[13] Sympathy is the quality that knits us together. Because of this quality, Smith says, we wish to maintain "the safe, respectable, and happy situation of our fellow-citizens."[14] It is thus both a moral and political emotion, one that underlies the possibility of all other emotions related to our communal endeavors. It need not rise to the level of "feeling sorry" for someone and thus spur fears of bias or lack of partiality. Instead, it should alert us to the need to take a second look, to slow down, to weigh carefully the need for expediency against the need for fairness. In Terry Lee Morris's case, a form of sympathy was at work, though it worked to Morris's detriment; everyone became agitated in response to Morris's agitation, so much that it seemed imperative to stop it. This sympathetic reaction (and here I speak of what modern theorists might call "emotional contagion"[15] or what neuroscientists call "mirror neurons") could have been, should have been, a trigger for heightened review rather than for electric shocks. Can we imagine a system in which when agitation is recognized through the operations of sympathy, it becomes the foundational feeling prompting us to take a second look, to step back, to review our proceedings for fairness?

Throughout the *Commentaries*, Blackstone attempted to shape legal emotions around the desire for harmonic justice. We are meant to desire harmonic justice, to mourn in ways that reinforce it, to be embarrassed if our bodies do not live up to its standards, to bolster its effects through allegiance to the book and to the rule of law, to submit to its claims under the threat of torture, to try to be happy, or at least not too unhappy, under its dictates. Our happiness, we are taught, depends on our acceptance of its gentle revolutions, its wheels within wheels turning without opposition. This understanding of justice requires us to banish the unhappy: unhappy "types" like the poor, the racially othered, the indecorous, the mentally ill, even the loquacious are silenced through banishment or torture. And this banishment occurs because harmonic justice is dependent on form, on formal operations that are attuned to each other, on formalities that typify our justice system today just as much as they did in Blackstone's time. Form is often taken to be restrictive, just as the "wheels within wheels" in Blackstone's fantasy of justice were. But, as Levine asks, "Are there potentialities that lie latent in a form?"[16] The potentiality in harmonic justice lies in its very rigidity, in its "wheels within wheels," because that rigidity throws unacceptable variances into high relief. It makes agitation visible, and thus allows us to engage in an analysis that marks an episode of extreme agitation as a moment that should trigger review rather than electric shocks.

Reworking legal emotions to recognize agitation as a formal sign of excessive subjectivity brings emotion to legal decision-making. It suggests a new understanding of legal subjectivity based in the agitation of the differently-abled, "rambling" subject, authorized not by decorum, respect for harmonic justice, or submission to its "wheels within wheels," but by the very agitation that makes this subject unacceptable. Sara Ahmed has taught us that "emotion [is] a form of cultural politics or world making."[17] We might consider Ahmed's recent argument that emotions are not so much "in either the individual or the social body but produce the very surfaces and boundaries that allow all kinds of objects to be delineated."[18] In this light, Morris's agitation in its expression of surfaces, boundaries, and boundaries breached can be reread as a sort of gift to us, one that should prompt us to rethink legal subjectivity, to articulate it as not simply a container for an unchanging set of rights and expectations, but as a form that designates certain emotions as legitimate (remorse, for instance) and others as illegitimate (agitation, for instance), and thus a form that can be changed.

ACKNOWLEDGMENTS

This is a book about emotions and law, two topics I've been thinking and talking about for most of my adult life. Thus, the word "acknowledgments" hardly seems adequate to describe the many debts of gratitude I've incurred as I have worked on this book. Georgetown colleagues have been extremely supportive, but I want to make special mention of Ricardo Ortiz, Sherry Linkon, M. Lindsay Kaplan, John Pfordresher, John Glavin, Wayne Davis, Terry Reynolds, Gay Cima, Patricia O'Connor, Sam Pinto, Eddie Maloney, Randy Bass, Jim O'Donnell, John Hirsh, Patrick O'Malley, Maggie Debelius, Jason Rosenblatt, Alex Sens, Peter Pfeiffer, Jane McAuliffe, and David Edelstein. My friend Lena Orlin intervened at a crucial moment that determined the book's direction. Friends and writing buddies like Nina Kushner, Pat Cahill, and Terese Schlachter offered companionship and moral support, and in Terese's case, her dining room table and a couple of Rhodesian Ridgebacks. Other colleagues and friends who deserve thanks include Lisa Freeman, Scott Krawczyk, Seth Lerer, Katie Barclay, Simon Stern, Alan Klima (thanks for the meditations, Alan!), Aaron Hanlon, Dennis Haarsager, Kris Straub, Toni Bowers, and Laura Rosenthal. To the folks at Chesapeake Health and Fitness, especially Kayla Schell, thanks for great conversations and for keeping me healthy. My dear friend Deborah Kaplan has provided delightful companionship and lively encouragement for over twenty-five years. Jessie Allen, author of the *Blackstone Weekly* and an unfailing source of vitality and spirit, reintroduced me to the idea of re-enchantment, and enchanted me with invigorating conversation. Patricia Meyer Spacks started me on this path in the late 1980s and has continued her unflagging support. I must mention Peter Goodrich as well. I first encountered his work in the mid-1990s. Without his scholarship and support, I could not have imagined writing this book. Wilf Prest first invited me to Australia to talk about Blackstone and later encouraged and urged me on during a difficult time. I doubt he realizes what a great and positive influence he has been.

Various organizations were important to this book's formation: the East-Central/American Society for Eighteenth-Century Studies has offered a warm, welcoming home for over twenty-five years. I will never forget those members who brought my young daughter gifts when we attended the conference the year after my husband died. The Association for the Study of Law, Culture and Humanities has provided wonderful occasions to mingle with like-minded theorists and scholars. More recently, I have thrived as a member of the Law and Society Association with its new Law and Emotions CRN. Thank you, Susan A. Bandes, Emily Kidd White, and Jody Madeira for welcoming me into the ranks. A number of chapters were written at Trudy Hale's lovely writing retreat in Norwood, Virginia, with Trudy always proving to be an interested and energizing companion. The NYU Press has offered support and counsel throughout the publication process. Thank you, Clara Platter, especially, and thanks also to my anonymous readers whose helpful suggestions have made this a better book.

I am grateful for the support I received from Georgetown in the form of multiple course releases, and from the American Council of Learned Societies, the National Endowment for the Humanities, the Folger Shakespeare Library, and the Australian Research Council Centre of Excellence for the History of Emotions in the form of fellowships. The Centre for the History of Emotions in Australia was especially influential, helping me re-envision the book in a warm, inviting atmosphere. Adelaide Director David Lemmings read and commented on the manuscript as a whole, for which I will be forever grateful. Claire Walker, Associate Investigator, arranged several opportunities for me to present papers. Most importantly, David and Claire and their children Tom and Charlotte invited me into their family during my several stays in Adelaide. With the eager assistance of their dog, Bede, they made me feel completely at home.

I could not have pursued this book while chairing the English Department at Georgetown without the assiduous support of Karen Lautman and Donna Even-Kesef. And I could not have finished it while running the Connected Academics Mellon Project without the help of Maria Snyder or the support of our Graduate School Dean Norberto Grzywacz and Vice Dean Sheila McMullan. Research assistants Liz

Carten, Larkin Postles Jago, Rachel Morota, Bridget McFarland, and Jacob Myers, among others, made many contributions. Joanne Muzak provided much-needed editorial help. My heartfelt thanks are owed to our highly tolerant and supportive Georgetown library professionals, especially Jeffrey Popovich, Sandy Hussey, and Jill Hollingsworth. I hope I don't hold the faculty record for most fines expunged, but it's possible.

The introduction, chapters 3 and 5, and the Coda include material that has appeared in print. Short sections of the introduction and of chapter 5 were drawn from "Sounds Couth and Uncouth: The Poetics of Harmonic Justice in William Blackstone's *Commentaries on the Laws of England*," *Law and Literature* 28, no. 2 (2016): 97–115. An abbreviated version of chapter 3 appeared in somewhat different form in "Blackstone's 'Stutter': The (Anti)Performance of the *Commentaries*," in *Reinterpreting Blackstone's* Commentaries: *A Seminal Text in National and International Contexts*, edited by Wilfrid Prest, 3–25 (Oxford: Hart Publishing, 2014). A few passages of chapter 5 first appeared as "What's Old Is New Again: William Blackstone's Theory of Happiness Comes to America," *Eighteenth Century* 55, no. 1 (Spring 2014): 129–34. Several paragraphs now in the Coda also appeared in "Heart of Agitation: Mary Wollstonecraft, Emotion, and Legal Subjectivity," *Eighteenth Century* 58, no. 3 (Fall 2017): 371–82. I thank these presses and publications for encouragement along the way and permission to reprint.

My brother, Bill Streever, a much-published nonfiction writer with a buoyant approach to the writing process, has been my companion throughout this journey. My sister, Kristyn Snedden, has amazing insight: she helped me be a better parent on untold occasions—a major concern if one is chairing a department, writing a book, and raising a child simultaneously. My niece, fellow academic Margaret Greaves-Ozgur, has been a wonderful reader and support while my nephew David Streever, a writer in his own right, has warmed me with his enthusiasm.

I am sorry that my husband, Jim Slevin, my parents, Don and Louise Streever, my brother, Don Streever, my nephew William Streever, and my close friend Donna Floyd did not live to see me complete this book. They are missed.

To my partner, Jim Mahshie, and my daughter, Lucy Slevin, I truly owe more than words can say. They have been daily sources of both stability and joy. Thank you.

NOTES

INTRODUCTION

1 Unless otherwise noted, all citations to Blackstone's work are included in paren-
theticals within the text and refer to the University of Chicago facsimile edition.
See Blackstone, *Commentaries: A Facsimile*.

2 The scholarship on Blackstone's influence is extensive and will be further addressed in chapter 5. For an excellent overview of Blackstone's influence in
America, see Hoeflich, "American Blackstones."

3 See Allen, "Reading Blackstone," 217.

4 For discussions of the relationship between emotion and reason in the eighteenth-
century context, see Maroney, "Persistent Cultural Script" and "Law and Emotion," as
well as Bandes and Blumenthal, "Emotion and the Law." For a critique of Enlightenment reason in the Law and the Humanities context, see Dayan, *Law is a White Dog*.

5 Vamik Volkan has written extensively about large group identity. See *Blind Trust*.
According to Volkan, group identity includes "shared tangible reservoirs from
images associated with positive emotion"; "shared 'good' identifications"; "chosen
glories"; and "formation of symbols that develop their own autonomy" (37). For
a psychoanalytic approach to group identity related directly to law, see Peter
Goodrich's introduction to *Law and the Unconscious*. There Goodrich writes, "To
establish the necessary bond between subject and law, the legal order depends
not simply upon fear of law's violence but much more generally upon a structure
of political love. The primary form of that bond . . . is constructed through the
textuality of law" (25). For discussions of myths about the common law and their
contribution to English national identity, see Goodrich, "Poor Illiterate Reason."
Blackstone assumed, as did most of his readers, that people had a natural affinity
for justice. Thus, his aim in the *Commentaries* was to connect English law to what
he probably believed was a universal human desire for justice.

6 For a helpful study of English legal history and jurisprudence before Blackstone,
see Berman, "Origins of Historical Jurisprudence." For more complete histories,
see Lemmings, *Professors of the Law*; Baker, *An Introduction to English Legal History*; and Langbein, Lerner, and Smith, *History of the Common Law*.

7 Lemmings, *Professors of the Law*, 20.

8 Lemmings, *Professors of the Law*, 19n38. See also Ross, "Memorial Culture," 229–
326 and 232–33, for a discussion of the relationship between the growth of print
and the culture of memory in the century preceding Blackstone's *Commentaries*.

9 Cromwell quoted in Simpson, *Legal History and Legal Theory*, 280.

10 Lobban, *Common Law and English Jurisprudence*, 9, 11.

11 Wood, *Institute of the Laws of England*, unpaginated preface.

12 Lemmings, *Professors of the Law*, 108.

13 Seipp, "Structure of English Common Law," 61, 71.

14 Boorstin, *Mysterious Science of the Law*, 3. The few who have written about Blackstone from a humanities perspective before the recent Blackstone revival spurred by Wilfrid Prest include Meehan, "Authorship and Imagination," and Smitten, "Blackstone's *Commentaries* as Constitutive Rhetoric."

15 Lieberman, *Province of Legislation Determined*, 179.

16 Ross, "Memorial Culture," 325.

17 Cosgrove, *Scholars of the Law*, 22.

18 William Meredith quoted in Lieberman, *Province of Legislation Determined*, 35–36.

19 Prest, *William Blackstone*, 1–2.

20 Quoted in Lemmings, *Professors of the Law*, 139n152.

21 [Anon.], *Literary Fly*, 308.

22 [Anon.], *British Critic*, 439.

23 Simpson, *Legal History and Legal Theory*, 296.

24 Prest, *William Blackstone*; Prest, *Re-Interpreting Blackstone's* Commentaries; Prest, *Blackstone and His Commentaries*; Blackstone, *Letters of Sir William Blackstone* (edited by Prest); Blackstone, *Commentaries* (Oxford edition, edited by Prest); Page, *Blackstone and His Critics*. All who work on Blackstone today are indebted to Prest's contribution to Blackstone scholarship.

25 See Allen's blog, *Blackstone Weekly*.

26 Prest, *William Blackstone*, 24–25.

27 For the poem, I rely on the version titled "The Lawyer's Farewel to His Muse," in *A Collection of Poems in Four Volumes. By Several Hands*, vol. 4, 1755, ed. Robert Dodsley. Later versions sometimes spell "Farewel" as "Farewell." Prest discusses the poem and Blackstone's literary interests in detail in *William Blackstone*, 58–60. See also Mauger, "'Observe how parts with parts unite'" and my essay, "Sounds Couth and Uncouth."

28 Pahl, "Logic of Emotionality," 1458.

29 See Reddy, *Navigation of Feeling*. Jan Plamper summarizes Reddy's work in *History of Emotions*, 251–64. Ahmed's *Cultural Politics of Emotion* has also been instrumental in advancing an understanding of emotions as acting on us, in us, but also on others.

30 In his interest in harmonic justice, Blackstone was influenced by Jean Bodin and Montesquieu. See Shaw, *Justice of Venice*, for a discussion of Bodin's understanding of harmonic justice as a flexible system that blended law and equity. For a detailed discussion of harmonic justice, see Engster, *Divine Sovereignty*.

31 Battestin, *Providence of Wit*, 7.

32 Hibbitts, "Making Sense of Metaphors," 249.

33 Battestin, *Providence of Wit*, 4.
34 Heninger Jr., *Touches of Sweet Harmony*, 256.
35 For a discussion of Aristotle's theory of the numerical equivalencies of justice, see Dimock, *Residues of Justice*, 2.
36 Blackstone, "Lawyer's Farewel," 230-231.
37 Denham, "Cooper's Hill: A Poem."
38 See Markley, "British Theory and Criticism." Markley notes the centrality of the metaphor of harmony to eighteenth-century criticism as representative of "efforts to transcend the complexities and contradictions of historical experience."
39 Wasserman, *Subtler Language*, 54.
40 Lemmings, *Professors of the Law*, 46.
41 Cowie, "Justice at Westminster Hall." See also Baker, "Westminster Hall," in *Common Law Tradition*, 247–62; Kyle, *Theater of State*.
42 Saunders, *Westminster Hall*, 240, 251.
43 Brown, *Amusements Serious and Comical*, 59–60.
44 For a discussion of the need to decode, to learn "to hear" the manuscript or print words that describe sounds in earlier eras, see Smith, "Listening to the Wild Blue Yonder."
45 See Mauger, "'Observe how parts with parts unite,'" for a detailed discussion of this passage and its relationship to Coke. While Mauger's methodology differs from that offered here, he provides a complementary analysis of the relationship between the poem and the *Commentaries*, emphasizing Blackstone's interest in creating a public, easily accessible compendium of law. In light of the poem, he argues, the *Commentaries* can be reread as "an exercise in what might now be termed 'legal transparency,' a democratizing watershed in the history of English law" (196).
46 Tom Tyler is the authority on this approach. See Tyler, *Why People Obey the Law*, 4.
47 Deigh, "Emotion and the Authority of Law."
48 No doubt these characterizations may seem like caricatures to some. For commentary on the anti-presentist bias in historical scholarship, see Wilson, "Historicizing Presentism." For an account of literary criticism that focuses on the struggle between analysis and intervention, see North, *Literary Criticism*. Robin West and Danielle Citron have recently discussed the normative emphasis in legal scholarship in "On Legal Scholarship." For two recent collections that define the field of study now referred to as the history of emotions, see Boddice, *History of Emotions*, and Rosenwein and Cristiani, *What Is the History of Emotions?* The field of law and emotion is developing quickly and may already be more capacious when this book is published than I represent it here. For early efforts to recognize the role of emotion in legal decision-making, see the oft-cited Cardozo, *Nature of the Judicial Process*, and Justice William Brennan Jr.'s famous essay "Reason, Passion, and 'The Progress of the Law.'" See Bandes, *Passions of Law*, for the collection of essays that launched law and emotion as a field of study in

the late twentieth century. See Bandes and Blumenthal, "Emotion and the Law," for a more recent survey of the field. In Robin West's even more recent "Law's Emotions," West points out that law and emotions scholarship has focused on the law's regulation of emotion and on emotion's impact on law but has paid little attention to the way law itself generates emotions. The forthcoming Elgar-published *Research Handbook on Law and Emotions* (eds. Susan A. Bandes, Jody Madeira, Emily Kidd White, and Kathryn D. Temple) will offer about forty essays that focus on methodology in law and emotions scholarship. For a survey of Law and Humanities approaches, see Sarat, Anderson, and Frank, *Law and the Humanities*. The Association of Law, Culture and the Humanities hosts conferences and a journal devoted to law and humanities scholarship, as does the *Yale Journal of Law & Humanities*.

49 The scholarship on this issue is vast and I have discussed it in my earlier book, *Scandal Nation*. Here I list a few central sources. See Temple, *Scandal Nation*; Colley, *Britons*; Anderson, *Imagined Communities*; and Gikandi, *Slavery and the Culture of Taste*.

50 I assume familiarity with the various well-known critiques of the Enlightenment. For an excellent summary of the critiques, see Bronner, "Great Divide." For accounts of the Enlightenment as a philosophical and cultural movement, see works by Peter Gay, Isaiah Berlin, and Jonathan Israel, and more recently, the much criticized book by Anthony Pagden, *The Enlightenment: And Why It Still Matters*.

51 Here I follow Darrin McMahon, who, in his important study of happiness, *Happiness: A History*, advocates methodological pluralism in studies of emotion, asserting that "there are infinite histories of happiness to be written" (xiii–xv).

52 Hensley, *Forms of Empire*, 17. See Williams, "From Reflection to Meditation," in *Marxism and Literature* for an early critique of claims that literature "reflects" culture. See Siskin and Warner, *This Is Enlightenment*, for applications of the concept of mediation to reading eighteenth-century texts.

53 See Felski, *Limits of Critique*, and Bennett, *Enchantment of Modern Life*.

54 Sedgwick, *Touching Feeling*.

55 Like many of his contemporaries, Blackstone used "it's" for the possessive. I have used the modern "its."

56 Hensley, "Curatorial Reading and Endless War," 60.

57 Here I am paraphrasing Bal in *Double Exposures*.

58 See Martinon, "Theses in the Philosophy of Curating," 30.

59 See Melville, *Billy Budd, Sailor*, 128.

60 For the debate around surface reading and close reading, see *Representations* 108, no. 1 (Fall 2009).

61 See Levine, *Forms*, and Brinkema, *Forms of the Affects*, xvi.

62 Hensley, *Forms of Empire*, 18.

63 Levine, *Forms*, 4–5.

64 Levine, *Forms*, 17.

65 See Dixon, "'Emotion,'" 339.

66 Brinkema, *Forms of the Affects*, xiv.

67 See Trigg, "Affect Theory," for the recognition that most emotion historians intentionally shift between "affect" and "emotion," using "affect" to refer to "the embodied, sensate aspect of mental and emotional activity" and "emotion" to refer to "linguistic or non-linguistic expression of feelings, emotions, passions, sentiments and drives" (11). See Brinkema, *Forms of the Affects*, for an argument against defining affect as prior to language, as an ineffable that cannot be described, does not have form, and thus cannot be critiqued or interpreted. See also Neuman, Marcus, Crigler, and Mackuen, *Affect Effect*, for a collection of essays on the relationship between affect, emotion, and political formations. See Ellison, *Cato's Tears*, for a discussion of these terms in relation to eighteenth-century studies of sensibility (4–9).

68 See Plamper, *History of Emotions*, for an introduction to the history of emotion; see Broomhall, *Early Modern Emotions*, for a general guide to history of emotions research in the early modern period, up to 1800.

69 See Reddy, *Navigation of Feeling*; Rosenwein, *Emotional Communities*; and Scheer, "Are Emotions a Kind of Practice?"

70 Scheer, "Are Emotions a Kind of Practice?," 220.

71 Scheer, "Are Emotions a Kind of Practice?," 200.

72 See Robinson, *Deeper than Reason*, 126.

73 See Rawls, *Theory of Justice*, for one of the great works of twentieth-century jurisprudence. Many have commented on Rawls's image of justice as decontextualized and idealized. See Dimock's *Residues of Justice* for an appreciative critique, 4, 102–6. In his "Postmodern Justice" in *Law and the Humanities*, Peter Goodrich is characteristically eloquent when he refers to "Rawls' city, the neo-Kantian architecture of the social," as "deserted of all human forms, a pure, but blank symmetry. The citizens are elsewhere . . . knowing nothing of themselves, existing as spectral forms, as hypotheses, they have no relation to each other, no conversation, and no actual amity or justice, but rather exist in the empty and weightless exigency of holding up the 'symmetry' of justice" (201).

74 Ahmed, *Cultural Politics of Emotion*, 13.

75 Young, *Judging the Image*, 11.

CHAPTER 1. WHAT'S LOVE GOT TO DO WITH IT?

1 Collins, *Armadale*, 453.

2 Collins, *Armadale*, 454.

3 Collins, *Armadale*, 455. I thank my colleague Nathan Hensley for drawing my attention to this passage. For discussions of Wilkie Collins and his contributions to the novel, see Costantini, *Armadale: Wilkie Collins and the Dark Threads of Life*; Taylor, *Cambridge Companion to Wilkie Collins*; and Sutherland's introduction to the 1995 Penguin edition of *Armadale* (vii–xxv).

4 Collins, *Armadale*, 457.

5 Collins, *Armadale*, 455.

6 Collins, *Armadale*, 456.

7 Collins, *Armadale*, 458.

8 Collins, *Armadale*, 458.

9 Legal scholarship on the relationship between love and law often takes the form of specific commentary related to contemporary events. For an interesting approach, see Calhoun, "Making Up Emotional People." For discussions of the law/love dichotomy, see Bankowski, *Living Lawfully*, and Grossi, *Looking for Love*. For a study of the laws related to love in Renaissance England, see Goodrich, *The Laws of Love*. Goodrich ends this rich study with the question "Does love have standing?" and a discussion of recent case law in light of the history of laws of love.

10 Collins, *Armadale*, 458, emphasis added.

11 Collins, *Armadale*, 455, emphasis added.

12 See Berlant, *Desire/Love*. Berlant argues that "there is no way definitively to capture desire. . . . The minute an object comes under analytic scrutiny, it bobs and weaves, becomes unstable, mysterious, and recalcitrant, seeing more like a fantasy than the palpable object it had seemed to be when the thinker/lover first risked engagement" (17). See Gorton, "Desire, Duras, and Melancholia," for a discussion of the various ways desire has been defined as "an emotion and an affect, and as the essence of human subjectivity" (18). There is, of course, a lengthy philosophical tradition.

13 Menninghaus, *Disgust*, 1.

14 Blackstone, "Lawyer's Farewell," 228.

15 For discussions of the imagery of justice, see Resnik and Curtis, *Representing Justice*, and Dimock, *Residues of Justice*.

16 Blackstone, "Lawyer's Farewell," 228.

17 The "thorny maze" appears frequently in references to justice. See Dent's play *The Lawyers' Panic*, where "virgins dressed in white, with black faces" "[strew] the ground with thorns and briars as emblematical of the ways of the law" (6). Twentieth-century lawyers were often introduced to law school by being assigned Karl N. Llewellyn's 1930 *The Bramble Bush*.

18 A version of this critique animates "The Gowns: A Tale from Westminster Hall," where we find a less thoughtful, more satiric image as women fight over their lover, Erskine. Justice takes both their purses and then distributes Erskine's clothes to them, saying, "I'll have Erskine myself; so dear ladies adieu" (9). Mr. L., "The Gowns," 5–9.

19 Blackstone, "Lawyer's Farewell," 231.

20 Berlant, *Desire/Love*, 18.

21 Blackstone, "Lawyer's Farewell," 231.

22 Blackstone, "Lawyer's Farewell," 231.

23 Lacan quoted in Olson, "Creative and Revolutionary Nature of Desire," 207. In "Courtly Love, or, Woman as Thing," Žižek, following Lacan, writes compellingly of this dynamic, arguing that while Freud constructed the object of desire as a void surrounded by artificial obstacles, Lacan argues that the object can be seen

"only when it is viewed from the side, in a partial, distorted form" (94). Desire is thus characterized by incessant postponement" and "the Object . . . is literally something that is created—whose place is encircled—through a network of detours, approximations and near-misses" (94).

24 See Felman, *Scandal*.

25 Blackstone, "Lawyer's Farewel," 231.

26 Blackstone, "Lawyer's Farewel," 230.

27 Warner, *Monuments and Maidens*, 154. Warner discusses the difficulties early modern philosophers and theorists had in representing justice. The familiar image of Lady Justice with scales and sometimes a sword was not necessarily the norm, although those elements were common. Many early images were explicitly violent, with Lady Justice depicted surrounded with tortured victims, chopping off limbs, etc. (157). Warner tells us that "the dilemmas posed by the concept of justice itself, social, legal, divine, are so immense that representation often wavers before them" (158). As Battista Fiera complained in 1515, "How can you represent Justice both with one eye and many eyes: and how can you depict her with one hand only, and yet measuring, and at the same time weighing, and simultaneously brandishing a sword?—unless, of course, they are all raving mad. Flatly, the thing can't be done" (Battista Fiera, *De Justicia Pingenda*, trans. and ed. James Wardrop [London: 1957], quoted in Warner, *Monuments and Maidens*, 158). Theorists across the centuries had grappled with what Jelica Sumic-Riha calls the "incalculability" of justice: "Justice is incalculable by definition. It is incalculable because it entails moments in which the decision between just and unjust cannot be ensured by a rule. Thus one could say that justice is the experience of incommensurability, of the impossible, of the undecidable." Sumic-Riha, "Fictions of Justice," 78.

28 Doody, *Daring Muse*, 165.

29 Sherwin, *Visualizing Law*, 2.

30 Hoeveler, "Female Captivity Narrative," 55.

31 Aikin, *General Biography*, 3:29.

32 Montagu, *Letters and Works of Lady Mary Wortley Montagu*, 345.

33 [Anon.], *Secret History of the Loose and Incestuous Loves of Pope Gregory VII*, 32; Manley, *Adventures of Rivella*, 59.

34 Wieland, *Oberon, a Poem*, 32.

35 Gentleman of the Middle Temple, *History of Lord Stanton*, 4:133.

36 Ballaster, *Fabulous Orients*, 61.

37 Blackstone, *Pantheon*, lines 90–94.

38 Haldar, *Law, Orientalism and Postcolonialism*, 57.

39 Johnson, "Disgust," in *Dictionary of the English Language*, facsimile of the 1755 ed., n.p.

40 See Nussbaum's *From Disgust to Humanity* and *Hiding from Humanity*. A robust debate about the positive and negative valences of disgust typifies the law and emotions scholarship, as the varied reactions to Nussbaum's work reveals. See, for instance, Kahan, "Progressive Appropriation of Disgust." For a recent approach

to disgust from a law and emotions standpoint, see Ashworth, "Affective Governmentality."

41 In *Anatomy of Disgust*, William Ian Miller makes the point that Adam Smith is primarily interested in "shame, disgust, and other wider-ranging moral sentiments, rather than . . . guilt and anger" (189). See Menninghaus, *Disgust*, for an insightful history and commentary on disgust. Eschenbaum and Correll's edited collection *Disgust in Early Modern English Literature* has also been helpful. See also Prinz, "The Moral Emotions." Other leading researchers on disgust as a moral emotion include Jonathan Haidt, Paul Rozin, and Clark McCauley. Mary Douglas's *Purity and Danger* and Julia Kristeva's *Powers of Horror* are both, of course, fundamental to this discussion. Blog posts on disgust by Daniel Kelly, Mark Bradley, Benedict Robinson, and Richard Firth-Godbehere in a series on *The History of Emotions Blog* have offered invaluable insights into the most current work in this area. See https://emotionsblog.history.qmul.ac.uk.

42 Miller, *Anatomy of Disgust*, 184.

43 Swift, "Description of a City Shower," 409.

44 Cockayne's *Hubbub: Filth, Noise and Stench in England, 1600–1770* offers a compelling account of the disgusting aspects of city life, with its overcrowding, open sewers, and industrial pollution.

45 Felman, *Scandal*, 86–89.

46 Goldberg, Musheno, and Bower, "Shake Yo' Paradigm," xii.

47 Burke quoted in Stern, "Editor's Introduction to Book II," xiii.

48 Johnson, *The Rambler*, 167.

49 These are unpaginated index entries from volume IV.

50 Arendt, *Human Condition*, 237.

51 See Gilbert Abbott à Beckett, *Comic Blackstone*, 80, for another version of the joke about marriage and reason.

52 Probert, *Marriage Law and Practice*.

53 Probert, *Marriage Law and Practice*, 343.

54 Probert, *Marriage Law and Practice*, 247, 249. See Lemmings, "Marriage and the Law," for a fascinating look at the "violent passions" that accompanied the passage of the act.

55 Probert, *Marriage Law and Practice*, 250, 249.

56 Act for the Better Prevention of Clandestine Marriage quoted in Probert, *Marriage Law and Practice*, 211.

57 Probert, *Marriage Law and Practice*, 212.

58 Sedgwick, *Touching Feeling*, 90.

59 See Felman, *Scandal*, 14.

60 Felman, *Scandal*, 15.

61 Felman, *Scandal*, 111.

62 Interestingly, Blackstone's biography provides another example of an unsuitable marriage: in his letters, he sets romance against law, entangling it all with racial difference, when he notes that while studying law he had met "a young lady of

extraordinary accomplishments & very ample fortune" who has "together with the riches, the complexion also of a jew" and thus was not "a very formidable rival to Coke upon Littleton." Blackstone, *Letters of Sir William Blackstone*, 65.

63 Cohen and Johnson, *Filth*.

64 Kolnai quoted in Menninghaus, *Disgust*, 16.

65 Cohen, "Introduction: Locating Filth," x.

66 Dabashi, *Post-Orientalism*, 277.

67 Wilson, *Hydra's Tale*, xxi.

68 Ballaster, *Fabulous Orients*, 146.

69 See Halliday, "Blackstone's King."

70 Halliday, "Blackstone's King," 177.

71 In Number 4 of *The Rambler*, Johnson writes, "Vice . . . should always disgust; nor should the graces of gaiety, or the dignity of courage, be so united with it, as to reconcile it to the mind."

72 Ngai, *Ugly Feelings*, 335.

73 Ballaster, *Fabulous Orients*, 80.

74 Ballaster, *Fabulous Orients*, 17.

75 Berlant, *Desire/Love*, 26.

76 Felman, *Scandal*, 15.

CHAPTER 2. BLACKSTONE'S "LAST TEAR"

1 Ahmed, *Cultural Politics of Emotion*, 13.

2 See Berlant, *Desire/Love*, for the idea that "melancholia mirrors inversely the idealizing narratives about merged souls more happily associated with love" (29).

3 See Brinkema, *Forms of the Affects*, 2. For an important early discussion of eighteenth-century melancholy, sensibility, and masculinity, see Ellison, *Cato's Tears*. Melancholy moods and sensibility were closely linked for eighteenth-century thinkers. See Todd, *Sensibility*, and Barker-Benfield, *Culture of Sensibility*. For a recent collection on the relationship between law and mourning, see Sarat, Douglas, and Umphrey, *Law and Mourning*.

4 See Dixon, "Tears of Mr. Justice Wilkes."

5 See Rosenwein, *Emotional Communities*, 29.

6 See Goodrich, *Oedipus Lex*, 1–16.

7 Prest, *William Blackstone*, 288–91.

8 Cheng, *Melancholy of Race*, 28.

9 See Brady and Haapala, "Melancholy as an Aesthetic Emotion."

10 Benjamin, *Selected Writings*, 4:390.

11 As Matthew Bell points out in *Melancholia*, studies of melancholia (and melancholy moods) generally rely on Klibansky, Panofsky, and Saxl, *Saturn and Melancholy*. See also Jackson, *Melancholia and Depression*, and Radden, *Nature of Melancholy*.

12 Warton, *Pleasures of Melancholy*. "Nor let me fail to cultivate my mind / With the soft thrillings of the tragic muse" (17).

13 For a full discussion of the elegiac tendency in mid-eighteenth-century verse, see Eric Parisot's *Graveyard Poetry*. See also the classic essays by Morris Golden in *Thomas Gray*. For a discussion of the different versions of the *Elegy* and access to an authoritative edition, see Alastair MacDonald's edition of the Eton manuscript and the first edition in *An Elegy Written in a Country Church Yard*, reproduced in facsimile, 1976. For the standard modern biography of Gray, see Mack, *Thomas Gray*.

14 Lawlor, "Fashionable Melancholy," 31.

15 See Daniel, *Melancholy Assemblage*, and the essays in Ingram et al., *Melancholy Experience in Literature*. As Daniel points out in his wonderful study of Burton, Burton's work, "through its encyclopedic reach, definitive status, and persistent popularity . . . sums up and completes the transmission of the melancholy archive from classical texts . . . into the examining rooms of physicians and onto the public stages of English popular culture." Daniel, *Melancholy Assemblage*, 166.

16 Bahun, *Modernism and Melancholia*, 3. The connection between melancholia and imagination is still invoked today; see, for instance, Kristeva, who argues in *Black Sun* that "loss, bereavement, and absence trigger the work of the imagination and nourish it permanently as much as they threaten it and spoil it" (9).

17 Quoted in Mack, *Thomas Gray*, 294. To offer only a few examples of other references to melancholy and melancholia, Ben Jonson mocked melancholy in his 1601 play *Every Man in His Humour* ("I am melancholy myself . . . and then do I no more but take pen and paper . . . and overflow you half a score, or a dozen of sonnets at a sitting" [III.i.80-84]); Milton recognized two melancholic traditions, the Galenic disease tradition and the Aristotelian creative tradition; Anne Finch associated melancholy with creativity in her dark 1709 poem *The Spleen*, and David Hume, David Hartley, and James Beattie tended to see melancholia as a "scholar's malady." Finally, George Cheyne, part of Blackstone's larger circle and famous for his medical treatises, treated melancholy as both a physical and spiritual disease, discussing such efforts in his work *The English Malady*.

18 Stukeley, *Of the Spleen*, [vi–ix].

19 See Adair, *Essays on Fashionable Diseases*. Matthew Bell suggests that modern melancholia owes more to fashion than capitalism (although untangling these two would seem to be impossible). See Bell, *Melancholia*, 121–23.

20 Ellis, *Politics of Sensibility*, 1. See Dixon, *Weeping Britannia*, especially chapter 12, "Damp Justice," 169–84. See also Vingerhoets, *Why Only Humans Weep*, for a fascinating account of the history, culture, and biology of tears.

21 See Cheng, *Melancholy of Race*.

22 See Clewell, "Mourning beyond Melancholia," 50; Flatley, *Affective Mapping*, 2.

23 Clewell, "Mourning beyond Melancholia," 51.

24 Gray, "Elegy Written in a Country Churchyard," 4:1–6.

25 There are numerous versions of the poem; see Parisot, *Graveyard Poetry*, for a discussion of the modern critical description of these. The version published in Dodsley's 1755 collection is entitled "An Elegy Written in a Country Church Yard." It includes the "Epitaph," familiar to contemporary readers. See Starr and Hen-

drickson, *Complete Poems of Thomas Gray*, 37–42, for a discussion of Gray's later changes.

26 Parisot, *Graveyard Poetry*, 153–54.

27 Woty, "The Pettyfogger, a Parody." See also [Anon.], "Elegy Written in Westminster-Hall," 2:77–82.

28 See Cheng, *Melancholy of Race*, 86, for one use of "encryption" that brings the idea of the tomb together with that of the way the lost object is "encrypted" or coded, leaving traces on body and psyche. Cheng refers to this as "endocryptic identification," relying on Abraham and Torok, who as Cheng points out, use the phrase to describe "melancholic identification with a lost love or unknowable inheritance." See Abraham and Torok, *Shell and the Kernel*.

29 Gray, "Elegy Written in a Country Churchyard," 4:1, l. 2, l. 13.

30 Gray, "Elegy Written in a Country Churchyard," 4:1, l. 8, l. 18, l. 10, l. 23.

31 Gray, "Elegy Written in a Country Churchyard," 4:1, l. 14.

32 Gray, "Elegy Written in a Country Churchyard," 4:4, l. 73.

33 Gray, "Elegy Written in a Country Churchyard," 4:3, l. 59.

34 Gray, "Elegy Written in a Country Churchyard," 4:4, l. 81–84.

35 Gray, "Elegy Written in a Country Churchyard," 4:3, l. 45–46.

36 Gray, "Elegy Written in a Country Churchyard," 4:1, l. 16; 4:3, l. 53–54.

37 Gray, "Elegy Written in a Country Churchyard," 4:4, l. 66.

38 Doody quoted in Parisot, *Graveyard Poetry*, 126.

39 Gray, "Elegy Written in a Country Churchyard," 4:6, l. 113, 115–16.

40 Cheng, "Melancholy of Race," 50.

41 Cheng, *Melancholy of Race*, 8.

42 Blackstone, "Lawyer's Farewel," 230.

43 Cheng, *Melancholy of Race*, 9.

44 See Stewart, *Poetry and the Fate of the Senses*, for a discussion of the way meter can be "a counter to the ceaselessness of all ceaseless things" (197). But while reminding us that things don't end, meter can also signify an end. Each downbeat closes down sound for an instant.

45 For a summary of the couplet's importance and uses, see Hunter, "Couplets."

46 Blackstone, "Lawyer's Farewel," 229, 230.

47 Stewart, *Poetry and the Fate of the Senses*, 79.

48 Blackstone, "Lawyer's Farewel," 229.

49 Blackstone, "Lawyer's Farewel," 230.

50 Blackstone, "Lawyer's Farewel," 231.

51 Blackstone, "Lawyer's Farewel," 231.

52 Blackstone, "Lawyer's Farewel," 232.

53 Luciano, *Arranging Grief*, 15.

54 For the oral origins of the common law, see Goodrich, "Poor Illiterate Reason," and Clanchy, *From Memory to Written Record*, 1–25. Ross's "Memorial Culture" offers a compelling account of late sixteenth- and early seventeenth-century legal efforts to integrate memory, customs, and print culture into a coherent whole.

55 Goodrich, "Poor Illiterate Reason," 16.
56 Alfred was on everyone's minds during Blackstone's youth. See Black, *Culture in Eighteenth-Century England*, for what he refers to as "the cult of King Alfred" (217), and for the idea that to simply mention Alfred "was to make a political point about the need for national integrity and the defence of national honour" (223).
57 Cheng, "Melancholy of Race," 53.
58 This complex area of legal history has been much discussed by legal historians. See Lieberman, "Property, Commerce, and the Common Law"; Willman, "Blackstone and the 'Theoretical Perfection'"; Gray, "Blackstone's History of English Law"; Cairns, "Eighteenth-Century Professorial Classification"; Rose, "Canons of Property Talk"; Harman, *Critical Commentaries on Blackstone*.
59 See Neu, *Tear Is an Intellectual Thing*.
60 Sartre, *Sketch for a Theory*, 61.
61 There is some evidence for Blackstone's depressive personality in the Charles Churchill poem of 1769, where he is referred to as the "scowling Blackstone," and in various descriptions, including self-descriptions, claiming that he was morose and irritable. See Prest, *William Blackstone*, 272–76. But my interest here lies in feelings of loss "as constituting social, political and aesthetic relations" (Butler, "Afterword," 467.) I am thus referring not to Blackstone's psychology, but to his representation of his own subjectivity and that of his time.
62 This history goes back to the classical tradition and is well documented as a medieval and Renaissance tradition. See Goodrich, *Oedipus Lex*; Lemmings, *Professors of the Law*.
63 Goodrich, *Oedipus Lex*, 12–13.
64 Roscoe, *Westminster Hall*, 2:8.
65 Lemmings, *Professors of the Law*, 228.
66 Hardwicke quoted in Lemmings, *Professors of the Law*, 135n128.
67 Holdsworth, "Some Aspects of Blackstone," 275.
68 Holdsworth, "Some Aspects of Blackstone," 275. Jeremy Bentham frequently repeated this criticism, summing it up as "everything-as-it-should-be-Blackstone." See Meehan, "Blackstone's *Commentaries*," 67.
69 Eng and Kazanjian, preface to *Loss*, ix.
70 Eng and Kazanjian, "Introduction," in *Loss*, 4.
71 Flatley, *Affective Mapping*, 2.
72 Goodrich suggests this possibility, arguing that "the negative dimension of loss inevitably has a positive representation," and that "the positive imagery of law" could be "the melancholic lawyer's projection to cover the lack of reason, system, and justice in a common law composed of infinite particulars" (*Oedipus Lex*, 7–8).
73 Margaret Jane Radin discusses this "personality theory of property" in her collection of essays, *Reinterpreting Property*. As Radin explains, Locke suggests that memory confirms our sense that we have a self-consciousness that persists over time and that this self-consciousness is essential to personhood. Radin's analysis

applies this idea to the history of property law: memory and continuity are crucial to a nation's claims of identity.

74 See Stern, "Editor's Introduction to Book II," xxiii.

75 This is, of course, one of the most famous and oft-quoted legal statements regarding property. As Rose points out, what she calls the "exclusivity axiom" is "in a sense a trope, a rhetorical figure describing an extreme or ideal type rather than reality" (Rose, "Canons of Property Talk," 604). In fact, property rights were not and are not now exclusive; all sorts of "social and political obligations" accompany any given right to property, as Blackstone well knew.

76 See Reichman, *Affective Life of Law*, for a discussion of this idea in the context of modernist fiction (439).

77 Rose, "Canons of Property Talk," 602. Rose has been much cited. Purdy's *Meaning of Property* discusses Rose's work in a larger discussion of Blackstone's emphasis on property law as the "first among institutions," and "the whole web of institutions, including sovereignty, law, and organized religion, as the children of property" (3).

78 Blackstone also quoted in Rose, "Canons of Property Talk," 601.

79 Blackstone repeats this sentiment in slightly different words in II:211. Here he shifts emphasis to the need to "prevent the mischiefs" that might result from cutting off property rights at the death of the owner and thus making every property up for grabs whenever an owner dies.

80 Rose, "Canons of Property Talk," 606, 609.

81 Kipling, of course, made use of this phrase in his *Just So Stories*, considered some of his finest work. Kipling's use of the phrase, however, is ironic, as he clearly marks his stories as fantasies. See, for example, "How the Elephant Got His Trunk" and "The Beginning of the Armadillos" in Kipling, *Just So Stories*.

82 Schmidgen, introduction to *Eighteenth-Century Fiction*, 5.

83 To say that a description of property law owes much to various narrative conventions is not to undermine its value. Contemporary theorists of property see narrative as fundamental to understanding property law: Jeremy Waldron in his influential entry on property in the *Stanford Encyclopedia of Philosophy* notes that even an untrue genealogy "can make an important contribution to our understanding," while in "Performing Property, Making the World," Nicholas Blomley argues that narratives about property persist because they are useful.

84 Rose, "Canons of Property Talk," 606, 609.

85 Rose, "Canons of Property Talk," 606. See Cairns, "Blackstone, the Ancient Constitution"; Willman, "Blackstone and the 'Theoretical Perfection'"; and Gray, "Blackstone's History of English Law," for Blackstone's treatment of the Norman Conquest as a consensual agreement among equals.

86 Gray, "Blackstone's History of English Law," 16.

87 Miller, *Communities in Fiction*, 16. Here, he is describing Raymond Williams's *Country and the City*.

88 See also II:344 where "the ingenuity of some, and the blunders of other practitioners" so "entangled" an estate with "a confusion unknown to the simple convey-
ances of the common law" that Parliament was increasingly asked to step in and
clean up the mess (II:345), causing the king "to wish, that men might not have too
much cause to fear, that the settlements which they make of their estates shall be
too easily unsettled when they are dead. . . ." (II:345).

89 Harbison, *The Built, the Unbuilt, and the Unbuildable*, 99.

90 Legendre, *Law and the Unconscious*, 110, 112.

91 Fetishes involve man-made objects that are believed to have power over others.
Jessie Allen has written eloquently about the power that "legal word acts" have
had over objects, particularly property: "Before legal word acts, what you have is
land, and after the words, magically, the land becomes property. . . . By legal word
magic, property survives us, and gives us a way of affecting a future in which we
no longer inhabit our own bodies." Allen, "Actions Speak Louder."

92 As Blackstone explains, a hotchpot is, in English, a pudding. "By this housewifely
metaphor our ancestors meant to inform us, that the lands . . . should be mixed
and blended together, and then divided in equal portions among all the daughters" (II:190). The proof required for "tenancy by the curtesy," Blackstone explains,
may have included an infant's cries. "Some have had a notion that it must be
heard to cry; but that is a mistake. Crying indeed is the *strongest* evidence of its
being born alive; but it is not the *only* evidence" (II:127). A baby born alive (even if
it died an instant later) had become a descendent, whereas a baby born dead had
not.

93 One notes the irony of this emphasis on the purity of genetic inheritability given
English legal history's attempts to trace a pure English legal descent from the
Saxon ancient constitution. It is not as clear to me as it was to legal historian
Charles M. Gray that Blackstone managed to rid English legal history of its
"fetter-like" aspects and demonstrate a pure, "progressive" path. See Gray, "Black-
stone's History of English Law," 4.

94 "Socage," Blackstone argued ("against the authority even of Littleton himself"),
was a Saxon word, one designating unrestricted ownership of property and one
of "the relicks of Saxon liberty" that had survived to the present day as a "grand
species of tenure" (II:81, 90).

95 Foucault, *Archaeology of Knowledge*, 53.

96 Hibbitts, "Making Sense of Metaphors," 248.

97 Smith, *Acoustic World*, 10.

98 See chapter 6 in Albert Lord's *Singer of Tales*. Lord considered this problem in
the context of the oral cultures of Macedonia and Albania between the 1930s
and 1950s. By the time he was writing, recording devices had made the scene he
describes obsolete.

99 See II:172 for another passage in which Blackstone apologizes for the "subtleties
and refinements, into which this doctrine, by the variety of cases which have
occurred in the course of many centuries, has been spun out and subdivided."

Despite apologizing here, he cannot resist a lengthy disquisition on "executory devises" (II:172).

100 Kermode, *Sense of an Ending*, 3.

101 See Allen, "Nothing Certain."

102 Rose, "Canons of Property Talk," 614.

103 Kennedy, "Structure of Blackstone's *Commentaries*," 210.

104 Kennedy, "Structure of Blackstone's *Commentaries*," 210.

105 Rose, "Canons of Property Talk," 609.

106 In *Sense of an Ending*, Kermode notes that modern fiction first appears when "the revealed, authenticated account of the beginning was losing its authority" (67). He associates "the fictions by which we order our world" with "the increasing complexity of what we take to be the 'real' history of that world" (67). Although he is speaking of an earlier period, the connection between a loss of an authoritative, unifying belief in beginnings and increasing complexity is helpful for understanding Blackstone's world as well.

107 Spargo, *Ethics of Mourning*, 5.

108 Spargo, *Ethics of Mourning*, 5.

CHAPTER 3. THE ORATOR'S DILEMMA

1 Gammerl quoted in Barclay, "New Materialism," 168.

2 Pope, *Essay on Criticism*, 305.

3 Bowring, [*Memoirs and Correspondence*], 10:45.

4 Clitherow, preface to *Reports of Cases*, xxvii.

5 Clitherow, preface to *Reports of Cases*, 7.

6 Prest refers to his "natural reticence and verbal inarticulacy" as a barrier to success in Parliament and quotes *House of Parliament* as recording Horace Walpole's judgment that Blackstone was "an indifferent speaker." See Prest, *William Blackstone*, 201.

7 Quoted in Prest, *Blackstone as a Barrister*, 15.

8 Prest, *William Blackstone*, 201.

9 Kadens, "Justice Blackstone's Common Law Orthodoxy," 1604.

10 Quoted in Kadens, "Justice Blackstone's Common Law Orthodoxy," 1604.

11 Blackstone, *Letters of Sir William Blackstone*, 29.

12 Prest, *William Blackstone*, 153.

13 Prest, *William Blackstone*, 22.

14 Phelan, *Unmarked*.

15 The legal scholarship on shame is extensive, but generally concerns criminal and, to a lesser extent, civil defendants. As Bandes and Blumenthal point out in their recent essay "Emotion and the Law," "the emotions of judges have generally received scant attention" (165). Although there is a recent interest in how judges deliberate, issues of judicial shame and embarrassment seem not to have come into play as yet. For recent work on shame in the law, see Nash and Kilday, *Cultures of Shame*; Maroney, "Law and Emotion"; and Massaro, "Show (Some)

Emotions." Most legal scholars recognize embarrassment and shame as related but distinct emotions.

16 See Evans, "Reputation Is the Modern Purgatory."

17 Johnson, *The Rambler* "No. 157," 180.

18 Johnson, *The Rambler* "No. 157," 182–83.

19 Johnson, *The Rambler* "No. 157," 184.

20 Johnson, *The Rambler* "No. 159," 197; Johnson, *The Rambler* "No. 159," 208; Johnson, *The Rambler* "No. 159," 201.

21 The *OED* notes that it appeared in John Cleland's *Memoir of a Coxcomb* in 1751: "My steadiness of gaze began to embarrass and give her pain" (*Oxford English Dictionary Online*, s.v. "embarrass," www.oed.com).

22 See Kay, "Trade in Feelings."

23 Johnson, *Dictionary of the English Language*, facsimile of the 1755 ed.

24 *OED Online*, s.v. "shame," accessed June 13, 2018, www.oed.com; Johnson, *Dictionary of the English Language*.

25 Nussbaum, *Hiding from Humanity*, 204; Crozier, "Blushing and the Private Self," 223. For the difficulties sorting out the differences between shame, embarrassment, "diffidence," and "bashfulness," see Nussbaum, *Hiding from Humanity*, 203–4, where Nussbaum refers to "shame and its relatives" and suggests that embarrassment is simply "a lighter matter than shame." Crozier settles on "a domain of shame, embarrassment and shyness" as related emotions with differences in intensity (223).

26 Goffman, "Embarrassment and Social Organization," 264.

27 Goffman, "Embarrassment and Social Organization," 264. R. S. Miller also lists stuttering as a symptom of embarrassment ("Is Embarrassment a Blessing or a Curse?," 248), as do other theorists of embarrassment.

28 Goffman, "Embarrassment and Social Organization," 266–67.

29 Johnson, *The Rambler* "No. 159," 198.

30 Westminster Hall was often referred to in theatrical terms. See Jobson, *Cobleriana*, 1:14–15, for a reference to "Westminster-Hall, that learned Theatre of the Law." Recent scholarship on theatricality and law includes Fawcett, "Overexpressive Celebrity." See also Roach, *Cities of the Dead*, 73–118; Rojek, *Celebrity*; and Wanko, *Roles of Authority*.

31 Felman, *Juridical Unconscious*, 162. See Robin Chapman Stacy, who has demonstrated that Irish medieval legal hearings, like theater, "functioned as entertainment in a world attuned to the pleasures of oral performance" (*Dark Speech*, 53). Theatrical courtroom scenes could preserve memory in oral cultures, but the court's power "lay as much in its ability to create and to transform as to record" (Stacy, *Dark Speech*, 2). Ball, "All the Law's a Stage," Hibbitts, "Making Sense of Metaphors," and Peters, "Theatricality," have all contributed to recent developments in understanding the nature of the relationship between law, performance, and theatricality.

32 See Read, *Theatre and Law*, 8–9, 32–33.

33 Venette, *Pleasures of Conjugal-Love Explain'd*, 54.

34 Saunders, *Westminster Hall*, 254–55.

35 Boswell, *Boswell, the English Experiment*, 222.

36 Saunders, *Westminster Hall*, 260.

37 More and Roberts, *Memoirs of the Life*, 1:55.

38 Wright and Smith, *Parliament Past and Present*, 160.

39 See Foote, *Trip to Calais.*

40 [Anon.], *Lindor & Adelaide*, 74–75. For accounts focused on the theatricality of the Hastings trial, see O'Quinn, *Staging Governance*; Marshall, *Impeachment of Warren Hastings*; and Peters, "Theatricality."

41 Sheridan, *General Dictionary*, vol. 1 preface, n.p.

42 Roscoe, *Westminster Hall*, 2:87.

43 Bentham, "Draught of a New Plan," 25.

44 See Peters, "Theatricality." See also Kinservik, *Sex, Scandal, and Celebrity.*

45 Fliegelman, *Declaring Independence*, 90.

46 [Anon.], "Wonderful Exhibition!!!"

47 Fliegelman, *Declaring Independence*, 31.

48 Fliegelman, *Declaring Independence*, 32.

49 Hortensius, *Deinology*, 1.

50 Cannon, *Letters of Junius*, 99, quoted in Prest, *William Blackstone*, 244.

51 Quoted in Fliegelman, *Declaring Independence*, 26.

52 Quoted in Fliegelman, *Declaring Independence*, 30.

53 Fliegelman, *Declaring Independence*, 1–2.

54 See Peters, "Theatricality."

55 Murphy, *Samuel Foote's Taste*, 53–55.

56 Murphy, *Samuel Foote's Taste*, xlix.

57 Murphy, *Samuel Foote's Taste*, 77.

58 Murphy, *Samuel Foote's Taste*, 78.

59 Foote uses this device to great effect in his *Treatise on the Passions*, where he ends a lengthy critique of a number of actors with a stuttering passage meant to exaggerate his sincerity and mock his own authorial labor (41).

60 Alter and Oppenheimer, "Uniting the Tribes of Fluency," 220.

61 Alter and Oppenheimer, "Suppressing Secrecy," 1415.

62 Fliegelman, *Declaring Independence*, 64–65.

63 As with embarrassment, which Greg Morgan, in "Give Me the Consideration of Being the Bondsman," connects to the new credit economy, libel during the eighteenth century became a matter related to credit and to the ability to sustain credibility. See Mitchell, *Making of the Modern Law.*

64 Lee, *Dictionary of National Biography*, 42:220.

65 Kadens, "Justice Blackstone's Common Law Orthodoxy," 1592.

66 Kadens, "Justice Blackstone's Common Law Orthodoxy," 1576.

67 Kadens, "Justice Blackstone's Common Law Orthodoxy," 1597, 1585, 1588.

68 Davis, "John Horne Tooke."

69 Quoted in Davis, "John Horne Tooke."

70 Davis, "John Horne Tooke."

71 Kadens, "Justice Blackstone's Common Law Orthodoxy," 1593.

72 Kadens, "Justice Blackstone's Common Law Orthodoxy," 1580n139.

73 [Gurney], *Trial of Frederick Calvert, Esq.*

74 [Gurney], *Whole Proceedings*; [Gurney], *Genuine Trial.*

75 [Gurney], *Whole Proceedings*, 44.

76 [Gurney], *Whole Proceedings*, 44.

77 [Gurney], *Whole Proceedings*, 6, 22.

78 [Gurney], *Whole Proceedings*, 45.

79 [Gurney], *Whole Proceedings*, 46.

80 [Gurney], *Whole Proceedings*, 44.

81 [Gurney], *Whole Proceedings*, 44–45.

82 [Gurney], *Whole Proceedings*, 45.

83 [Gurney], *Whole Proceedings*, 45.

84 [Gurney], *Whole Proceedings*, 47.

85 [Gurney], *Whole Proceedings*, 47.

86 [Gurney], *Whole Proceedings*, 47.

87 [Gurney], *Whole Proceedings*, 47–48.

88 [Gurney], *Whole Proceedings*, 47.

89 Kadens, "Justice Blackstone's Common Law Orthodoxy," 1605.

90 [Anon.], *Monthly Review*, 42, 409.

91 [Anon.], *Beauties of Biography*, 2:35.

92 Allen, "Theater of the Invisible."

93 See Allen, "Performing Justice."

94 Fawcett, "Overexpressive Celebrity," 952.

95 Roach, *Cities of the Dead*, 6.

96 Roach, *Cities of the Dead*, 79.

97 See Deutsch, *Resemblance and Disgrace*, for a discussion of the relationship between body and text in Pope's career. For the larger context, see McKenzie, *Bibliography*, and especially Finkelstein and McCleery, *Introduction to Book History*, which consolidates forty years of scholarship on the history of the book as a cultural artifact.

98 Johnson, *Dictionary of the English Language.*

99 Milton, "Areopagitica," in *Works of John Milton*, 4:298.

100 Of course, books could prompt other forms of embarrassment, even shame, but those embarrassed moments tend to be located in the imagination rather than in public arenas. Books, unlike oral speech, operate at a remove from the embarrassed body. See Probyn, "Writing Shame."

101 Ricks, *Keats and Embarrassment*, 1.

102 Frye, *Collected Works*, 233.

103 Fliegelman, *Declaring Independence*, 21.

CHAPTER 4. TERROR, TORTURE, AND THE TENDER HEART OF THE LAW

1 Derrida, "Law of Genre," 81.

2 Derrida's take on law and justice has been much discussed. See, for instance, De Ville, "Madness and the Law."

3 See Stern, "Blackstone's Legal Actors," for an interesting and related discussion of the personification of the law in the *Commentaries*.

4 For background on the form, see Terry Castle's essay "The Gothic Novel."

5 See Ahmed, *Cultural Politics of Emotion*, for her discussion of fear and "technologies of governance" (71). The idea that law was founded in violence was a commonplace in eighteenth-century political writing, and is usually attributed to Bodin and Hobbes. See Bourdieu, "Force of Law," and Cover, "Supreme Court, 1982 Term" and "Violence and the Word," for further discussions of this issue. Quema's *Power and Legitimacy* makes the case that law and literature are both instruments of power and violence in that they are "social practices with varying performative effects of symbolic power and authoritative means of legitimizing" (7).

6 Ahmed, *Cultural Politics of Emotion*, 12.

7 Ahmed, *Cultural Politics of Emotion*, 13.

8 For some examples of how various literary critics have treated Blackstone's castle imagery, see Watt, *Contesting the Gothic*; Duggett, *Gothic Romanticism*; Postema, *Bentham*; and Chaplin's *Gothic and the Rule of Law* and "'Written in the Black Letter.'" Schmidgen offers a brilliant discussion of this "darling figure: the Gothic castle" in *Eighteenth-Century Fiction*, 171. See Chiu, "Faulty Towers," for the evolution of the castle metaphor. Prest, in "Blackstone as Architect," connects Blackstone's architectural interests to the *Commentaries*. See also Matthews, "Model of the Old House."

9 Jessie Allen has pointed out that a much more logical position for this metaphor would have been in volume II, chapters 4–5, where Blackstone describes the feudal origins of English inheritable property (personal correspondence [email], June 6, 2016).

10 This idea, of course, is not original with Blackstone. The statement can be interpreted in two ways: naïve readers (this defines many of the readers in Blackstone's intended audience) could be excused if they understand it as awarding ultimate authority to the king. More sophisticated readers might see it as suggesting that the king is not permitted to do wrong. I thank Susan Bandes for offering this interpretation. For an interesting discussion of Blackstone's understanding of royal authority, see Halliday, "Blackstone's King," with Ruth Paley's accompanying commentary, in *Re-Interpreting Blackstone's Commentaries*.

11 Reddy, *Navigation of Feeling*.

12 Punter and Byron, *The Gothic*, 262.

13 Volume 3, where the castle image appears, was first published in 1768; volume 4, the criminal law volume, in 1769.

14 Walpole, *Castle of Otranto*, 23.

15 Miles, *Gothic Writing*, 32. See also Williams, "Monstrous Pleasures." Williams
points out that a French gothic tradition preceded Walpole and an English novel
called *Longsword* had preempted *Castle of Otranto*. Terry Halle, in "French and
German Gothic," and E. J. Cleary, in "Genesis of 'Gothic' Fiction," both in *The
Cambridge Companion to Gothic Fiction*, offer illuminating discussions of the
origins of the literary gothic, arguing that it far preceded the publication date of
the *Commentaries*. A well-known earlier example of the literary gothic that must
have drawn Blackstone's attention is William Collins's 1746 "Ode to Fear," in *The
Works of William Collins*: "Ah Fear! Ah Frantic Fear! / I see, I see Thee near" (27).
See also Punter and Byron, *The Gothic*, xvii.

16 Blackstone, "Lawyer's Farewell," 228.

17 Blackstone, "Lawyer's Farewell," 230.

18 Blackstone, "Lawyer's Farewell," 231.

19 Blackstone, "Lawyer's Farewell," 232.

20 See Sedgwick, *Coherence of Gothic Conventions*, especially 9–10.

21 Botting, *Gothic*, 3.

22 Blackstone's letter is quoted in Prest, *William Blackstone*, 66–67.

23 See Miles, *Gothic Writing*, for the proposition that gothic fiction involves the dis-
ciplining of youthful desire (27) and is "predicated on the discipline of the young"
(38).

24 William Meredith quoted in Lieberman, *Province of Legislation Determined*, 35–
36.

25 Gibbon, "Remarks," 5:545.

26 Quoted in Lemmings, *Professors of the Law*, 139.

27 Wollstonecraft, *Rights of Men*, 42. Wollstonecraft is quoted in Townshend, "Improvement and Repair," 727.

28 Miles, *Gothic Writing*, 42–43.

29 Bentham, *Fragment on Government*, 410.

30 Townshend, "Improvement and Repair," 725.

31 See Townshend, "Improvement and Repair," for a full discussion.

32 See Prest, "Blackstone as Architect."

33 Carter, *Builder's Magazine*, 100; Gomme, *Sacred and Medieval Architecture*, 9.

34 See Volkan, *Blind Trust*, for a discussion of this concept in the context of group
psychology.

35 Volkan, *Blind Trust*, 37, 12.

36 Walpole, *Castle of Otranto*, 23.

37 Walpole, *Castle of Otranto*, 25.

38 Walpole, *Castle of Otranto*, 5. See Wall, *Prose of Things*, 114–22, for a sensitive
reading of the "things" like the helmet and sword as humorous and ironically
presented in *Castle of Otranto*. Whether they were perceived as humorous or
terrifying might have been dependent on the sophistication of the reader; in
"Disoriented," Peter Otto points out that Walpole's "impossible objects that appear

at those limits where everyday procedures for organizing time and space . . . begin to break down" became a common trope in the gothic (694).

39 Walpole, *Castle of Otranto*, 11–12.

40 Walpole, *Castle of Otranto*, 11.

41 Not much is known about exactly what Blackstone read. However, I thank Wilfrid Prest for sharing his copy of *Bibliotheca Blackstoneiana, A Catalogue of a Library of 4,500 Volumes* with me. This volume gives us some insight to Blackstone's holdings as it catalogues books collected by Blackstone and his son, sold by auction in 1845. It lists "Walpole's Castle of Otranto" along with the "Vicar of Wakefield" and "Rasselas," all published in the 1750s and 1760s and sold as miscellaneous volumes in Lot 73 (7).

42 See Lake, "Bloody Records," for a discussion of the ongoing debate about Walpole's historical methods and their seriousness. Given my concerns with the overlap of the literary gothic and the "real" in the last section of this chapter, it is interesting to note that Walpole relied on at least some verifiable historical details in writing the novel.

43 Prest, *William Blackstone*, 165–67. See also Chaplin, "Spectres of Law," 178, for this information about Walpole.

44 For Blackstone's position on capital punishment for minor crimes, see Lemmings, "Editor's Introduction to Book I." The literature on crime and punishment during this period is extensive. See, for example, Linebaugh, *London Hanged*; McLynn, *Crime and Punishment*; Sharpe, *Judicial Punishment in England*; Gladfelder, *Eighteenth-Century England*; King and Ward, "Rethinking the Bloody Code."

45 Foucault, of course, argues convincingly that this new leniency is simply another attempt at control: "Beneath the humanization of the penalties, what one finds are all those rules that authorize, or rather demand, 'leniency', as a calculated economy of the power to punish" (*Discipline and Punish*, 101).

46 See Massumi, "Future Birth of the Affective Fact": "The mass affective production of felt threat-potential engulfs the (f)actuality of the comparatively small number of incidents where danger materialized. They blend together in a shared atmosphere of fear" (61).

47 Tiffany, *Infidel Poetics*, 15.

48 Arraignment has been so naturalized in criminal procedure as to seldom be the subject of analysis. It is a procedure meant to ensure the proper identity of the defendant as the person accused of a crime, to inform the court and the defendant of the charges against him, and in its later use to inform the defendant of his rights. But it also establishes jurisdiction in that it establishes the rights of the court to adjudicate the defendant's case. As J. H. Baker points out in *An Introduction to English Legal History* (3rd ed.), the defendant who refused to plead was labelled "one who refuses the common law" (580). In *The History of English Law*, Frederick Pollack and F. W. Maitland place a high value on jurisdiction as "one of the main ties which keeps society together." Chillingly, they trace jurisdictional

issues to those of slavery: speaking of the medieval period, they note that "if we examine the rights of the lord over his villain we find it difficult to decide where ownership leaves off and where jurisdiction begins" (527). There is evidence that eighteenth-century defendants saw arraignment as a moment when jurisdiction could be challenged because they believed themselves to be in the wrong court. See McKenzie, "'This Death,'" for the case of David Pearce and William Stoaks, 1673, who believed they should not be tried at the Old Bailey for robberies they had committed in Rutlandshire. To extrapolate from Daniel Matthews's comment that "the law speaks only to itself," arraignment recruits the legal subject into the common law and thus allows that speaking-to-itself to occur. See Matthews, "From Jurisdiction to Juriswriting." I view jurisdiction here as Matthews does, "broadly, as a set of practices and techniques that give voice to legal authority" (3) and, I might add, deny a voice to those who oppose it.

49 In "'This Death,'" McKenzie documents a few cases where prisoners pretended to be unable to speak. The history of the practice includes references to prisoners with hearing and speech defects who were treated as if they are "'obstinately' or naturally mute" (285).

50 One might wonder if the phrase was a common one in eighteenth-century England, so common that it needed no explanation. But a thorough ECCO search of English fiction and nonfiction prose, as well as poetry, reveals only a few mentions before the publication of the *Commentaries*.

51 Theobald Mathew points out that as early as Edward III's reign, Law French had been rejected in favor of "the English Tongue" (although Coke was known for preferring French, as he felt that ignorant people reading their own laws in English might misinterpret them). It had lingered on despite various anti-French movements, until the early 1730s when it was banned by statute. See Mathew, "Law French," 360–62. Thus, Blackstone usually translates Law French when he uses it; the *Commentaries* is so full of examples of his etymological explications that I will not list all of them here. See *Commentaries* I:129, "An infant *in ventre sa mere*, or in the mother's womb," for a typical example. I am indebted to my research assistant, Rachel Morota, for cataloguing Blackstone's numerous uses of Law French with their accompanying translations. The "Gothic black letter" that so terrorized law students was a typeface that began to go out of style in the seventeenth century.

52 Walpole, *Castle of Otranto, A Story*, unpaginated.

53 Ironically, critics of *peine forte et dure* tended to see England as no better than Europe. See Kames, *Sketches of the History of Man*, vol. III, 261, for the negative comparison of England to Holland. He argues that *peine forte et dure* "is no less absurd" than Holland's practices of torture.

54 Punter, *Gothic Pathologies*, 9.

55 Whether *peine forte et dure* constituted torture turns on one's definition of torture. Although I greatly respect his work, John Langbein's evaluation of *peine forte et dure* in *Torture and the Law of Proof* as "best regarded as a special kind of guilty

plea. The defendant underwent a different mode of capital punishment in order to save his estate" (76) seems almost as ludicrous as the US courts' redefinition of water boarding as "enhanced interrogation." For a study of the history of torture in English common law, see Friedman, "Torture and the Common Law." Particularly of interest is a 1684 case Friedman discusses in which the victim was removed from England to Scotland ("extraordinary rendition") to skirt England's anti-torture stance (193–94). For a general discussion of the history of European torture, see Peters, *Torture*. For the history of English torture through the Stuarts, see Heath, *Torture and English Law*. J. Jeremy Wisnewski, in *Understanding Torture*, argues that considering types of torture is more productive than developing one generalizable definition. His typography includes "judicial/evidential," "punitive," "interrogational," and, important to our discussion, "dehumanizing." Wisnewski points out that the purpose of dehumanizing torture is to attack the prisoner's identity (351). Equally important for our discussion is "terroristic/deterrent" torture: "torture which aims to deter future incidents of certain sorts" (6). In email correspondence (February 21, 2016) with the author, Wisnewski distinguished "institutional" torture from "judicial" torture, and "interrogational" torture from torture motivated by terrorism or sadism. In his 1927 essay "Torture under English Law," Ernest G. Black clearly construes *peine forte et dure* as torture. Lastly, Lynn Hunt, in *Inventing Human Rights*, makes little effort to distinguish judicial torture from practices like *peine forte et dure*, extreme punishments, and other forms of brutality that typified every European legal system in the eighteenth century.

56 Punter, *Gothic Pathologies*, 121. Blackstone's winding narrative replicates the gothic tendency to imply mysterious horrors while delaying explicit details. This tendency is what eighteenth-century literary critic Anna Laetitia Aikin (later Barbauld) points to as providing the perverse "pleasure" of the gothic. Although such pleasures (and by extension, the sadistic pleasures of observing another's pain) are beyond the scope of this chapter, Aikin does note that the more a frightening scene adheres to the real, the less pleasure we take in it. Scenes of horror accompanied by occult, fantastic occurrences, such as those in *Castle of Otranto* are more productive of pleasure than realistic scenes. See Aikin (Barbauld), "On the Pleasures Derived."

57 McKenzie writes that *peine forte et dure* ended in 1772 when the courts began to interpret the refusal to plead as "equivalent to a guilty verdict," and was formally abolished by act of Parliament in 1827. "'This Death,'" 282.

58 Baker, *Introduction to English Legal History*, 580.

59 Baker, *Introduction to English Legal History*, 580.

60 See Sedgwick, *Coherence of Gothic Conventions*, for the gothic convention of "unintelligible writings" (9).

61 Paulson, *Representations of Revolution*, 534.

62 McKenzie, "'This Death.'"

63 This description is quoted in McKenzie, "'This Death,'" 288.

64 McKenzie, "'This Death,'" 288.

65 See [Anon.], *Anecdotes*, 173–77; [Anon.], *Lives of the Most Remarkable Criminals*, 106; Jackson, *New and Complete Newgate Calendar*, 1:271; and Montagu, *Old Bailey Chronicle*, vol. 1.

66 See Punter, *Gothic Pathologies*, for the pleasure we take in the resistant body, the "monster" who thwarts the law and thus suggests its dismantling (45).

67 [Anon.], *Lives of the Most Remarkable Criminals*, 103.

68 [Anon.], *Lives of the Most Remarkable Criminals*, 105.

69 [Anon.], *Lives of the Most Remarkable Criminals*, 106.

70 [Anon.], *Lives of the Most Remarkable Criminals*, 107.

71 [Anon.], *Lives of the Most Remarkable Criminals*, 105.

72 [Anon.], *Anecdotes*, 175.

73 Jackson, *New and Complete Newgate Calendar*, 271.

74 [Anon.], *Lives of the Most Remarkable Criminals*, 109.

75 [Anon.], *Lives of the Most Remarkable Criminals*, 110.

76 [Anon.], *Anecdotes*, 176.

77 [Anon.], *Lives of the Most Remarkable Criminals*, 111.

78 [Anon.], *Anecdotes*, 176.

79 Wisnewski, *Understanding Torture*, 56.

80 See Scarry, *Body in Pain*, who notes how this concept plays out in the metaphoric language of the "knifelike pain" (even when there is no knife, but only internal pain) as well as in the confession (when the victim is blamed for his own pain as he has not confessed), or in forced exercise or postures (where the victim's actions create his pain) (53). Similarly, the use of loud music as torture is thought to be effective because the victim cannot help but internalize the unwanted stimulation.

81 Foucault, *Discipline and Punish*, 54–55.

82 Bourke, in *The Story of Pain*, discusses how pain itself (even outside of torture) estranges victims from their communities because of its impact on our ability to communicate. In cases of torture, the deliberate infliction of pain through torture changes the victim's psyche so that "the sufferer's body comes to occupy the whole world" (30). On the other hand, pain can also create communities, as we see when pain creates bonds between victim and sympathetic observers.

83 Sedgwick, *Coherence of Gothic Conventions*, 7.

84 Ahmed, *Cultural Politics of Emotion*, 70.

85 Sussman, "What's Wrong with Torture?," 7. Philosophical debates regarding the symbolic significance of punishment would position my argument here as an expressionist one. Blackstone's treatment of *peine forte et dure* goes beyond the usual communication of what Igor Primoratz refers to as "resentment and indignation" to deliver a much more complex message related to the civilizing and harmonizing intents of the English legal system. See Primoratz, "Punishment as Language," and Skillen, "How to Say Things with Walls," among others who have discussed these issues.

86 Ahmed, *Cultural Politics of Emotion*, 6.

87 Blackstone, "Lawyer's Farewel," 243.

88 Marshall, *Transatlantic Gothic Novel*.

89 Marshall, *Transatlantic Gothic Novel*, 459.

90 See Bourke's *Story of Pain* for a historicized introduction to pain and a discussion of Scarry's *Body in Pain*.

91 Sedgwick, *Coherence of Gothic Conventions*, 14.

92 Scarry, *Body in Pain*, 14.

93 Scarry, *Body in Pain*, 3.

94 Phillips, *Terrors and Experts*, 56.

95 Phillips, *Terrors and Experts*, 57.

96 Phillips, *Terrors and Experts*, 53.

97 Miles, *Gothic Writing*, 2nd ed., 3.

98 Scarry, *Body in Pain*, 6.

99 Bourke, *Story of Pain*, 6–7.

100 Bourke, *Story of Pain*, 30.

101 This "tenderness" is obviously related to sympathy, empathy, and compassion and to the moral emotions, all of which have been the subject of much study. Works that have been particularly helpful to this project include Berlant, *Compassion*; Schliesser, *Sympathy*; and Frazer, *Enlightenment of Sympathy*. There is a long line of legal scholarship on compassion and empathy much indebted to Martha Minow. See, for instance, Minow, "Forgiveness, Law, and Justice."

102 Ahmed, *Cultural Politics of Emotion*, 14.

103 See Ahmed, where she argues that to articulate a feeling makes the feeling capable of shaping action. The example she offers involves the nation: "To say 'the nation mourns' is to generate the nation, *as if it were a mourning subject*. The 'nation' becomes a shared 'object of feeling' through the orientation that is taken towards it" (*Cultural Politics of Emotion*, 13).

104 See Blackstone, *Commentaries*, III:15, 16, 101, 151, 213, for examples.

105 This, of course, has come down to us as the "tender years" doctrine, as what Martha E. Ertman, in "Legal Tenderness," describes as a legal "solicitude towards a particularly vulnerable person, such as a child" (551). The gendered implications of tenderness are beyond the scope of this chapter, but see Cope, "Evelina's Peculiar Circumstances," for a discussion of the way feminine tenderness performs as a sort of legal tender.

106 Johnson, *Dictionary of the English Language*, "Tenderness."

107 Smith, "Of the Amiable and Respectable Virtues," in *Theory of Moral Sentiments*, 45. Smith framed these comments with what Laura J. Rosenthal astutely recognizes as "a dramatic public scene," one of torture, in which the anonymous "we" views someone being tortured on the rack. Rosenthal, "Adam Smith and the Theatre," 123.

108 Fielding, *Enquiry*, 106. When warning "prosecutors," Fielding is actually warning victims who were responsible for prosecuting crimes in eighteenth-century Eng-

land. Other emotional traits that might lead victims not to prosecute include fear, delicacy (too "delicate" to appear in court), indolence, and avarice (an unwillingness to expend funds to prosecute).

109 Johnson, "Tender," in *A Dictionary of the English Language*, facsimile of the 1755 ed., n.p.

110 Rayner, *Digest of the Law*, 16, emphasis added.

111 [Anon.], *Tryals*, 5, emphasis added. See also Howell, *Complete Collection of State Trials*.

112 Paley, *Works of William Paley*, 3:303.

113 See chapter 2, "Bone of Their Bone: Abolishing Torture," of Lynn Hunt's *Inventing Human Rights* for a discussion of Voltaire's and Beccaria's responses to legalized brutality and for the argument in favor of a new focus on individuality and the "advent of the self-enclosed individual" (83).

114 Punter and Byron, *The Gothic*, 310.

115 Sedgwick, *Coherence of Gothic Conventions*, 13. That the boundaries between gothic fiction and the "real" were porous can be demonstrated variously, but see in particular *Llewellin: A Tale* (London, 1798–99), in which the hero refuses the jurisdiction of a villainous court and dies during *peine forte et dure*. Otto, in "Disoriented," fruitfully suggests the connections between Walpole's gothic and the "early twenty-first" century when "real-unrealities, or, as they are more commonly called, virtual realities, have become a part of everyday experience" (706). See Baldick and Mighall, "Gothic Criticism," for this argument: "Misconceiving Gothic fictions as examples of anti-realist 'fantasy' or dream-writing . . . has repeatedly overlooked their manifest temporal, geographical and ideological referents while constructing increasingly implausible models of their supposed latent fears, desires and revolutionary impulses" (209–10). Punter and Byron, *The Gothic*, also note that actual eighteenth-century conditions, such as in prisons, resembled those in gothic fiction (29). See Belsey's *Culture and the Real* for a discussion of the real as "not reality, which is what we do know, the world picture that culture represents to us. . . . The real, as culture's defining difference, does not form part of our culturally acquired knowledge, but exercises its own, independent determinations even so" (xii). In a post-fact world, the fictional, the real, and the "true" are so relativized as to be indistinguishable at times, but we still have to try.

116 Foucault, "Eye of Power." Foucault, of course, made the connection between fiction and the real explicit in "The Eye of Power," but he presented these cultural twins in opposition to each other, at least in this interview, arguing that to the extent that the Enlightenment "sought to break up the patches of darkness that blocked the light," gothic novels offered "imaginary spaces . . . like the negative of the transparency and visibility which it aimed to establish" (12–13). There is some evidence that even *Castle of Otranto* was based in real events.

117 Emerson, "Did Blackstone Get the Gallic Shrug?," 188.

118 Emerson, "Did Blackstone Get the Gallic Shrug?," 188.

119 Sedgwick, *Coherence of Gothic Conventions*, 153.

120 Sedgwick, *Coherence of Gothic Conventions*, 153.

121 Ahmed, *Cultural Politics of Emotion*, 191.

122 See Kahn, *Sacred Violence*, for useful background on torture and sovereignty; see Butler, *Guantanamo Bay*, for thoughtful approaches to the moral and judicial issues raised by US practices related to Guantanamo Bay.

123 See Leung, "Torture, Cover-Up at Gitmo?"

124 Foster, "CIA 'Tortured Al-Qaeda Suspects.'" A 2009 headline in the UK's *Independent* referred to the torture of Binyam Mohamed as "medieval"; see Verkaik, "'I Was a Victim of Medieval Torture.'"

125 See Nieminen, "Forever Again." The essay offers an illuminating discursive analysis of governmental discussions of torture.

126 Van Natta, Bonner, and Waldman, "Threats and Responses"; Ghoshray, "On the Judicial Treatment of Guantanamo Detainees," 81.

127 As I write, President Trump has announced his belief that "torture works," and a draft of an executive order reopening black sites has been leaked to the press. See Mazzetti and Savage, "Leaked Draft of Executive Order." Secret documents, tyrants, and remote, mysterious locations are all operative in this latest effort to resume US-sponsored brutality.

128 Wisnewski, *Understanding Torture*, 66.

129 There are references to a "special tenderness doctrine" in contemporary Anglo-American law. See Ertman, "Legal Tenderness"; *Royal Bank of Scotland v. Etridge* (no. 2) UKHL 44 (2001); MacKinnon, "Law and Tenderness." In the law of equity, tenderness is often mentioned.

130 Miller, "Wall of Ideas." Miller argues that the late eighteenth century was "the crucial era of attack on the sentimental" where "the baby of tenderness tended to be thrown out with the bathwater of fashionable sentimentality" (674).

131 See Fineman, "Vulnerable Subject"; Sen, *Commodities and Capabilities*; and Nussbaum, *Creating Capabilities*. See also Ertman, who in her review of Mulcahey and Wheeler's *Feminist Perspectives on Contract Law* focuses on the "three senses of tender" (money, solicitude, independence) to make a case for a renewed focus on tenderness in cases of special vulnerability, while also issuing a warning as to the possible misuses of such an approach ("Legal Tenderness," 554). Ertman notes that "tenderness for systemically vulnerable parties . . . is an integral part of contract doctrine" (561).

132 See Cock, "'Off Dropped the Sympathetic Snout,'" for a discussion of "medical sympathy" or the idea that one could "feel" another's pain without being similarly afflicted. Cock documents more bizarre beliefs, such as that a physician could cure a patient from a distance, or that "a corpse would bleed in the presence of his or her murderer" (150–51).

133 Scarry, *Body in Pain*, 57–58. This sensitivity to the pain of others is discussed frequently in the literature on sympathy and empathy, and in twenty-first-century

neuroscience is explained in terms of "mirror neurons," a much-debated concept, as Bourke points out (*Story of Pain*). See also Preston and de Waal, "Empathy."

134 McKenzie, "'This Death,'" 286.

135 Bourke, *Story of Pain*, 34–39.

136 See Ahmed, among others, for the notion of "affective economies" and the argument that feelings "are produced as effects of circulation" (*Cultural Politics of Emotion*, 8).

137 Swanson, "'Tender Instinct,'" 81.

138 Kalawski, "Is Tenderness a Basic Emotion?," 158.

139 Langdon and Mackenzie, *Emotions, Imagination, and Moral Reasoning*, 6.

140 Fineman, "Vulnerable Subject," 8. Emphasis added.

CHAPTER 5. BLACKSTONE'S LONG TAIL

1 Helms, Vishmidt, and Berlant, "Affect and the Politics of Austerity."

2 See Davies, *Happiness Industry*. Darrin McMahon offers an authoritative overview of the history of happiness in *Happiness: A History*. For histories of happiness that focus on eighteenth-century Britain, see Potkay, *Passion for Happiness*; Norton, *Fiction and the Philosophy of Happiness*; and "Happiness (and Unhappiness) in Eighteenth-Century English Literature," special issue, *English Literature* 2, no. 1 (2015), especially Gregori's introduction.

3 See Bronsteen, Buccafusco, and Masur, *Happiness and the Law*, for a helpful review of research into both public and private happiness and their relationship(s) to law. Definitions of happiness in the legal arena tend to merge the hedonic and the "flourishing" or "well-being" definitions of happiness. For instance, in this excellent study of recent social science research and its influence on the American legal system, the authors explain that "happiness means feeling good on a moment-by-moment basis, and it is such good feeling that constitutes the quality of life" (6). Eric Posner and Cass R. Sunstein's 2010 collection *Law and Happiness* offers a mix of essays, some more philosophical, others more focused on public policy.

4 Bronsteen, Buccafusco, and Masur, *Happiness and the Law*, 3.

5 McMahon, *Happiness: A History*, 212.

6 McKendrick, Brewer, and Plumb, *Birth of a Consumer Society*.

7 *Black's Law Dictionary*, 9th ed., s.v. "happiness," ed. Bryan A. Garner (Eagan, MI: West Group, 2009), 717. See also, *The Law Dictionary, Featuring Black's Law Dictionary*, "What Is Happiness?," accessed March 5, 2018, https://thelawdictionary.org.

8 For the classic account of how this relationship between happiness and liberty evolved, see Jones, *Pursuit of Happiness*. This property-oriented understanding of liberty is somewhat inconsistent with the Founders' views. James Madison, among others, included in the concept of "property" a wide range of non-material, non-commercial intangibles, including "life, freedom, one's stake in society," and other conceptions that relate to our concepts of self. See Cahn, "Madison and the Pursuit of Happiness."

9 McMahon, *Happiness: A History*, 206. McMahon's chapter 4 is devoted to demonstrating a shift from the belief that happiness could only be attained in the hereafter to the idea that we could be happy here on earth.

10 In the eighth edition, Blackstone changed "his own happiness" to "his own true and substantial happiness," suggesting an effort to distinguish between the sort of happiness achieved as the result of immediate pleasure and a more meaningful, authentic happiness. See *Commentaries*, Oxford edition (2016), vol. I, 318.

11 See also II:8 where Blackstone notes how "graciously has providence woven our duty and our happiness together." This idea is generally related to but not exactly the same as views expressed in Locke's and Hutcheson's works. Locke believed that happiness was part of a divine order in which we were led by our pleasurable feelings to do the right thing; Hutcheson, that we had an additional sense, a "moral sense akin to touch, taste, sight, sound, a capacity to respond pleasurably to goodness in others and in ourselves" (McMahon, *Happiness: A History*, 326).

12 McMahon, *Happiness: A History*, 317.

13 Angner, "Natural Law," 2.

14 In associating harmony with natural law and with human reason, Blackstone followed Grotius and Pufendorf. See Angner, "Natural Law," 3.

15 On the point that by using the phrase "real happiness," Blackstone indicated that he means more than simply happiness as feeling good while acknowledging that those good feelings help motivate us to uphold virtue and justice, see Conklin, "Origins of the Pursuit of Happiness," 253.

16 Conklin, "Origins of the Pursuit of Happiness," 200.

17 Soni, *Mourning Happiness*. Soni focuses on a very particular understanding of Eudaimonia associated with the "poet, lawgiver, and sage" Solon, who helped found the Athenian understanding of law (34). Soni highlights the issues involved in trying to equate happiness with Eudaimonia in that "there is a gap in our language obscured by the fact that 'happiness' masquerades as a translation of *Eudaimonia*. The problem, then, is not that we have gained a new concept we dislike, it is rather that we have lost one without realizing it and do not even have the language to describe what is missing" (256).

18 Soni, *Mourning Happiness*, 177.

19 Soni struggles with the issue of whether sympathy (in Adam Smith's sense) for another's happiness is simply a response to particular narratives or "the experience of an affect" (*Mourning Happiness*, 302).

20 A full exposition of Soni's complex argument is beyond the scope of this chapter. For two stimulating reviews of Soni's *Mourning Happiness*, see Thorne, "Time without Happiness," and Saccamano, review of *Mourning Happiness*.

21 Ahmed, *Promise of Happiness*, 5.

22 Ahmed, *Promise of Happiness*, 7.

23 McMahon, *Happiness: A History*, 11.

24 In the *Dictionary of the English Language*, Johnson illustrates this definition of happiness by quoting Pope's *Essay on Criticism*: "Some beauties yet no precepts can declare; For there's a *happiness* as well as care."

25 Johnson, *Dictionary of the English Language*.

26 Ahmed, *Promise of Happiness*, 199.

27 Soni, *Mourning Happiness*, 260.

28 Soni, *Mourning Happiness*, 280.

29 Soni, *Mourning Happiness*, 254.

30 Potkay, "Narrative Possibilities of Happiness," 524.

31 Soni, *Mourning Happiness*, 59.

32 Rawls, *Theory of Justice*, 409.

33 Rawls, *Theory of Justice*, 550.

34 Canuel, *Justice, Dissent and the Sublime*, 19.

35 Johnson, "Happiness," in *A Dictionary of the English Language*, facsimile of the 1755 ed., n.p.

36 See Boorstin, *Mysterious Science of Law*, for an analysis of Blackstone's focus on harmony on the macro level. He comments at length throughout his study on Blackstone's determined effort to present English law as a system in equilibrium, balanced and proportional.

37 For only one of many examples, see volume III, where Blackstone shifts back and forth from various types of offenses against property to the processes whereby such offenses could be remedied.

38 Palladian style derived from Andrea Palladio's sixteenth-century architectural theory, heavily reliant on harmonic ratios. For discussions of the Palladian style in eighteenth-century literature, see Battestin, *Providence of Wit*; Van Ghent, *English Novel*; Hilles, "Art and Artifice"; and Varey, *Space*. In his 2008 biography of Blackstone, Prest reprints Blackstone's syllabus for his law lectures; when turned on its side, it resembles a Palladian building. See *William Blackstone*, Illustration 15, "Printed Syllabus of Blackstone's first law lectures," following 174.

39 W. S. Holdsworth recognized this in his 1932 article, "Some Aspects of Blackstone and His *Commentaries*," noting that "all Blackstone's literary works show the capacity for reducing to order and system even the most intractable material" (266).

40 Boorstin provides numerous examples of Blackstone's faith in "the beauty of a pattern of numbers" (*Mysterious Science of the Law*, 93, 213).

41 For an analysis of Aristotle's justice formulas, see Dimock, *Residues of Justice*, 2–4.

42 Meehan, "Authorship and Imagination," 118.

43 For a helpful discussion of the uses of mixture in eighteenth-century thought, see Schmidgen, *Exquisite Mixture*.

44 See Kennedy, one of Blackstone's most astute modern critics, "Structure of Blackstone's *Commentaries*," for the argument that any effort to analyze law is "an effort to discover the conditions of social justice." But it is also "an attempt to deny the truth of our painfully contradictory feelings about the actual state of relations between persons in our social world" (210–12).

45 Soni, *Mourning Happiness*, 235.

46 Rawls, *Theory of Justice*, 550.

47 Kent, *Commentaries on American Law*, 512.

48 See Jessie Allen's blog *Blackstone Weekly* for an example of the pleasures that may be found in Blackstone: https://blackstoneweekly.wordpress.com.

49 Ahmed, *Promise of Happiness*, 6.

50 See Abel, "Political Ethics of Paul Ricoeur."

51 Johnson, "Machine," in *A Dictionary of the English Language*, facsimile of the 1755 ed., n.p.

52 See Davis, *Problem of Slavery*.

53 Gikandi, *Slavery and the Culture of Taste*, 93.

54 McMahon, *Happiness: A History*, 215.

55 For the distinction between abolitionists who took a gradualist approach to ending slavery and emancipationists who advocated for an immediate end to the institution, see Gigantino, *Ragged Road to Abolition*, 5. After 1830, a group of emancipationists "appropriated the term 'abolitionist' . . . and claimed that the gradualists were actually not abolitionists" (5), so the two terms have developed some confusing overlaps.

56 See Oldham, *English Common Law*, 318.

57 Van Cleve, "Somerset's Case."

58 Paley, "Imperial Politics and English Law," 661.

59 Mansfield quoted in Michals, "'That Sole and Despotic Dominion,'" 205.

60 Michals, "'That Sole and Despotic Dominion,'" 209.

61 Abel, "Political Ethics of Paul Ricoeur."

62 Ahmed, *Promise of Happiness*, 68–69.

63 Ferguson, *Law and Letters*, 11.

64 Blackstone's influence on US black letter law can and has been debated at length. For a study of Blackstone's impact on the United States, see Hoeflich, "American Blackstones." See also Nolan, "Sir William Blackstone"; Alschuler, "Rediscovering Blackstone"; and Allen, "Reading Blackstone."

65 See Allen, "Reading Blackstone," 218–19.

66 Nolan notes that the first professor of law at Columbia College (1793–98), later a judge of the New York Supreme Court, credited Blackstone for inspiring him to study law. In another anecdote, we learn that William Wirt of Culpeper, VA, the United States Attorney General from 1817 to 1829, opened his practice with only "a rapid and indistinct enunciation, a considerable degree of shyness, a copy of Blackstone, two volumes of don Quixote, and a copy of *Tristram Shandy*." Nolan, "Sir William Blackstone," citing Howell Heaney, "Advice to a Law Student: A Letter of William Wirt in the Free Library of Philadelphia," *American Journal of Legal History* 2, no. 3 (1958): 319–20. Nolan chronicles the spread of Blackstone from the East Coast westward.

67 Gilmore, *Ages of American Law*, 5.

68 Adams, "Thoughts on Government," 4.

69 See Cahn, "Madison and the Pursuit of Happiness."

70 Johnson, *Understanding* To Kill a Mockingbird, xi.

71 Pauli, "Harper Lee Tops Librarians' Must-Read List."

72 Description of *To Kill a Mockingbird*, Amazon.com, accessed March 6, 2018.

73 See Gibbons, To Kill a Mockingbird *in the Classroom*, 13. For treatments of the novel, see Johnson, To Kill a Mockingbird: *Threatening Boundaries* and *Understanding* To Kill a Mockingbird; Petry, *On Harper Lee*. For Lee's biography, see Shields, *Mockingbird*. For a more recent and more nuanced reading of *To Kill a Mockingbird*, see Jay, "Queer Children and Representative Men."

74 Jay explains that this popularity is due to the novel's "well-crafted use of a pedagogical narrative that positions the reader as the addressee of moral lessons, lifting the confrontation with racism out of a historical and political context and placing it within a more consoling story" (490). In other words, critics have signed onto the ideological work of the novel.

75 See Papantonio, *In Search of Atticus Finch*, which encourages attorneys to model themselves after the novel's hero.

76 See Petry's introduction in *On Harper Lee* for a review of the criticism. See also Jay, who asks us to "imagine the effect in the conversation . . . if asked to discuss *Mockingbird* as an analysis of white supremacy or white privilege, much less as an exploration of queer desire, rather than a novel of empathy, moral courage, bigotry, or intolerance" (498). See also Menarndt, "Forget Atticus," and Ako-Adjei, "Why It's Time."

77 Lee, *To Kill a Mockingbird*, 142.

78 Berlant, *Cruel Optimism*.

79 Lee, *To Kill a Mockingbird*, 1.

80 Lee, *To Kill a Mockingbird*, 152.

81 Lee, *To Kill a Mockingbird*, 289.

82 Allen, "Reading Blackstone," 233.

83 Lee, *To Kill a Mockingbird*, 5.

84 Lee, *To Kill a Mockingbird*, 63.

85 Jay, "Queer Children and Representative Men," 499.

86 Berlant, *Cruel Optimism*, 101.

87 Lee, *To Kill a Mockingbird*, 112–17.

88 Jones, *Pursuit of Happiness*, 75.

89 Jones, *Pursuit of Happiness*, 73.

90 Lee, *To Kill a Mockingbird*, 280.

91 Berlant, *Cruel Optimism*, n.p.

92 Jay, "Queer Children and Representative Men," 509.

93 Lee, *To Kill a Mockingbird*, 1.

94 Faflek, "Persuasion of Happiness," 15.

CODA

1 Flynn, "'Barbarism.'"
2 Flynn, "'Barbarism.'"
3 *Morris v. State of Texas.*
4 *Morris v. State of Texas*, 1.
5 Wollstonecraft, *Rights of Men*, 42.
6 Temple, "Heart of Agitation."
7 Boyle, "Is Subjectivity Possible?," 511.
8 Boyle, "Is Subjectivity Possible?," 514.
9 See Fineman, *Vulnerability.*
10 See Finkelde, *Excessive Subjectivity*, 206.
11 Finkelde, *Excessive Subjectivity*, 206.
12 See Hume, *Treatise of Human Nature*, 3.3.1.7. See also Pitson's discussion in *Hume's Philosophy of the Self*, 152–53. Schliesser's collection of essays *Sympathy: A History* offers an excellent overview of various approaches to sympathy. Sympathy and its related emotions, compassion and empathy, have been much discussed in law and emotion circles. See Zipursky, "*Deshaney* and the Jurisprudence of Dispassion"; Bandes and Blumenthal, "Emotion and the Law," 170; and Maroney, "Persistent Cultural Script" for representative examples.
13 See Smith, *Theory of Moral Sentiments*, 331.
14 Smith, *Theory of Moral Sentiments*, 405.
15 Bandes and Blumenthal, "Emotion and the Law," 170.
16 Levine, *Forms*, 6.
17 Ahmed, *Cultural Politics of Emotion*, 12.
18 Ahmed, *Cultural Politics of Emotion*, 10.

BIBLIOGRAPHY

Abel, Olivier. "The Political Ethics of Paul Ricoeur: Happiness and Justice." Paper presented at Conference of the Union Theological Seminary, New York, October 30, 1992. Accessed March 6, 2018. http://olivierabel.fr.

Abraham, Nicolas, and Maria Torok. *The Shell and the Kernel*. Trans. Nicholas T. Rand. Chicago: University of Chicago Press, 1994.

Abrams, Kathryn, and Hila Keren. "Who's Afraid of the Law and the Emotions." *Minnesota Law Review* 94 (2010): 1997–2074.

Adair, James Makittrick. *Essays on Fashionable Diseases*. London: NP, 1790.

Adams, John. "Thoughts on Government." Philadelphia: Printed by John Dunlap, 1776.

Ahmed, Sara. *The Cultural Politics of Emotion*. New York: Routledge, 2004.

———. *The Promise of Happiness*. Durham, NC: Duke University Press, 2010.

Aikin (Barbauld), Anna Laetitia. "On the Pleasures Derived from Objects of Terror." 1773. Accessed January 17, 2017. www.english.upenn.edu.

Aikin, John. *General Biography, or Lives, Critical and Historical, of the Most Eminent Persons of All Ages, Countries, Conditions, and Professions, Arranged According to Alphabetical Order*. 10 vols. London: Printed for G. G. and J. Robinson; G. Kearsley; R. H. Evans [successor to Mr. Edwards]; and J. Wright, 1802. Eighteenth Century Collections Online (Range 913).

Ako-Adjei, Naa Baako. "Why It's Time Schools Stopped Teaching *To Kill a Mockingbird*." *Transition* 122 (2017): 182–200.

Allen, Jessie. "Actions Speak Louder." *Blackstone Weekly* (blog). June 10, 2016. https://blackstoneweekly.wordpress.com.

———. *Blackstone Weekly* (blog). https://blackstoneweekly.wordpress.com.

———. "Nothing Certain." *Blackstone Weekly* (blog). September 28, 2015. https://blackstoneweekly.wordpress.com.

———. "Performing Justice." Paper presented at Association for the Study of Law, Culture and the Humanities conference, Stanford University, March 2017.

———. Personal correspondence (email). June 9, 2016.

———. "Reading Blackstone in the Twenty-First Century and the Twenty-First Century through Blackstone." In *Re-Interpreting Blackstone's* Commentaries: *A Seminal Text in National and International Contexts*, edited by Wilfrid Prest, 215–37. Oxford: Hart Publishing, 2014.

———. "Theater of the Invisible." *Blackstone Weekly* (blog). May 23, 2011. https://blackstoneweekly.wordpress.com

Alschuler, Albert W. "Rediscovering Blackstone." *University of Pennsylvania Law Review* 45 (1996): 1–43.

Alter, Adam L., and Daniel M. Oppenheimer. "Suppressing Secrecy through Metacognitive Ease." *Psychological Science* 20, no. 11 (2009): 1414–20.

———. "Uniting the Tribes of Fluency to Form a Metacognitive Nation." *Personality and Social Psychology Review* 13, no. 3 (2009): 219–35.

Anderson, Benedict. *Imagined Communities: Reflections on the Origin and Spread of Nationalism.* London: Verso Books, 1983.

Angner, Eric. "Natural Law and the Science of Happiness." Paper prepared for Natural Law and Economics Consultation, Princeton University, May 2009. www.researchgate.net.

[Anon.] *Anecdotes, Bon Mots, Traits, Stratagems and Biographical Sketches of the Most Remarkable Highwaymen, Swindlers and Other Daring Adventurers.* London: Printed for D. Brewman, no. 45, Old Bailey, 1797. Eighteenth Century Collections Online (Range T088946).

———. *The Beauties of Biography, A Selection of the Lives of Eminent Men.* 2 vols. London: Printed for G. Riebau, 1792.

———. *Bibliotheca Blackstoneiana. A Catalogue of a Library of 4,500 Volumes . . . The Greater Part Having Been Collected by the Celebrated Judge Blackstone and Dr. Blackstone of Oxford . . . Sold by Auction, by Mr. Price . . . 10th of Sept., 1845* (1845).

———. *The British Critic*, vol. II. [London]: Printed for J. Mawman, Ludgate Street, 1826.

———. "Elegy Written in Westminster-Hall During the Long Vacation." In *The Repository: A Select Collection of Fugitive Pieces of Wit and Humour, in Prose and Verse*, 2:77–82. 4 vols. London: Edward and Charles Dilly, 1777. Eighteenth Century Collections Online (Range 9578).

———. *Lindor & Adelaide: A Moral Tale.* London: Printed for John Stockdale, 1791.

———. *The Literary Fly.* [London]: Printed and published by [Christopher] Etherington, 1779.

———. *The Lives of the Most Remarkable Criminals.* 3 vols. London: Printed and sold by John Osborn, at the Golden-Ball in Pater-Noster-Row, 1735. Eighteenth Century Collections Online (Range T088946).

———. *The Monthly Review or Literary Journal* 42. London: Printed for R. Griffiths, 1770.

———. *The Secret History of the Loose and Incestuous Loves of Pope Gregory VII, Commonly Call'd St. Hildebrand: and of the Cardinal de Richelieu, Collected from Several French and Italian Manuscripts Written in Their Time.* London: Printed for T. Warner, 1722.

———. *Tryals.* 1679. Ann Arbor: University of Michigan, 2012.

———. "Wonderful Exhibition!!! Signor Gulielmo Pittachio the sublime wonder of the world!!! Condescends to inform the public at large." [London], [1794].

Arendt, Hannah. *The Human Condition.* 2nd ed. Chicago: University of Chicago Press, 1998.

Ashworth, Michael. "Affective Governmentality: Governing through Disgust in Uganda." *Social & Legal Studies* 26, no. 2 (2017): 188–207.

Bahun, Sanja. *Modernism and Melancholia: Writing as Countermourning*. Oxford: Oxford University Press, 2014.

Baker, J. H. *The Common Law Tradition: Lawyers, Books and the Law*. London: Hambledon Press, 2000.

———. *An Introduction to English Legal History*. 3rd ed. London: Butterworths, 1990.

Bal, Mieke. *Double Exposures: The Subject of Cultural Analysis*. New York: Routledge, 1996.

Baldick, Chris, and Robert Mighall. "Gothic Criticism." In *A Companion to the Gothic*, edited by David Punter, 209–28. Oxford: Blackwell Publishers, 2000.

Ball, Milner S. "All the Law's a Stage." *Cardozo Studies in Law and Literature* 11, no. 2 (Winter 1999): 215–21.

Ballaster, Ros. *Fabulous Orients: Fictions of the East in England 1662–1785*. Oxford: Oxford University Press, 2005.

Bandes, Susan, ed. *The Passions of Law*. New York: NYU Press, 2000.

Bandes, Susan, and Jeremy A. Blumenthal. "Emotion and the Law." *Annual Review of Law and Social Science* 8 (2012): 161–81.

Bankowski, Zenon. *Living Lawfully: Love in Law and Law in Love*. Dordrecht, Netherlands: Springer, 2001.

Barclay, Katie. "New Materialism and the New History of Emotions." *Emotions: History, Culture, Society* 1, no. 1 (2017): 161–83.

Battestin, Martin C. *The Providence of Wit: Aspects of Form in Augustan Literature and the Arts*. Charlottesville: University of Virginia Press, 1974.

Beckett, Gilbert Abbott à. *The Comic Blackstone*. Philadelphia: J. B. Lippincott & Co., 1876.

Bell, Matthew. *Melancholia: The Western Malady*. Cambridge: Cambridge University Press, 2014.

Belsey, Catherine. *Culture and the Real: Theorizing Cultural Criticism*. New York: Routledge, 2005.

Benfield, C. J. Barker. *The Culture of Sensibility*. Chicago: University of Chicago Press, 1995.

Benjamin, Walter. *Selected Writings*, Volume 4, *1938–1940*. Edited by Howard Eiland and Michael W. Jennings. Cambridge, MA: Belknap Press, 1996.

Bennett, Jane. *The Enchantment of Modern Life: Attachments, Crossings, and Ethics*. Princeton: Princeton University Press, 2016.

Bentham, Jeremy. "Draught of a New Plan for the Organisation of the Judicial Establishment in France: Proposed as a Succedaneum to the Draught Presented, for the Same Purpose, by the Committee of Constitution, to the National Assembly, December 21st, 1789." London, 1790.

———. *A Fragment on Government*. 1823. Oxford: Oxford University Press, 2008.

Berlant, Lauren. *Cruel Optimism*. Durham, NC: Duke University Press, 2011.

———. *Desire/Love*. Brooklyn, NY: Punctum Books, 2012.

Berlant, Lauren, ed. *Compassion: The Culture and Politics of an Emotion*. New York: Routledge, 2004.

Berman, Harold J. "The Origins of Historical Jurisprudence: Coke, Selden, Hale." *Yale Law Journal* 103, no. 7 (May 1994): 1651–738.

Black, Ernest G. "Torture under English Law." *Pennsylvania Law Review* 75, no. 4 (1927): 344–48.

Black, Jeremy. *Culture in Eighteenth-Century England: A Subject for Taste*. London: Bloomsbury Academic, 2007.

Blackstone, William. *Commentaries on the Laws of England*. 4 vols. General Editor: Wilfrid Prest. Oxford: Oxford University Press, 2016.

———. *Commentaries on the Laws of England: A Facsimile of the First Edition of 1765–1769*. 4 vols. Chicago: University of Chicago Press, 1979.

———. "The Lawyer's Farewell to His Muse." In *A Collection of Poems in Four Volumes. By Several Hands*, 228–32. London: Printed by J. Hughs, for R. and J. Dodsley, 1755. Eighteenth Century Collections Online (Range 1916).

———. *The Letters of Sir William Blackstone 1744–1780*. Edited by Wilfrid Prest. London: Selden Society, 2006.

———. *The Pantheon: A Vision*. London: Printed for R. Dodsley, 1747. Eighteenth Century Collections Online (Range 6813).

Blomley, Nicholas. "Performing Property, Making the World." *Canadian Journal of Law and Jurisprudence* 27, no. 1 (2013): 23–48.

Boddice, Rob. *The History of Emotions*. Manchester: Manchester University Press, 2018.

Boorstin, Daniel. *The Mysterious Science of the Law: An Essay on Blackstone's Commentaries*. Chicago: University of Chicago Press, 1941, 1996.

Boswell, James. *Boswell, the English Experiment, 1785–1789*. Edited by Irma S. Lustig and Frederick A. Pottie. New York: McGraw-Hill, 1986.

Botting, Fred. *Gothic*. New York: Routledge, 1996.

Bourdieu, Pierre. "The Force of Law: Toward a Sociology of the Juridical Field." *Hastings Law Journal* 38, no. 5 (1987): 805–53.

Bourke, Joanna. *The Story of Pain: From Prayer to Painkillers*. Oxford: Oxford University Press, 2014.

Bowring, John. [*Memoirs and Correspondence.*] In *The Works of Jeremy Bentham*. Vol. 10. Edinburgh: William Tait, 1843.

Boyle, James. "Is Subjectivity Possible? The Post-Modern Subject in Legal Theory." *University of Colorado Law Review* 62 (1991): 489–524.

Brady, Emily, and Arto Haapala. "Melancholy as an Aesthetic Emotion." *Contemporary Aesthetics* 1 (2003). http://hdl.handle.net/2027/spo.7523862.0001.006.

Brennan, William J., Jr. "Reason, Passion, and 'The Progress of the Law.'" *Cardozo Law Review* 10 (1988): 3–23.

Brinkema, Eugenie. *The Forms of the Affects*. Durham, NC: Duke University Press, 2014.

Broomhall, Susan, ed. *Early Modern Emotions: An Introduction*. New York: Routledge, 2017.

Bronner, Stephen Eric. "The Great Divide: The Enlightenment and Its Critics." *New Politics* 5, no. 3 (Summer 1995): 65–86.

Bronsteen, John, Christopher Buccafusco, and Jonathan S. Masur. *Happiness and the Law*. Chicago: University of Chicago Press, 2014.

Brown, Thomas. *Amusements Serious and Comical, Calculated for the Meridian of London*. London, 1702.

Butler, Clark, ed. *Guantanamo Bay and the Judicial-Moral Treatment of the Other*. West Lafayette, IN: Purdue University Press, 2007.

Butler, Judith. "Afterword: After Loss, What Then?" In *Loss: The Politics of Mourning*, edited by David Eng and David Kazanjian, 467–74. Berkeley: University of California Press, 2002.

Cahn, Edmond N. "Madison and the Pursuit of Happiness." *New York University Law Review* 27 (April 1952): 265–76.

Cairns, John W. "Blackstone, the Ancient Constitution and the Feudal Law." *Historical Journal* 28, no. 3 (1985): 711–17.

———. "Eighteenth-Century Professorial Classification of the English Common Law." *McGill Journal of Law* 33 (1987): 318–60.

Calhoun, Cheshire. "Making Up Emotional People: The Case of Romantic Love." In *Passions of Law*, edited by Susan Bandes, 217–40. New York: NYU Press, 2000.

Cannon, John, ed. *The Letters of Junius*. Oxford: Clarendon Press, 1978.

Canuel, Mark. *Justice, Dissent and the Sublime*. Baltimore: Johns Hopkins University Press, 2012.

Cardozo, Benjamin N. *The Nature of the Judicial Process*. New Haven, CT: Yale University Press, 1921.

Carter, John. *The Builder's Magazine: Or, A Universal Dictionary for Architects, Carpenters, Masons, Bricklayers &c*. London: Printed for E. Newbery, 1788.

Castle, Terry. "The Gothic Novel." In *The Cambridge History of English Literature 1660–1780*, edited by John Richetti, 673–706. Cambridge: Cambridge University Press, 2005.

Chaplin, Sue. *The Gothic and the Rule of Law, 1764–1820*. New York: Palgrave Macmillan, 2007.

———. "Spectres of Law in *The Castle of Otranto*." *Romanticism: The Journal of Romantic Culture and Criticism* 12, no. 6 (2006): 177–88.

———. "'Written in the Black Letter': The Gothic and/in the Rule of Law." *Law and Literature* 17, no. 1 (2005): 47–68.

Cheng, Anne Anlin. "The Melancholy of Race." *Kenyon Review* 19, no. 1 (1997): 49–61.

———. *The Melancholy of Race: Psychoanalysis, Assimilation, and Hidden Grief*. Oxford: Oxford University Press, 2000.

Cheyne, George. *The English Malady*. London: Printed for G. Strahan and J. Leake, 1733.

Chiu, Frances A. "Faulty Towers: Reform, Radicalism and the Gothic Castle 1760–1800." *Romanticism on the Net* 44 (2006). http://id.erudit.org/iderudit/013996ar.

Clanchy, M. T. *From Memory to Written Record: England 1066–1307.* West Sussex, UK: Wiley-Blackwell, 2012.

Cleary, E. J. "The Genesis of 'Gothic' Fiction." In *The Cambridge Companion to Gothic Fiction,* edited by Jerrold E. Hogle, 21–40. Cambridge: Cambridge University Press, 2002.

Clewell, Tammy. "Mourning beyond Melancholia: Freud's Psychoanalysis of Loss." *Journal of the American Psychoanalytic Association* 52, no. 1 (2004): 43–67.

Clitherow, James. Preface to *Reports of Cases Determined in the Several Courts of Westminster-Hall, from 1746–1779.* London: Printed by His Majesty's Law Printers, 1781.

Cock, Emily. "'Off Dropped the Sympathetic Snout': Shame, Sympathy, and Plastic Surgery at the Beginning of the Long Eighteenth Century." In *Passions, Sympathy and Print Culture,* edited by Heather Kerr, David Lemmings, and Robert Phiddian, 145–64. London: Palgrave Macmillan UK, 2016.

Cockayne, Emily. *Hubbub: Filth, Noise and Stench in England, 1600–1770.* New Haven, CT: Yale University Press, 2007.

Cohen, William A. "Introduction: Locating Filth." In *Filth: Dirt, Disgust, and Modern Life,* edited by William A. Cohen and Ryan Johnson, vii–xxxviii. Minneapolis: University of Minnesota Press, 2004.

Cohen, William A., and Ryan Johnson, eds. *Filth: Dirt, Disgust, and Modern Life.* Minneapolis: University of Minnesota Press, 2004.

Colley, Linda. *Britons: Forging the Nation, 1707–1837.* New Haven, CT: Yale University Press, 2005.

Collins, Wilkie. *Armadale.* Cambridge: Penguin Classics, 2011.

Collins, William. *The Works of William Collins.* Edited by Richard Wendorf and Charles Ryskamp. Oxford: Clarendon Press, 1979.

Conklin, Carli N. "The Origins of the Pursuit of Happiness." *Washington University Jurisprudence Review* 7, no. 2 (2015): 195–262. https://openscholarship.wustl.edu.

Cope, Virginia H. "Evelina's Peculiar Circumstances." *Eighteenth-Century Fiction* 18, no. 1 (2003): 59–78.

Cosgrove, Richard A. *Scholars of the Law: English Jurisprudence from Blackstone to Hart.* New York: NYU Press, 1996.

Costantini, Mariaconcetta, ed. *Armadale: Wilkie Collins and the Dark Threads of Life.* Rome: Aracne, 2009.

Cover, Robert M. "The Supreme Court, 1982 Term—Foreword: Nomos and Narrative." *Harvard Law Journal* 97, no. 4 (1983): 4–69.

———. "Violence and the Word." *Yale Law Journal* 95, no. 8 (1986): 1601–29.

Cowie, Leonard W. "Justice at Westminster Hall." *History Today* 21, no. 3 (March 1971): 178–86.

Crozier, W. Ray. "Blushing and the Private Self." In *The Psychological Significance of the Blush,* edited by W. Ray Crozier and Peter J. de Jong, 222–41. Cambridge: Cambridge University Press, 2013.

Dabashi, Hamid. *Post-Orientalism: Knowledge and Power in a Time of Terror*. New Brunswick, NJ: Transaction Publishers, 2009.

Daniel, Drew. *The Melancholy Assemblage: Affect and Epistemology in the English Renaissance*. New York: Fordham University Press, 2013.

Davies, William. *The Happiness Industry: How the Government and Big-Business Sold Us Well-Being*. London: Verso, 2015.

Davis, David Brion. *The Problem of Slavery in the Age of Emancipation*. New York: Vintage Books, 2015.

Davis, Michael T. "John Horne Tooke [formerly John Horne] (1736–1812)." In *Oxford Dictionary of National Biography*. Online ed., edited by David Cannadine, October 2009. www.oxforddnb.com.

Dayan, Colin. *The Law is a White Dog: How Legal Rituals Make and Unmake Persons*. Princeton: Princeton University Press, 2011.

Deigh, John. "Emotion and the Authority of Law: Variation on Themes in Bentham and Austin." In *The Passions of Law*, edited by Susan Bandes, 285–308. New York: NYU Press, 2000.

Denham, John. "Cooper's Hill: A Poem." Edited by Jack Lynch. Accessed March 15, 2018. https://andromeda.rutgers.edu.

Dent, John. *The Lawyers' Panic, or, Westminster Hall in an Uproar, A Prelude, Acted at the Theatre Royal, Covent Garden, with Universal Applause*. London: Printed for S. Bladon, 1785. Eighteenth Century Collections Online (Range 12407).

Derrida, Jacques. "The Law of Genre." *Critical Inquiry* 7, no. 1 (1980): 55–81.

Deutsch, Helen. *Resemblance and Disgrace: Alexander Pope and the Deformation of Culture*. Cambridge, MA: Harvard University Press, 1996.

De Ville, Jacques. "Madness and the Law." In *Jacques Derrida: Law as Absolute Hospitality*, 95–112. New York: Routledge, 2011.

Dimock, Wai Chee. *Residues of Justice: Literature, Law, Philosophy*. Berkeley: University of California Press, 1996.

Dixon, Thomas. "'Emotion': History of a Keyword in Crisis." *Emotion Review* 4, no. 4 (2012): 338–44.

———. "The Tears of Mr. Justice Wilkes." *Journal of Victorian Culture* 17, no. 1 (2012): 1–23.

———. *Weeping Britannia: Portrait of a Nation in Tears*. Oxford: Oxford University Press, 2015.

Doody, Margaret Anne. *The Daring Muse: Augustan Poetry Reconsidered*. Cambridge: Cambridge University Press, 1985.

Douglas, Mary. *Purity and Danger: An Analysis of Concepts of Pollution and Taboo*. New York: Routledge, 1966.

Duggett, Tom. *Gothic Romanticism: Architecture, Politics and Literary Form*. New York: Palgrave Macmillan, 2010.

Elias, Norbert. *The Civilizing Process: Sociogenetic and Psychogenetic Investigations*. 2nd ed. Oxford: Wiley-Blackwell, 2000.

Ellis, Markman. *The Politics of Sensibility: Race, Gender and Commerce in the Sentimental Novel*. Cambridge: Cambridge University Press, 2004.

Ellison, Julie. *Cato's Tears and the Making of Anglo-American Emotion*. Chicago: University of Chicago Press, 1999.

Emerson, John. "Did Blackstone Get the Gallic Shrug?" In *Blackstone and His Commentaries: Biography, Law, and History*, edited by Wilfrid Prest, 185–98. Oxford: Hart Publishing, 2009.

Eng, David, and David Kazanjian, eds. *Loss: The Politics of Mourning*. Berkeley: University of California Press, 2002.

Engster, Daniel. *Divine Sovereignty: The Origins of Modern State Power*. DeKalb: Northern Illinois University Press, 2001.

Ertman, Martha E. "Legal Tenderness." A Review of *Feminist Perspectives on Contract Law*, edited by Linda Mulcahy and Sally Wheeler. *Yale Journal Law & Feminism* 18, no. 542 (2006): 545–71.

Eschenbaum, Natalie K., and Barbara Correll, eds. *Disgust in Early Modern English Literature*. New York: Routledge, 2016.

Evans, Jules. "Reputation is the Modern Purgatory." *History of Emotions Blog*, February 7, 2012. https://emotionsblog.history.qmul.ac.uk.

Faflek, Joel. "The Persuasion of Happiness." Paper presented at Washington Romanticists Group, Spring 2013.

Fawcett, Julia H. "The Overexpressive Celebrity and the Deformed King: Recasting the Spectacle as Subject in Colley Cibber's *Richard III*." *PMLA* 126, no. 4 (2011): 950–65.

Felman, Shoshana. *The Juridical Unconscious: Trials and Traumas in the Twentieth Century*. Cambridge, MA: Harvard University Press, 2002.

——. *Scandal of the Speaking Body: Don Juan with J.L. Austin, or Seduction in Two Languages*. Stanford, CA: Stanford University Press, 2003.

Felski, Rita. *The Limits of Critique*. Chicago: University of Chicago Press, 2015.

Ferguson, Robert A. *Law and Letters in American Culture*. Cambridge, MA: Harvard University Press, 1984.

Fielding, Henry. *An Enquiry into the Causes of the Late Increase of Robbers, &c*. Dublin: Printed for G. Faulkner in Essex-Street, P. Wilson, R. James, and M. Williamson in Dame-Street, Booksellers, 1751. Eighteenth Century Collections Online (Range T089872).

Fiera, Battista. *De Justicia Pingenda*. Translated and edited by James Wardrop. [London, 1957].

Fineman, Martha. "The Vulnerable Subject: Anchoring Equality in the Human Condition." *Yale Journal of Law and Feminism* 20, no. 1 (2008): 1–24.

Fineman, Martha, ed. *Vulnerability: Reflections on a New Ethical Foundation for Law and Politics*. Burlington, VT: Ashgate, 2013.

Finkelde, Dominik. *Excessive Subjectivity: Kant, Hegel, Lacan, and the Foundations of Ethics*. New York: Columbia University Press, 2017.

Finkelstein, David, and Alistair McCleery. *An Introduction to Book History*. New York: Routledge, 2005.

Flatley, Jonathan. *Affective Mapping: Melancholia and the Politics of Modernism*. Cambridge, MA: Harvard University Press, 2008.

Fliegelman, Jay. *Declaring Independence: Jefferson, Natural Language, and the Culture of Performance*. Stanford, CA: Stanford University Press, 1993.

Flynn, Meagan. "'Barbarism': Texas Judge Ordered Electric Shocks to Silence Man on Trial." *Washington Post*, March 7, 2018. www.washingtonpost.com.

Foote, Samuel. *A Treatise on the Passions, So Far as They Regard the Stage*. London: Printed for C. Corbet, 1747.

———. *A Trip to Calais: A Comedy, in Three Acts*. London: Printed by J. Jarvis, 1794.

Foster, Peter. "CIA 'Tortured Al-Qaeda Suspects Close to the Point of Death by Drowning Them in Water-Filled Baths.'" *Telegraph* (UK), September 7, 2014. www.telegraph.co.uk.

Foucault, Michel. *The Archaeology of Knowledge*. Translated by A. M. Sheridan Smith. London: Routledge, 1991.

———. *Discipline and Punish*. Translated by Alan Sheridan. New York: Vintage Books, 1995.

———. "The Eye of Power." In *The Impossible Prison: A Foucault Reader* (exhibition catalog), edited by Alex Farquharson, 8–15. Nottingham, UK: Nottingham Contemporary, 2008. www.aelab.ifilnova.pt.

Frazer, Michael. *The Enlightenment of Sympathy: Justice and the Moral Sentiments in the Eighteenth Century and Today*. Oxford: Oxford University Press, 2010.

Friedman, Danny. "Torture and the Common Law." *European Human Rights Law Review* 2 (2006): 180–99.

Frye, Northrop. *Collected Works of Northrop Frye*. Vol. 19, *The Great Code: The Bible and Literature*. Edited by Alvin A. Lee. Toronto, ON: University of Toronto Press, 2006.

Gentleman of the Middle Temple. *The History of Lord Stanton. A Novel. By a Gentleman of the Middle Temple, Author of The Trial, or History of Charles Horton*. 5 vols. London: Printed for T. Vernor, [1775?]. Eighteenth Century Collections Online (Range 1107).

Ghoshray, Saby. "On the Judicial Treatment of Guantanamo Detainees in International Law." In *Guantanamo Bay and the Judicial-Moral Treatment of the Other*, edited by Clark Butler, 80–118. West Lafayette, IN: Purdue University Press, 2007.

Gibbon, Edward. "Remarks on Blackstone's Commentaries, Referred to in Mr. Gibbon's Memoirs." In *The Miscellaneous Works of Edward Gibbon, Esq. with Memoirs of His Life and Writings*. 5 vols., 5:545–47. London, 1814.

Gibbons, Louel C. To Kill a Mockingbird *in the Classroom: Walking in Someone Else's Shoes*. Urbana, IL: National Council of Teachers of English, 2009.

Gigantino, James J. *The Ragged Road to Abolition: Slavery and Freedom in New Jersey, 1775–1865*. Philadelphia: University of Pennsylvania Press, 2014.

Gikandi, Simon. *Slavery and the Culture of Taste*. Princeton: Princeton University Press, 2014.

Gilmore, Grant. *The Ages of American Law*. 2nd ed. New Haven, CT: Yale University Press, 2014.

Gladfelder, Hal. *Eighteenth-Century England: Beyond the Law*. Baltimore: Johns Hopkins University Press, 2003.

Goffman, Erving. "Embarrassment and Social Organization." *American Journal of Sociology* 62, no. 3 (November 1956): 264–71.

Goldberg, David Theo, Michael Musheno, and Lisa C. Bower. "Shake Yo' Paradigm: Romantic Longing and Terror in Contemporary Sociolegal Studies." In *Between Law and Culture: Relocating Legal Studies*, edited by David Theo Goldberg, et al., ix–xxv. Minneapolis: University of Minnesota Press, 2001.

Golden, Morris. *Thomas Gray*. New York: Grosset & Dunlap, 1964.

Gomme, George Laurence, ed. *Sacred and Medieval Architecture*. Vol. 1. London: The Gentleman's Magazine, 1890.

Goodrich, Peter. Introduction to *Law and the Unconscious: A Legendre Reader*, by Pierre Legendre, edited by Peter Goodrich, 1–36. London: Macmillan, 1997.

———. *The Laws of Love: A Brief Historical and Practical Manual*. New York: Palgrave Macmillan, 2006.

———. *Oedipus Lex: Psychoanalysis, History, Law*. Berkeley: University of California Press, 1995.

———. "Poor Illiterate Reason: History, Nationalism and Common Law." *Social and Legal Studies* 1, no. 1 (1992): 7–28.

———. "Postmodern Justice." In *Law and the Humanities: An Introduction*, edited by Austin Sarat, Matthew Anderson, and Cathrine O. Frank, 188–96. Cambridge: Cambridge University Press, 2010.

Gorton, Kristyn. "Desire, Duras, and Melancholia: Theorizing Desire after the 'Affective Turn.'" *Feminist Review* 89 (2008): 16–33.

Gray, Charles Montgomery. "Blackstone's History of English Law." *Publications*, Paper 3 (2009): 1–31. http://chicagounbound.uchicago.edu.

Gray, Thomas. "An Elegy Written in a Country Churchyard." In *A Collection of Poems in Four Volumes. By Several Hands*, edited by Robert Dodsley. Vol. 4, 1–6. London: Printed by J. Hughs, For R. and J. Dodsley, at Tully's Head in Pall-Mall, 1755.

———. *An Elegy Written in a Country Church Yard: The Eton Manuscript & the First Edition, 1751*. Reproduced in facsimile. Edited by Alastair MacDonald. Ilkey, Yorkshire, UK: The Scolar Press, 1976.

Gregori, Flavio. Introduction to "Happiness (and Unhappiness) in Eighteenth-Century English Literature." Special issue *English Literature* 2, no. 1 (2015). www.academia.edu.

Grossi, Renata. *Looking for Love in the Legal Discourse of Marriage*. Acton, Australia: ANU Press, 2014.

[Gurney, Joseph.] *The Genuine Trial between The Rt. Hon. Geo. Onslow, Esq; and The Rev. Mr. John Horne, tried at Guildford the 1st of August, 1770*. London: Printed for J. Williams and J. Godwin, 1770.

———. *The Trial of Frederick Calvert, Esq; Baron of Baltimore in the Kingdom of Ireland*. London: Printed for William Owen, 1768.

———. *The Whole Proceedings in the Cause on the Action Brought by The Rt. Hon. Geo. Onslow, Esq. against The Rev. Mr. Horne*. London: Printed for T. Davies and J. Gurney, 1770.

Haldar, Piyel. *Law, Orientalism and Postcolonialism: The Jurisdiction of the Lotus Eaters.* New York: Routledge, 2013.

Halle, Terry. "French and German Gothic: The Beginnings." In *The Cambridge Companion to Gothic Fiction*, edited by Jerrold E. Hogle, 63–84. Cambridge: Cambridge University Press, 2002.

Halliday, Paul D. "Blackstone's King." In *Re-Interpreting Blackstone's* Commentaries*: A Seminal Text in National and International Contexts*, edited by Wilfrid Prest, 169–87. Oxford: Hart Publishing, 2014.

Harbison, Robert. *The Built, the Unbuilt, and the Unbuildable: In Pursuit of Architectural Meaning.* Cambridge, MA: MIT Press, 1991.

Harman, Charles E. *Critical Commentaries on Blackstone.* Brookings, OR: Old Court Press, 2002.

Heath, James. *Torture and English Law: An Administrative and Legal History from the Plantagenets to the Stuarts.* Westport, CT: Greenwood Press, 1982.

Heinzelman, Susan Sage. *Riding the Black Ram: Law, Literature, and Gender.* Stanford, CA: Stanford University Press, 2010.

Helms, Gesa, Marina Vishmidt, and Lauren Berlant. "Affect and the Politics of Austerity: An Interview Exchange with Lauren Berlant." *Variant* 39/40 (Winter 2010). www.variant.org.uk.

Heninger, S. K., Jr. *Touches of Sweet Harmony: Pythagorean Cosmology and Renaissance Poetics.* San Marino, CA: Huntington Library Press, 1974.

Hensley, Nathan K. "Curatorial Reading and Endless War." *Victorian Studies* 56, no. 1 (2013): 59–83.

———. *Forms of Empire: The Poetics of Victorian Sovereignty.* Oxford: Oxford University Press, 2016.

Hibbitts, Bernard J. "Coming to Our Senses: Communication and Legal Expression in Performance Cultures." *Emory Law Journal* 41, no. 4 (1992): 873–960.

———. "De-scribing Law: Performance in the Constitution of Legality." Paper presented at the 1996 Performance Studies Conference, Northwestern University, March 1996. http://law.pitt.edu/archive/hibbitts/describ.htm.

———. "Making Sense of Metaphors: Visuality, Aurality, and the Reconfiguration of American Legal Discourse." *Cardozo Law Review* 16, no. 2 (1994): 229–356.

Hilles, Frederick W. "Art and Artifice in *Tom Jones*." In *Imagined Worlds: Essays on Some English Novels in Honor of John Butt*, edited by Maynard Mack and Ian Gregor, 91–110. London: Methuen, 1968.

Hoeflich, Michael. "American Blackstones." In *Blackstone and His Commentaries: Biography, Law, History*, edited by Wilfrid Prest, 171–84. Oxford: Hart Publishing, 2009.

Hoeveler, Diane Long. "The Female Captivity Narrative: Blood, Water, and Orientialism." In *Interrogating Orientalism: Contextual Approaches and Pedagogical Practices*, edited by Diane Hoeveler Long and Jeffrey Cass, 46–71. Columbus: Ohio State University Press, 2006.

Holdsworth, W. S. "Some Aspects of Blackstone and His *Commentaries*." *Cambridge Law Journal* 4, no. 3 (1932): 261–85.

Hortensius. *Deinology: or, The Union of Reason and Elegance*. London: Printed for G. G. J. and J. Robinson, 1789.

Howell, T. B., Compiler. *A Complete Collection of State Trials and Proceedings for High Treason*. 21 vols. London: Printed by T. C. Hensard, Peterborough-Court, Fleet-Street, 1816.

Hume, David. *Treatise of Human Nature: Being an Attempt to Introduce the Experimental Method of Reasoning into Moral Subjects*. 3 vols. London: Printed for John Noon, 1739–40. Eighteenth Century Collections Online (Range 2084).

Hunt, Lynn. *Inventing Human Rights*. New York: W. W. Norton & Company, 2008.

Hunter, J. Paul. "Couplets." In *The Oxford Handbook of British Poetry, 1660–1800*, edited by Jack Lynch, 373–85. Oxford: Oxford University Press, 2016.

Ingram, Allan, Stuart Sim, Clark Lawlor, Richard Terry, John Baker, and Leigh Wetherall Dickson. *Melancholy Experience in Literature of the Long Eighteenth Century: Before Depression, 1660–1800*. London: Palgrave Macmillan UK, 2011.

Jackson, Stanley. *Melancholia and Depression: From Hippocratic Times to Modern Times*. New Haven, CT: Yale University Press, 1990.

Jackson, William. *The New and Complete Newgate Calendar; or Villany Displayed in All its Branches. Containing Accounts of the Most Notorious Malefactors from the Year 1700 to the Present Time*. London: Alexander Hogg, [1795?]. Eighteenth Century Collections Online (Range T117003).

Jay, George. "Queer Children and Representative Men: Harper Lee, Racial Liberalism, and the Dilemma of *To Kill a Mockingbird*." *American Literary History* 27, no. 3 (Fall 2015): 487–522.

Jobson, Cobler of Drury Lane. *Cobleriana; or, the Cobler's Medley*. 2 vols. London: Printed for J. Wilkie, 1768.

Johnson, Claudia Durst. To Kill a Mockingbird: *Threatening Boundaries*. New York: Twayne Publishers, 1994.

———. *Understanding* To Kill a Mockingbird: *A Student Casebook to Issues, Sources, and Historic Documents*. Westport, CT: Greenwood Press, 1994.

Johnson, Samuel. *A Dictionary of the English Language*. Facsimile of 1755 ed. Printed by W. Strahan, London. New York: Arno Press, 1979.

———. *The Rambler*. 6 vols. Printed for J. Payne, at Popoe's Head, in Pater-Noster-Row, 1752.

Jones, Howard Mumford. *The Pursuit of Happiness*. Cambridge, MA: Harvard University Press, 1953.

Jonson, Ben. *Every Man in His Humour*. https://www.gutenberg.org/files/5333/5333-h/5333-h.htm.

Kadens, Emily. "Justice Blackstone's Common Law Orthodoxy." *Northwestern University Law Review* 103, no. 4 (Fall 2009): 1553–605.

Kahan, Dan M. "The Progressive Appropriation of Disgust." In *The Passions of Law*, edited by Susan Bandes, 63–79. New York: NYU Press, 2001.

Kahn, Paul W. *Sacred Violence: Torture, Terror, and Sovereignty*. Ann Arbor: University of Michigan Press, 2008.

Kalawski, Juan Pablo. "Is Tenderness a Basic Emotion?" *Motivation and Emotion* 34, no. 2 (2010): 158–67. doi: 10.1007/s11031-010-9164-y.

Kames, Henry Home. Sketches of the *History of Man*. Vol. III of IV. Edinburgh: Printed for A. Strahan and T. Cadell, London; and for William Creech, Edinburgh, 1788.

Kay, Ailsa. "Trade in Feelings: Shame in Eighteenth-Century Britain." PhD diss., McMaster University, 2012. https://macsphere.mcmaster.ca.

Kennedy, Duncan. "The Structure of Blackstone's *Commentaries*." *Buffalo Law Review* 28, no. 2 (1979): 205–382.

Kent, James. *Commentaries on American Law*. 4 vols. New York: O. Halsted, 1826.

Kermode, Frank. *The Sense of an Ending: Studies in the Theory of Fiction*. New ed. Oxford: Oxford University Press, 2000.

King, Peter, and Richard Ward. "Rethinking the Bloody Code in Eighteenth-Century Britain: Capital Punishment at the Centre and on the Periphery." *Past and Present* 228, no. 1 (2015): 159–205. doi: 10.1093/past/gtv026.

Kinservik, Matthew J. *Sex, Scandal, and Celebrity in Late Eighteenth-Century England*. New York: Palgrave Macmillan, 2007.

Kipling, Rudyard. *Just So Stories*. London: Macmillan Publishers, 1902.

Klibansky, Raymond, Erwin Panofsky, and Fritz Saxl. *Saturn and Melancholy: Studies in the History of Natural Philosophy, Religion, and Art*. New York: Basic Books, 1964.

Kristeva, Julia. *Black Sun: Depression and Melancholia*. Translated by Leon S. Roudiez. New York: Columbia University Press, 1992.

———. *Powers of Horror: An Essay on Abjection*. Translated by Leon S. Roudiez. New York: Columbia University Press, 1980.

Kyle, Chris R. *Theater of State: Parliament and Political Culture in Early Stuart England*. Stanford, CA: Stanford University Press, 2012.

Lake, Crystal B. "Bloody Records: Manuscripts and Politics in *The Castle of Otranto*." *Modern Philology* 4, no. 110 (2013): 489–512.

Langbein, John. *Torture and the Law of Proof*. Chicago: University of Chicago Press, 2006.

Langbien, John, Renée Lettow Lerner, and Bruce P. Smith. *History of the Common Law: The Development of Anglo-American Legal Institutions*. New York: Aspen Publishers, 2009.

Langdon, Robyn, and Catriona Mackenzie. *Emotions, Imagination, and Moral Reasoning*. New York: Taylor & Francis Group, 2012.

Lawlor, Clark. "Fashionable Melancholy." In *Melancholy Experience in Literature of the Long Eighteenth Century: Before Depression, 1660–1800*, by Allan Ingram, Stuart Sim, Clark Lawlor, Richard Terry, John Baker, and Leigh Wetherall-Dickson, 25–53, London: Palgrave Macmillan UK, 2011.

Lee, Harper. *To Kill a Mockingbird*. 1960. New York: Harper Perennial Classics, 2002.

Lee, Sidney, ed. *Dictionary of National Biography*. 63 vols. London: Smith, Elder & Co., 1895.

Legendre, Pierre. *Law and the Unconscious: A Legendre Reader*. Edited by Peter Goodrich. Translated by Peter Goodrich with Alain Pottage and Anton Schüz. New York: St. Martin's Press, 1997.

Lemmings, David. "Editor's Introduction to Book I." In *The Oxford Edition of Black-stone's* Commentaries on the Laws of England: *Book II: Of the Rights of Things*, edited by David Lemmings, xvii–xl. Oxford: Oxford University Press, 2016.

———. "Marriage and the Law in the Eighteenth Century: Hardwicke's Marriage Act of 1753." *Historical Journal* 39, no. 2 (1996): 339–60.

———. *Professors of the Law: Barristers and English Legal Culture in the Eighteenth Century*. Oxford: Oxford University Press, 2000.

Leung, Rebecca. "Torture, Cover-Up at Gitmo?" *CBS News*, April 28, 2005. www.cbsnews.com.

Levine, Caroline. *Forms: Whole, Rhythm, Hierarchy, Network*. Princeton: Princeton University Press, 2015.

Lieberman, David. "Property, Commerce, and the Common Law." In *Early Modern Conceptions of Property*, edited by John Brewer and Susan Staves, 144–58. London: Routledge, 1996.

———. *The Province of Legislation Determined: Legal Theory in Eighteenth-Century Britain*. Cambridge: Cambridge University Press, 1989.

Linebaugh, Peter. *The London Hanged: Crime and Civil Society in the Eighteenth Century*. 2nd ed. London: Verso, 2006.

Lobban, Michael. *The Common Law and English Jurisprudence, 1760–1850*. Oxford: Clarendon, 1991.

Lord, Albert. *Singer of Tales*. Cambridge, MA: Harvard University Press, 1960.

Luciano, Dana. *Arranging Grief: Sacred Time and the Body in Nineteenth-Century America*. New York: NYU Press, 2007.

Mack, Robert L. *Thomas Gray: A Life*. New Haven, CT: Yale University Press, 2000.

MacKinnon, John E. "Law and Tenderness in Bernhard Schlink's *The Reader*." *Law and Literature* 16, no. 2 (2004): 179–201.

Manley, Delarivier. *The Adventures of Rivella*. Edited by Katherine Zelinsky. Peterborough, ON: Broadview Press, 1999.

Markley, Robert. "British Theory and Criticism: Early Eighteenth Century." In *The Johns Hopkins Guide to Literary Theory & Criticism*, 2nd ed., edited by Michael Groden, Martin Kreiswirth, and Imre Szeman. Baltimore, MD: Johns Hopkins University Press, 1994, 2005. Online edition accessed June 8, 2013. http://litguide.press.jhu.edu.

Maroney, Terry. "Law and Emotion: A Proposed Taxonomy of an Emerging Field." *Law and Human Behavior* 30, no. 2 (2006): 119–42.

———. "The Persistent Cultural Script of Judicial Dispassion." *California Law Review* 99, no. 2 (2011): 629–82.

Marshall, Bridget M. *The Transatlantic Gothic Novel and the Law, 1790–1860*. Burlington, VT: Ashgate, 2011.

Marshall, P. J. *The Impeachment of Warren Hastings*. London: Oxford University Press, 1965.

Martinon, Jean-Paul. "Theses in the Philosophy of Curating." In *The Curatorial: A Philosophy of Curating*, edited by Jean-Paul Martinon, 25–34. London: Bloomsbury Publishing, 2013.

Massaro, Toni M. "Show (Some) Emotions." In *Passions of Law*, edited by Susan Bandes, 80–120. New York: NYU Press, 2000.

Massumi, Brian. "The Future Birth of the Affective Fact: The Political Ontology of Threat." In *The Affect Theory Reader*, edited by Melissa Gregg and Gregory J. Seigworth, 52–70. Durham, NC: Duke University Press, 2010.

Mathew, Theobald. "Law French." *Law Quarterly Review* 54, no. 3 (1938): 358–69.

Matthews, Carol. "A Model of the Old House: Architecture in Blackstone's Life and *Commentaries*." In *Blackstone and His Commentaries: Biography, Law, History*, edited by Wilfrid Prest, 15–34. Oxford: Hart Publishing, 2009.

Matthews, Daniel. "From Jurisdiction to Juriswriting: At the Expressive Limits of the Law." *Law, Culture and the Humanities* 13, no. 3 (2017): 425–45. doi: 10.1177/1743872114525745.

Mauger, Matthew. "'Observe how parts with parts unite / In one harmonious rule of right': William Blackstone's Verses on the Laws of England." *Law and Humanities* 6, no. 2 (2012): 179–96.

Mazzetti, Mark, and Charlie Savage. "Leaked Draft of Executive Order Could Revive C.I.A. Prisons." *New York Times*, January 25, 2017. www.nytimes.com.

McKendrick, Neil, John Brewer, and J. H. Plumb. *The Birth of a Consumer Society: The Commercialization of Eighteenth-Century England*. London: Europa Publications, 1982.

McKenzie, Andrea. "'This Death Some Strong and Stout Hearted Man Doth Choose': The Practice of Peine Forte et Dure in Seventeenth- and Eighteenth-Century England." *Law and History Review* 23, no. 2 (2005): 279–313.

McKenzie, D. F. *Bibliography and the Sociology of Texts*. Cambridge: Cambridge University Press, 1999.

McLynn, Frank. *Crime and Punishment in Eighteenth-Century England*. New York: Routledge, 1989.

McMahon, Darrin. *Happiness: A History*. New York: Grove Press, 2006.

Meehan, Michael. "Authorship and Imagination in Blackstone's *Commentaries on the Laws of England*." *Eighteenth-Century Life* 16, no. 1 (1992): 111–26.

———. "Blackstone's *Commentaries*: England's Legal Georgic?" In *Re-Interpreting Blackstone's Commentaries: A Seminal Text in National and International Contexts*, edited by Wilfrid Prest, 59–69. Oxford: Hart Publishing, 2014.

Melville, Herman. *Billy Budd, Sailor*. Edited by Harrison Hayford and Merton M. Sealts Jr. Chicago: University of Chicago Press, 1962.

Menarndt, Will. "Forget Atticus: Why We Should Stop Teaching 'To Kill a Mockingbird.'" *The Establishment*, January 24, no year. Accessed March 6, 2018. https://medium.com.

Menninghaus, Winfried. *Disgust: The Theory and History of a Strong Sensation*. Translated by Howard Eiland and Joel Golb. New York: SUNY Press, 2003.

Michals, Teresa. "'That Sole and Despotic Dominion': Slaves, Wives, and Game in Blackstone's *Commentaries*." *Eighteenth-Century Studies* 27, no. 2 (Winter 1993–94): 195–216.

Miles, Robert. *Gothic Writing 1750–1820: A Genealogy*. New York: Routledge, 1993.

———. *Gothic Writing 1750–1820: A Genealogy*. 2nd ed. London: Routledge, 2002.

Miller, Gavin. "A Wall of Ideas: The 'Taboo on Tenderness' in Theory and Culture." *New Literary History* 38, no. 4 (2007): 667–81.

Miller, J. Hillis. *Communities in Fiction*. New York: Fordham University Press, 2015.

Miller, R. S. "Is Embarrassment a Blessing or a Curse?" In *The Self-Conscious Emotions: Theory and Research*, edited by Jessica L. Tracy, Richard W. Robins, and June Price Tangney, 245–62. New York: Guilford Press, 2007.

Miller, William Ian. *The Anatomy of Disgust*. Cambridge, MA: Harvard University Press, 1997.

Milton, John. *The Works of John Milton*. 18 vols. Edited by Frank Allen Patterson. New York: Columbia University Press, 1934–38.

Minow, Martha. "Forgiveness, Law, and Justice." *California Law Review* 103, no. 6 (2015): 1615–45.

Mitchell, Paul. *The Making of the Modern Law of Defamation*. Oxford: Hart Publishing, 2005.

Montagu, James. *The Old Bailey Chronicle*. 4 vols. London: Printed by authority, for S. Smith, Paternoster-Row, 1788. Eighteenth Century Collections Online (Range N010965).

Montagu, Mary Wortley. *The Letters and Works of Lady Mary Wortley Montagu*. Edited by Lord Wharncliffe with additions by W. Moy Thomas. 2 vols. London: Swan Sonnenschein & Co; New York: Macmillan & Co., 1893. Digital access provided by Library of the University of California–Riverside. https://archive.org/stream/.

More, Hannah, and William Roberts. *Memoirs of the Life and Correspondence of Hannah More*. New York: Harper and Brothers, 1835.

Morgan, Greg. "Give Me the Consideration of Being the Bondsman: Embarrassment and the Figure of the Bond in the Sentimental Fiction of Samuel Richardson." *Eighteenth-Century Fiction* 28, no. 4 (Summer 2016): 667–90.

Morris v. State of Texas, 2018 Tex.App.Lexis 1568, February 28, 2018.

Mr. L. "The Gowns: A Tale from Westminster Hall in Trinity Term, 1783." In *An Asylum for Fugitive Pieces, in Prose and Verse, Not in Any Other Collection: With Several Pieces Never Before Published*. London: Printed for J. Debrett, 1875. Eighteenth Century Collections Online (Range 765).

Murphy, Mary C. *Samuel Foote's Taste and the Orators: A Modern Edition with Five Essays*. Annapolis, MD: United States Naval Academy, 1982.

Nash, David, and Anne-Marie Kilday. *Cultures of Shame: Exploring Crime and Morality in Britain, 1600–1900*. Basingstoke, UK: Palgrave Macmillan UK, 2010.

Neu, Jerome. *A Tear Is an Intellectual Thing: The Meanings of Emotions*. Oxford: Oxford University Press, 2002.

Neuman, W. Russell, George E. Marcus, Anne N. Crigler, and Michael Mackuen, eds. *The Affect Effect: Dynamics of Emotion in Political Thinking and Behavior*. Chicago: University of Chicago Press, 2007.

Ngai, Sianne. *Ugly Feelings*. Cambridge, MA: Harvard University Press, 2007.

Nieminen, Kati. "Forever Again: How Discursive Strategies Re-Legitimate Torture in the US Senate Select Committee's 'Torture Report' and the CIA's Response." *No Foundations: An Interdisciplinary Journal of Law and Justice* 13 (2016): 70–95.

Nolan, Dennis R. "Sir William Blackstone and the New American Republic: A Study of Intellectual Impact." *New York University Law Review* 51 (1976): 731–68.

North, Joseph. *Literary Criticism: A Concise Political History*. Cambridge, MA: Harvard University Press, 2017.

Norton, Brian Michael. *Fiction and the Philosophy of Happiness: Ethical Inquiries in the Age of Enlightenment*. Lewisburg, PA: Bucknell University Press, 2012.

Nussbaum, Martha. *Creating Capabilities: The Human Development Approach*. Cambridge, MA: Harvard University Press, 2011.

———. *From Disgust to Humanity: Sexual Orientation and Constitutional Law*. Oxford: Oxford University Press, 2010.

———. *Hiding from Humanity: Disgust, Shame, and the Law*. Princeton: Princeton University Press, 2004.

Oldham, James. *English Common Law in the Age of Mansfield*. Chapel Hill: University of North Carolina Press, 2004.

Olson, Carl. "The Creative and Revolutionary Nature of Desire: A Critical Comparison of Some Postmodern Viewpoints." *Philosophy Today* 47, no. 2 (2003): 205–17.

O'Quinn, Daniel. *Staging Governance: Theatrical Imperialism in London, 1770–1800*. Baltimore: Johns Hopkins University Press, 2005.

Otto, Peter. "Disoriented, Twice Removed from the Real, Racked by Passion in Walpole's Protean Theatres of Sensation." *Eighteenth-Century Fiction* 27, no. 3/4 (2015): 681–706.

Pagden, Anthony. *The Enlightenment: And Why It Still Matters*. Oxford: Oxford University Press, 2013.

Page, Anthony, and Wilfrid Prest, eds. *Blackstone and His Critics*. Oxford: Hart Publishing, 2018.

Pahl, Katrin. "The Logic of Emotionality." *PMLA* 130, no. 5 (October 2015): 1457–66.

Paley, Edmund, ed. *The Works of William Paley*. 4 vols. London, 1838.

Paley, Ruth. "Imperial Politics and English Law: The Many Contexts of Somerset." *Law and History Review* 24, no. 3 (Fall 2006): 659–64.

Papantonio, Mike. *In Search of Atticus Finch: A Motivational Book for Lawyers*. N.p.: Seville Publishing, 1996.

Parisot, Eric. *Graveyard Poetry: Religion, Aesthetics and the Mid-Eighteenth-Century Poetic Condition*. Newark: Ashgate, 2013.

Pauli, Michelle. "Harper Lee Tops Librarians' Must-Read List." *The Guardian*, March 2, 2006. www.theguardian.com.

Paulson, Ronald. *Representations of Revolution, 1789–1820*. New Haven, CT: Yale University Press, 1983.

Peters, Edward. *Torture*. Philadelphia: University of Pennsylvania Press, 1985.

Peters, Julie Stone. "Theatricality, Legalism, and the Scenography of Suffering: The Trial of Warren Hastings and Richard Brinsley Sheridan's *Pizarro*." *Law and Literature* 18, no. 1 (Spring 2006): 15–45.

Petry, Alice Hall, ed. *On Harper Lee: Essays and Reflections*. Knoxville: University of Tennessee Press, 2007.

Phelan, Peggy. *Unmarked: The Politics of Performance*. London: Routledge, 1993.

Phillips, Adam. *Terrors and Experts*. Cambridge, MA: Harvard University Press, 1995.

Pitson, Tony. *Hume's Philosophy of the Self*. New York: Routledge, 2005.

Plamper, Jan. *The History of Emotions: An Introduction*. New York: Oxford University Press, 2017.

Pollack, Frederick, and F. W. Maitland. *The History of English Law before the Time of Edward I*. 2nd ed. Vol. 1. 1898. Cambridge: Cambridge University Press, 1968.

Pope, Alexander. *An Essay on Criticism*. In *Pastoral Poetry and an Essay in Criticism*, edited by E. Audra and Aubrey Williams. New Haven, CT: Yale University Press, 1961.

Posner, Eric, and Cass R. Sunstein, eds. *Law and Happiness*. Chicago: University of Chicago, 2010.

Postema, Gerald J. *Bentham and the Common Law Tradition*. Oxford: Oxford University Press, 1986.

Potkay, Adam. "Narrative Possibilities of Happiness, Unhappiness, and Joy." *Social Research* 77, no. 2 (Summer 2010): 523–44. http://wmpeople.wm.edu.

———. *The Passion for Happiness: Samuel Johnson and David Hume*. New York: Cornell University Press, 2000.

Prest, Wilfrid. "Blackstone as Architect: Constructing the *Commentaries*." *Yale Journal of Law and the Humanities* 15, no. 1 (2003): 103–34.

———. *Blackstone as a Barrister: Selden Society Lecture Delivered in Lincoln's Inn Old Hall, July 10th, 2007*. London: Selden Society, 2010.

———. *William Blackstone: Law and Letters in the Eighteenth Century*. Oxford: Oxford University Press, 2008.

Prest, Wilfrid, ed. *Blackstone and His Commentaries: Biography, Law, History*. Oxford: Hart Publishing, 2009.

———. *Re-Interpreting Blackstone's* Commentaries: *A Seminal Text in National and International Contexts*. Oxford: Hart Publishing, 2014.

Preston, Stephanie D., and Frans B. M. de Waal. "Empathy: Its Ultimate and Proximate Bases." *Behavioral and Brain Sciences* 25, no. 1 (2002): 1–71.

Primoratz, Igor. "Punishment as Language." *Philosophy* 64, no. 248 (1989): 187–205.

Prinz, Jesse J. "The Moral Emotions." In *The Oxford Handbook of Philosophy of Emotion*, edited by Peter Goldie, 519–38. Oxford: Oxford University Press, 2013.

Probert, Rebecca. *Marriage Law and Practice in the Long Eighteenth Century: A Reassessment*. Cambridge: Cambridge University Press, 2009.

Probyn, Elspeth. "Writing Shame." In *The Affect Theory Reader*, edited by Melissa Gregg and Gregory J. Seigworth, 71–90. Durham, NC: Duke University Press, 2010.

Punter, David. *Gothic Pathologies: The Text, the Body, and the Law.* New York: Palgrave Macmillan, 1998.

Punter, David, and Glennis Byron. *The Gothic.* Malden, MA: Blackwell Publishing, 2004.

Purdy, Jedediah. *The Meaning of Property: Freedom, Community, and the Legal Imagination.* New Haven, CT: Yale University Press, 2010.

Quema, Anne. *Power and Legitimacy: Law, Culture, and Literature.* Toronto: University of Toronto Press, 2015.

Radden, Jennifer, ed. *The Nature of Melancholy: From Aristotle to Kristeva.* New York: Oxford University Press, 2000.

Radin, Margaret Jane. *Reinterpreting Property.* Chicago: University of Chicago Press, 1993.

Rawls, John. *A Theory of Justice.* Cambridge, MA: Harvard University Press, 1971.

Rayner, John. *A Digest of the Law Concerning Libels.* London: Printed for the Author by H. Woodfall and W. Strahan, 1765.

Read, Alan. *Theatre and Law.* London: Palgrave Macmillan UK, 2016.

Reddy, William M. *The Navigation of Feeling: A Framework for the History of Emotions.* Cambridge: Cambridge University Press, 2001.

Reichman, Ravit. *The Affective Life of Law: Legal Modernism and the Literary Imagination.* Stanford, CA: Stanford University Press, 2009.

Resnik, Judith, and Dennis Curtis. *Representing Justice: Invention, Controversy, and Rights in City-States and Democratic Courtrooms.* New Haven, CT: Yale University Press, 2011.

Ricks, Christopher. *Keats and Embarrassment.* Oxford: Clarendon Press, 1974.

Roach, Joseph. *Cities of the Dead: Circum-Atlantic Performance.* New York: Columbia University Press, 1996.

Robinson, Jenefer. *Deeper than Reason: Emotion and Its Role in Literature, Music, and Art.* Oxford: Oxford University Press, 2007.

Rojek, Chris. *Celebrity.* London: Reaktion Books, 2004.

Roscoe, Thomas. *Westminster Hall: Or, Professional Relics and Anecdotes of the Bar, Bench, and Woolsack.* 2 vols. London: J. Knight & H. Lacey, 1825.

Rose, Carol M. "Canons of Property Talk, or, Blackstone's Anxiety." *Yale Law Journal* 108, no. 3 (1999): 601–32.

Rosenthal, Laura J. "Adam Smith and the Theatre in *Moral Sentiments.*" In *Passions, Sympathy and Print Culture: Public Opinion and Emotional Authenticity in Eighteenth-Century Britain,* edited by Heather Kerr, David Lemmings, and Robert Phiddian, 122–41. London: Palgrave Macmillan UK, 2016.

Rosenwein, Barbara. *Emotional Communities in the Early Middle Ages.* New York: Cornell University Press, 2006.

Rosenwein, Barbara, and Riccardo Cristiani. *What Is the History of Emotions?* Cambridge: Polity Press, 2018.

Ross, Richard J. "The Memorial Culture of Early Modern English Lawyers: Memory as Keyword, Shelter, and Identity, 1560–1640." *Yale Journal of Law and Humanities* 10, no. 2 (1998): 229–326.

Saccamano, Neil. Review of *Mourning Happiness: Narrative and the Politics of Modernity*, by Vivasvan Soni. *Eighteenth-Century Fiction* 25, no. 3 (Spring 2013): 615–19.

Sarat, Austin, Lawrence Douglas, and Martha Merrill Umphrey, eds. *Law and Mourning*. Boston: University of Massachusetts Press, 2017.

Sarat, Austin, Matthew Anderson, and Cathrine O. Frank, eds. *Law and the Humanities: An Introduction*. Cambridge: Cambridge University Press, 2010.

Sartre, Jean-Paul. *Sketch for a Theory of Emotions*. Translated by Philip Mainet. London: Routledge, 2003.

Saunders, Hilary Aidan St. George. *Westminster Hall*. London: M. Joseph, 1951.

Scarry, Elaine. *The Body in Pain*. Oxford: Oxford University Press, 1985.

Scheer, Monique. "Are Emotions a Kind of Practice (And Is That What Makes Them Have a History)? A Bourdieuian Approach to Understanding Emotion." *History and Theory* 51, no. 2 (May 2012): 193–220.

Schliesser, Eric, ed. *Sympathy: A History*. Oxford: Oxford University Press, 2015.

Schmidgen, Wolfram. *Eighteenth-Century Fiction and the Law of Property*. Cambridge: Cambridge University Press, 2002.

———. *Exquisite Mixture: The Virtues of Impurity in Early Modern England*. Philadelphia: University of Pennsylvania Press, 2013.

Sedgwick, Eve Kosofsky. *The Coherence of Gothic Conventions*. New York: Methuen, 1986.

———. *Touching Feeling: Affect, Pedagogy, Performativity*. Durham, NC: Duke University Press, 2003.

Seipp, David J. "The Structure of English Common Law in the Seventeenth Century." In *Legal History in the Making: Proceedings of the Ninth British Legal History Conference, Glasgow 1989*, edited by W. M. Gordon and T. D. Fergus, 61–83. London: Hambledon Press, 1989.

Sen, Amartya. *Commodities and Capabilities*. Amsterdam: North-Holland, 1985.

Sharpe, J. A. *Judicial Punishment in England*. London: Faber and Faber, 1990.

Shaw, James E. *The Justice of Venice: Authorities and Liberties in the Urban Economy, 1550–1700*. Oxford: Oxford University Press, 2006.

Sheridan, Thomas. *A General Dictionary to the English Language*. 2 vols. London: Printed for J. Dodsley, 1780.

Sherwin, Richard K. *Visualizing Law in the Age of the Digital Baroque: Arabesques and Entanglements*. New York: Routledge, 2011.

Shields, Charles J. *Mockingbird: A Portrait of Harper Lee*. New York: Henry Holt and Company, 2006.

Simpson, A. W. B. *Legal History and Legal Theory: Essays on the Common Law*. London: Hambledon Press, 1987.

Siskin, Clifford, and William Warner, eds. *This Is Enlightenment*. Chicago: University of Chicago Press, 2010.

Skillen, A. J. "How to Say Things with Walls." *Philosophy* 55, no. 214 (1980): 509–23.

Smith, Adam. *Theory of Moral Sentiments*. London, 1759. Eighteenth Century Collections Online (Range 45).

Smith, Bruce. *The Acoustic World of Early Modern England: Attending to the O-Factor*. Chicago: University of Chicago Press, 1999.

———. "Listening to the Wild Blue Yonder: The Challenges of Acoustic Ecology." In *Hearing Cultures: Essays on Sound, Listening, and Modernity*, edited by Veit Erlmann, 21–41. Oxford: Berg, 2004.

Smitten, Jeffrey. "Blackstone's *Commentaries* as Constitutive Rhetoric." *Studies in Eighteenth-Century Culture* 17 (1987): 173–89.

Soni, Vivasvan. *Mourning Happiness: Narrative and the Politics of Modernity*. New York: Cornell University Press, 2010.

Spargo, R. Clifton. *The Ethics of Mourning: Grief and Responsibility in Elegiac Literature*. Baltimore: Johns Hopkins University Press, 2004.

Stacy, Robin Chapman. *Dark Speech: The Performance of Law in Early Ireland*. Philadelphia: University of Pennsylvania Press, 2007.

Stark, Helen, Sarah Chaney, Thomas Dixon, and Jules Evans, eds. *The History of Emotions Blog*. The Queen Mary Centre for the History of the Emotions. https://emotionsblog.history.qmul.ac.uk.

Starr, H. W., and J. R. Hendrickson, eds. *The Complete Poems of Thomas Gray, English, Latin and Greek*. Oxford: Clarendon Press, 1966.

Stern, Simon. "Blackstone's Legal Actors: The Passions of a Rational Jurist." In *Impassioned Jurisprudence: Law, Literature and Emotion, 1760-1841*, edited by N. Johnson, 1–19. Lewisburg, PA: Bucknell University Press, 2015.

———. "Editor's Introduction to Book II." In *The Oxford Edition of Blackstone's Commentaries on the Laws of England: Book II: Of the Rights of Things*, edited by Simon Stern, vii–xxvi. Oxford: Oxford University Press, 2016.

Stewart, Susan. *Poetry and the Fate of the Senses*. Chicago: University of Chicago Press, 2002.

Stukeley, William. *Of the Spleen, Its Description and History*. London: Printed for the author, 1724.

Sumic-Riha, Jelica. "Fictions of Justice." *Filozofski vestnik* 19, no. 2 (1994): 67–80.

Sussman, David. "What's Wrong with Torture?" *Philosophy and Public Affairs* 33, no. 1 (2005): 1–33.

Sutherland, John. Introduction to *Armadale*, by Wilkie Collins, vii–xxv. London: Penguin Books, 1995.

Swanson, Gillian. "'The Tender Instinct Is the Hope of the World': Human Feeling and Social Change before Empathy." *New Formations* 79 (Autumn 2013): 126–50.

Swift, Jonathan. "Description of a City Shower." In *Miscellanies in Prose and Verse*. London: Printed for John Morphew, 1711. Eighteenth Century Collections Online (Range 2583).

Taylor, Jenny Bourne. *The Cambridge Companion to Wilkie Collins*. Cambridge: Cambridge University Press, 2006.

Temple, Kathryn. "Heart of Agitation: Mary Wollstonecraft, Emotion, and Legal Subjectivity." *Eighteenth Century* 58, no. 3 (Fall 2017): 371–82.

———. *Scandal Nation: Law and Authorship in Britain, 1750–1832*. New York: Cornell University Press, 2003.

———. "Sounds Couth and Uncouth: The Poetics of Harmonic Justice in William Blackstone's *Commentaries on the Laws of England*." *Law and Literature* 28, no. 2 (2016): 97–115.

Thorne, Christian. "The Time without Happiness." *Eighteenth-Century Life* 37, no. 2 (Spring 2013): 140–50.

Tiffany, Daniel. *Infidel Poetics: Riddles, Nightlife, Substance*. Chicago: University of Chicago Press, 2009.

Todd, Janet M. *Sensibility: An Introduction*. London: Methuen, 1986.

Townshend, Dale. "Improvement and Repair: Architecture, Romance and the Politics of Gothic, 1790–1817." *Literary Compass* 8, no. 10 (2011): 712–38.

Trigg, Stephanie. "Affect Theory." In *Early Modern Emotions: An Introduction*, edited by Susan Broomhall, 10–13. New York: Routledge, 2017.

Tyler, Tom R. *Why People Obey the Law*. Princeton: Princeton University Press, 2006.

Van Cleve, George. "Somerset's Case and its Antecedents in Imperial Perspective." *Law and History Review* 24, no. 3 (Fall 2006): 601–46.

Van Ghent, Dorothy. *The English Novel: Form and Function*. New York: HarperCollins, 1953.

Van Natta, Don, Jr., Raymond Bonner, and Amy Waldman. "Threats and Responses: Interrogations; Questioning Terror Suspects in a Dark and Surreal World." *New York Times*, March 9, 2003. www.nytimes.com.

Varey, Simon. *Space and the Eighteenth-Century Novel*. Cambridge: Cambridge University Press, 1990.

Venette, Nicolas. *The Pleasures of Conjugal-Love Explain'd*. London: Printed for P. Meighan, 1740?

Verkaik, Robert. "'I Was a Victim of Medieval Torture,' Says Freed Guantanamo Detainee." *Independent* (UK), February 24, 2009. www.independent.co.uk.

Vingerhoets, Ad. *Why Only Humans Weep: Unravelling the Mysteries of Tears*. Oxford: Oxford University Press, 2013.

Volkan, Vamik. *Blind Trust: Large Groups and Their Leaders in Times of Crisis and Terror*. Los Angeles: Pitchstone Publishing, 2004.

Waldron, Jeremy. "Property and Ownership." In *Stanford Encyclopedia of Philosophy*, Winter 2016 ed., edited by Edward N. Zalta. https://plato.stanford.edu.

Wall, Cynthia Sundberg. *The Prose of Things: Transformations of Description in the Eighteenth Century*. Chicago: University of Chicago Press, 2006.

Walpole, Horace. *The Castle of Otranto, A Story*. 1st ed. London: Printed for Tho. Lownds, 1765.

Wanko, Cheryl. *Roles of Authority: Thespian Biography and Celebrity in Eighteenth-Century Britain*. Lubbock: Texas Tech University Press, 2003.

Warner, Marina. *Monuments and Maidens: The Allegory of the Female Form*. Berkeley: University of California Press, 2000.

Warton, Thomas. *The Pleasures of Melancholy: A Poem*. London: Printed for R. Dodsley; and sold by M. Cooper, 1747.

Wasserman, Earl. *The Subtler Language: Studies in Neoclassic and Romantic Poetry.* Baltimore: Johns Hopkins University Press, 1959.

Watt, James. *Contesting the Gothic: Fiction, Genre and Cultural Conflict, 1764–1832.* Cambridge: Cambridge University Press, 1999.

West, Cornel. "Justice Is What Love Looks Like in Public." Lecture delivered at Howard University, April 17, 2011. YouTube, www.youtube.com/watch?v=nGqP7S_WO6o.

West, Robin. "Law's Emotions." *Richmond Journal of Law and the Public Interest* 19, no. 4 (2016): 339–62. https://scholarship.richmond.edu.

West, Robin, and Danielle Citron. "On Legal Scholarship." Association of American Law Schools, August 2014. Accessed July 3, 2018. www.aals.org.

Wieland, Christoph Martin. *Oberon, a Poem, from the German of Wieland.* London: Printed for Cadell and Davies; Edwards; Faulder; and Hatchard, 1798. Eighteenth Century Collections Online (Range 1290).

Williams, Anne. "Monstrous Pleasures: Horace Walpole, Opera and the Conception of Gothic." *Gothic Studies* 2, no. 1 (2000): 104–18.

Williams, Raymond. *Country and the City.* Oxford: Oxford University Press, 1975.

———. *Marxism and Literature.* Oxford: Oxford University Press, 1978.

Willman, Robert. "Blackstone and the 'Theoretical Perfection' of English Law in the Reign of Charles II." *Historical Journal* 26, no. 1 (1983): 39–70.

Wilson, Jeffrey R. "Historicizing Presentism: Toward the Creation of *Humanities Now,* a Journal of the Public Humanities." Unpublished manuscript, July 2018.

Wilson, Robert Rawdon. *The Hydra's Tale: Imagining Disgust.* Edmonton: University of Alberta Press, 2002.

Wisnewski, J. Jeremy. Personal correspondence (email). February 21, 2016.

———. *Understanding Torture.* Edinburgh: Edinburgh University Press, 2010.

Wollstonecraft, Mary. *Vindication of the Rights of Men and a Vindication of the Rights of Women.* Edited by Sylvana Tomaselli. Cambridge: Cambridge University Press, 1995.

Wood, Thomas. *An Institute of the Laws of England.* London, 1754. Eighteenth Century Collections Online (Range No. 5038).

Woty, William. "The Pettifogger, a Parody. Written in Westminster Hall in the Long Vacation." 1770. English Poetry 1579–1830: Spenser and the Tradition. Accessed July 21, 2018. http://spenserians.cath.vt.edu.

Wright, Arnold, and Philip Smith. *Parliament Past and Present: A Popular and Picturesque Account of a Thousand Years in the Palace of Westminster.* London: Hutchinson, ~1920.

Young, Alison. *Judging the Image: Art, Value, Law.* New York: Routledge, 2005.

Zipursky, Benjamin. "*DeShaney* and the Jurisprudence of Compassion." *New York University Law Review* 65, no. 4 (1990): 1101–47.

Žižek, Slavoj. "Courtly Love, or, Woman as Thing." In *The Metastases of Enjoyment: Six Essays on Women and Causality,* 89–112. London: Verso, 1994.

INDEX

Abel, Olivier, 169

Adair, James Makittrick, 64

affect, as term, 20, 197n67. *See also* emotion

African Americans: racism in *Mockingbird*, 25, 173–79, 224n76. *See also* slavery

agitation, 25, 183–88. *See also* resistance

Ahmed, Sara: emotions, 22–23, 60, 137, 142, 188, 194n29, 217n103, 220n136; fear, 132, 211n5; happiness, 153, 154, 155, 165, 169

Aikin, John, 35–36

Alfred, King: in "Lawyer's Farewel," 33, 68–69, 73, 77–78, 204n56. *See also* history of English law; monarchy

Allen, Jessie, 5, 85, 110, 175, 206n91, 211n9, 223n48

Alter, Adam, 102

Angner, Erik, 151

anxiety about modernity. *See* modernity

architecture, 117, 119–20, 160, 184, 211n8, 222n38. *See also* gothic tradition

Arendt, Hannah, 44

Aristotle, 10, 63, 195n35, 202n17, 222n41

Armadale (Collins): *Commentaries* in, 27–31; desire and disgust for marriage law, 23, 27–32, 42–45, 50

artificial sentiments, 60–61

Austin, J. L., 39, 44, 47, 111

Bahun, Sanja, 63

Baker, J. H., 128, 213–14n48

Ballaster, Ros, 36, 53

Bandes, Susan, 195–96n48, 207n15

bashfulness, 93–94, 208n25

Beattie, James, 167

Belcher, Jonathan, 70

Bell, Matthew, 201n11, 202n19

Benjamin, Walter, 63

Bentham, Jeremy, 90, 96, 98, 119, 204n68

Berlant, Lauren, 22, 25, 30, 33, 58, 147–48, 174, 176, 179, 198n12, 201n2

Bible: Genesis, 75–76

Billy Budd (Melville), 5, 19

Blackstone, William: about, 6; architectural interests, 119, 211n8; as a barrister, 96, 111; on the bench, 91, 100, 103, 104, 111; early life, 6, 92; his library, 213n41; as lecturer, 70–71, 90–92, 100, 111, 117; literary interests, 6, 61; personal qualities, 90–92, 100, 103, 105–7, 108–10, 204n61; as surrogate for *Commentaries*, 110–11

Blackstone, William, performance and speech: about, 24, 90–91, 103, 111–12; authenticity, 103, 110–11; consistency of oral vs. written, 100–103, 111–12; disfluency in speech, 24, 90–91, 100, 102–5, 110–12; embarrassment, 24, 90–91, 103; interruptive style, 105–8; in *Onslow* case, 24, 103–8; Vinerian lectures, 90–91. *See also* courts; oral culture; theatricality of law

Blackstone, works: about, 5; Magna Carta edition, 122; "The Pantheon" (poem), 36–37; on Shakespeare, 61; Vinerian lectures, 90–91, 117. See also *Commentaries on the Laws of England*; "Lawyer's Farewel to His Muse"

See also courts; "Lawyer's Farewel to His Muse"; legal education; tenderness of the law; Westminster Hall

"Lawyer's Farewel to His Muse": about, 6–14, 38, 68–69, 149; aesthetic losses, 7, 60–61, 70; *Concordia discors*, 9–12, 40; "countless wheels" in harmony, 11, 33–35, 37, 39–40, 51, 185, 188; couplets and caesuras, 8–10, 67–68, 162; death of poet-lawyer, 8, 51, 68, 117; desire vs. disgust, 32–37, 39–40, 51–56; discordances and noise, 2, 8, 10, 12–13, 68; disgust for law, 7, 34, 38, 40, 50–51; "eastern queen," 7, 10, 32–37, 39–40, 50–56; emotions, 6–8, 149; ghosts, 68–69; gothic imagery, 116–17; happiness, 149–50, 164; harmonic justice, 8–13, 31–35, 37–38, 40, 51, 68–69, 149, 164; idealization of literature and harmonic justice, 31–32; influence of Gray's *Elegy*, 65–67; King Alfred and legal history, 33, 68–69, 73, 77–78, 204n56; law as "mystic, dark, discordant," 38, 50, 68, 117, 133; law as "thorny maze," 10, 32–33, 37, 198n17; melancholia, 60–62, 67–69; moral sentiment, 7–8, 38; obstacles to justice, 32–33; Orientalism, 53–54; pratfalls, 39–40; publication, 65; retirement of poet-lawyer, 8, 13, 67–69, 178; sexualized metaphors, 7, 10–11, 32–34; sound and sense, 8–9, 67–69; at Westminster Hall, 12–14, 68. *See also* harmonic justice

Lee, Harper. See *To Kill a Mockingbird* (Lee)

legal education: about, 16; *Commentaries* in law schools, 1, 170; dullness, 38; Gothic black letter typeface, 125, 214n51; legal studies before *Commentaries*, 2–5, 70–71, 118; melancholia in students, 70; "On the Study of Law," 40–42, 70–71, 117, 149–50; Vinerian lectures, 90–91, 117

legal emotions. *See* law and emotion

legal history. *See* history and law; history of English law; interdisciplinary methodology; Law and Humanities

legal practice. *See* law practice and lawyers

legal studies and humanities. *See* Law and Humanities

Legendere, Pierre, 79

Lemmings, David, 12–13, 190, 200n54

Levine, Caroline, 19–20, 188

libel: embarrassment, 103–4, 209n63; *Onslow* case, 24, 92, 103–9

liberty: about, 24–25, 163–70; ambivalence about, 25, 165–66, 168–70; in *Commentaries*, 163–64, 167–70; contrarieties in law, 17–18; cruel optimism about, 25, 174; free markets, 148; happiness, 148, 167–70, 220n8; harmonic justice, 163–64, 169, 174; in *Mockingbird*, 174; vs. slavery, 167–70

literature and law: form and style, 19–20; genres, 21; happiness turn, 147; key questions, 15; Law and Humanities, 15; and real experience, 215n56, 218nn115–16; scholarship on, 15, 195–96n48; ways of reading, 16–22

Locke, John, 150–51, 204–5n73

Lord, Albert, 84, 206n98

loss. *See* melancholia and loss

love and law: about, 54; emotional bonds to law, 18, 20, 73, 87–88, 120, 149, 164–65, 193n5; Freud on, 58; grief for loss of, 60; love for justice, 14–15, 195n46; obedience to the law, 14–15, 195n46; processes for community building, 54; scholarship on, 198n9

Luciano, Dana, 69

Macpherson, James, 63

Maria (Wollstonecraft), 119, 184–85

marriage law: about, 41–50; in *Armadale*, 27–32, 42–45, 50; clandestine mar-

diversity of oral origins, 162; as embodied emotion, 8; vs. harmonic justice, 12–13; in "Lawyer's Farewel," 2, 8, 10, 12–13, 68, 178; as legal incoherence, 2, 8, 12–13; and torture, 134, 216n80. *See also* harmonic justice; sound

Nolan, Dennis R., 223n66

novels. See *The Castle of Otranto* (Walpole); *To Kill a Mockingbird* (Lee)

Nussbaum, Martha, 37–38, 94, 144, 199n40, 208n25

obedience to the law, 14–15

Onslow v. Horne (1770), 24, 92, 103–9

Oppenheimer, Daniel, 102

oral culture, 62, 68–69, 77–87, 92, 99–112, 162, 203n54. *See also* print culture; theatricality of law

The Orators (Foote), 101–2

Orientalism, 32–37, 51–56

Otranto. See *The Castle of Otranto* (Walpole)

Pahl, Katrin, 6

pain: communicability of, 187, 219nn132–33; governmental inflictions of, 140; and language, 136–37; and tenderness of the law, 144; by torture, 131–32, 134, 136–37, 139–40, 216n82. *See also* tenderness of the law; torture

Paley, Ruth, 168–69

Paley, William, 139

Pamela (Richardson), 33, 152, 153, 156

"The Pantheon" (Blackstone), 36–37

Parisot, Eric, 65

parody, 65

passion, as term, 20, 197n67. *See also* emotion

Paulson, Ronald, 129

peine forte et dure (pressing), 24, 113–14, 126–45, 213–14n48, 214n51, 214–15n55, 215n57, 216n85, 218n115. *See also* torture

performance and speech. *See* Blackstone, William, performance and speech; courts; oral culture; theatricality of law

Perrin v. Blake (1772), 104

personal property law, 74. *See also* property law

"The Pettyfogger, a Parody," 65

Phelan, Peggy, 92

Phillips, Adam, 134–35

philosophy and law, 15. *See also* interdisciplinary methodology; Law and Humanities

plays: *The Orators*, 101–2

pleas, 127

poetry: Blackstone's "The Pantheon," 36–37; couplets and caesuras, 8–10, 67–68; elegies, 23–24, 65, 202n13; Gray's *Elegy*, 23–24, 65–67, 86, 202n13, 202n25; and law, 25; meter, 8, 10, 67, 203n44; orality of, 68; sound and sense, 7–9, 66, 67–69. *See also* "Lawyer's Farewel to His Muse"

politics. *See* government and politics

Pope, Alexander, 5, 6, 11, 61, 90, 99, 111, 171, 210n97, 222n24

Potkay, Adam, 156

Prest, Wilfrid, 5, 91, 122, 194n24, 194n27, 207n6, 211n8, 213n41, 222n38

Primoratz, Igor, 216n85

print culture: about, 3, 92, 111–12; *Commentaries* as symbol of, 24, 111–12; court reviews and reports, 96–98, 106, 109; Declaration of Independence as, 112; embarrassment and books, 210n100; errors in records, 105–9, 128–29, 133–34; in Gray's *Elegy*, 66; idealization of writing, 66; legal studies before *Commentaries*, 2–3, 70–71; *Onslow* case, 105–8; vs. oral culture, 83–84, 92, 102–4, 105–12; priority of, 92, 102–4, 106–12; property deeds, 80. *See also* oral culture

Probert, Rebecca, 46–47, 48

ABOUT THE AUTHOR

Kathryn D. Temple, J.D., Ph.D., Associate Professor and former Chair of the English Department at Georgetown University, is the author of *Scandal Nation: Law and Authorship in Britain*. The recipient of numerous fellowships, including the NEH and the ACLS Burkhardt, she has published widely on the history of legal culture and legal emotions.